D0216529

Jean Sibelius

COMPOSER RESOURCE MANUALS
VOLUME 41
GARLAND REFERENCE LIBRARY OF THE HUMANITIES
VOLUME 1664

Composer Resource Manuals

Guy A. Marco, *General Editor*

Carl Maria von Weber
A Guide to Research
by Donald G. Henderson
and Alice H. Henderson

Alessandro and
Domenico Scarlatti
A Guide to Research
by Carole F. Vidali

Guillaume de Machaut
A Guide to Research
by Lawrence Earp

Edward Elgar
A Guide to Research
by Christopher Kent

Alban Berg
A Guide to Research
by Bryan R. Simms

Benjamin Britten
A Guide to Research
by Peter J. Hodgson

Béla Bartók
A Guide to Research,
Second Edition
by Elliott Antokoletz

Jean Sibelius
A Guide to Research
by Glenda D. Goss

Jean Sibelius
A Guide to Research

Glenda D. Goss

Garland Publishing, Inc.
A member of the Taylor & Francis Group
New York and London
1998

Library of Congress Cataloging-in-Publication Data

Goss, Glenda Dawn.
Jean Sibelius : a guide to research / by Glenda D. Goss.
p. cm. — (Composer resource manuals ; vol. 41) (Garland reference library of the humanities ; v. 1664)
Includes index.
ISBN 0-8153-1171-0 (alk. paper)
1. Sibelius, Jean, 1865–1957—Bibliography. I. Title. II. Series: Garland composer resource manuals ; v. 41. III. Series: Garland reference library of the humanities ; vol. 1664.
ML134.S49G67 1998
016.78'092—dc21 97-33019
CIP
MN

Cover photograph of Jean Sibelius from his 1919 passport provided courtesy of Jean Sibelius Family Archives, National Archives of Finland.

Printed on acid-free, 250-year-life paper
Manufactured in the United States of America

Composer Resource Manuals

In response to the growing need for bibliographic guidance to the vast literature on significant composers, Garland is publishing an extensive series of research guides. This ongoing series encompasses more than 50 composers; they represent Western musical tradition from the Renaissance to the present century.

Each research guide offers a selective, annotated list of writings, in all European languages, about one or more composers. There are also lists of works by the composers, unless these are available elsewhere. Biographical sketches and guides to library resources, organizations, and specialists are presented. As appropriate to the individual composer, there are maps, photographs, or other illustrative matter, glossaries, and indexes.

To Sibelius lovers everywhere
this volume is warmly dedicated

Everything and everybody is sooner or later identified, defined, and put in perspective . . . the truth as always is simultaneously better and worse than what the popular mythmaking has it.

William Saroyan, "Memories of the Depression," *The Literary Review*, Fall, 1983

Contents

Introduction

There is no shortage of literature on Jean Sibelius (1865–1957). Thousands of articles, monographs, reviews, interviews, encyclopedia entries, analytical notes, and essays have been written about this composer and his music. When Fred Blum compiled his admirable *Jean Sibelius: An International Bibliography on the Occasion of the Centennial Celebrations* in 1965, he listed more than 1,400 items. In the last thirty years the world-wide information explosion has inevitably rocked the area of Sibelius studies, and Blum's figure has been multiplied many times over.

Therein, of course, lies the rub. How does one begin to make one's way through the labyrinth of bibliographic material, some of which is anecdotal, some pure gold, and much of which is buried in the deep, and for many, the inaccessible mine of the Finnish language? That one man's trash may be another man's treasure compounds the difficulties: a third-hand life and works summary of little value as a biographical document may be the very evidence needed by the person writing a history of musical reception. And in the hundreds of impressions left in print by all those who met the composer or wrote to the composer or simply viewed the composer from afar, one occasionally comes upon a nugget worth saving.

The present volume, therefore, was planned with several goals in mind, none of which included trying to annotate everything ever written about Jean Sibelius. Instead, the generic title of "guide," a person or a book whose chief purpose is to show the way, has been taken to heart. Those who want to investigate aspects of Sibelius's music or simply to read and learn more about the composer must travel the paths for themselves. Of foremost importance for undertaking such a journey, however, is the identification of essential literature that might serve as a starting point. Perhaps equally consequential is knowing which items are reliable, or scholarly, in the sense of being carefully researched through consultation of original documents, and which are of value for being impressions by contemporaries or opinions symptomatic of Sibelius's wider reputation. And grateful is the traveller who discovers that material in Finnish or Swedish, Finland's two official but little-known languages, may also be found in one of the more familiar European tongues, which rather often is the case.

These needs shaped the contents of the present book and led to the following limitations:

1) The *Guide* contains only published material, with the year 1994 serving as the *terminus ad quem*. A single exception has been made to this delimitation: the group of studies published as *The Sibelius Companion* that appeared in 1996. Because this volume represents the state of research as of 1994 and also contains so much new and important information, it was considered essential to include. As for manuscript materials and archival documents, their sheer quantity and the present condition of Sibelius research, in many ways still in its infancy, make it impractical to list primary sources. When inventories to these materials have been published, however, they are cited.

2) No attempt has been made to locate and annotate the seemingly endless numbers of Sibelius-related articles in newspapers and magazines that have appeared throughout the world. Devising parameters for articles to be included has been particularly troublesome. In the United States, pieces in such magazines as *Time* and the old and fondly remembered *Life* would not be considered appropriate for a bibliography like the present one. While of interest if one is casting a wide net for the writing of a reception history, these types of magazines are current-events publications, not scholarly journals. Finland, however, has a long and respected tradition whereby scholars publish new findings in newspapers and illustrated magazines such as *Suomen Kuvalehti* (Finland's equivalent to *Life*). The articles appear without supporting notes or bibliography, but they may contain essential material and significant illustrations, including facsimiles of music

manuscripts and letters. Although later the author may bring out the research in an academic publication, this does not always happen, with the result that important information exists in weeklies or popular magazines that is unavailable elsewhere.

Nor is the dividing line between scholarly and journalistic as clear as in the United States. Some of Finland's musicological periodicals also publish articles without documenting notes. And there has been no system of what is known in American academic circles as "refereed journals," whereby articles are vetted by an independent authority before being accepted for publication (although since 1995 *Musiikki* has implemented this system). While the setup may seem all too casual to the American observer, it has the great advantage of avoiding delays in communicating new findings and of cultivating a wide audience for musical matters.

In order to make manageable a task that has threatened to grow out of all proportion, the American periodicals inventoried here have been limited to those considered learned music journals. Current-events and non-music magazines, from *Musical America* to *The New Yorker*, and performing media journals (*Clarinet*, *The Strad*) have been excluded. Among Finland's publications, house journals such as Helsinki University Library's *Helsingin yliopiston kirjaston tiedotuslehti* and Sibelius Academy's *Sibis* and *Finaali* have been omitted. No independent articles from any newspapers have been annotated unless they happen also to be published in book or journal form. The reader will, however, find printed guides to Finland's newspapers and magazines; anthologies of newspaper reviews and magazine essays in various languages when they include a substantial number of writings about Sibelius; important articles from the more popular Finnish music journals such as *Rondo*; and annotations of all kinds of journal issues devoted wholly or in significant part to Jean Sibelius. Yet there remains enough further reading for a lifetime in one's favorite armchair. Those undaunted by the nearly fifty-page list of journals and magazines, both music and non-music, in more than half a dozen languages whose Sibelius-related contents are analyzed in Blum's still valuable *Bibliography* will find there an ideal place to begin.

3) While doctoral dissertations have been considered within the scope of the *Guide*, papers written either as master's theses or for the

European degree of licentiate and for university seminars have been omitted. Over the last century, Helsinki University has been the most important sponsor of this kind of research on Sibelius, almost all of it in Finnish; for a list of the resulting titles, the reader should consult Erkki Salmenhaara's "Bibliografia: Sibelius-tutkimusta Helsingin yliopistossa" [Bibliography: Sibelius Research at Helsinki University]. *Musiikki* 20 (1990): 34–38.

4) Also omitted are reviews of concerts and recordings, although in continuation of Blum's excellent model, book reviews since 1965 have been mentioned wherever possible. There are no armchair concert guides with chatty program notes or program notes of any kind; no liner notes to recordings, publishers' or auction catalogues, letters to editors, congratulatory birthday letters, popular accounts of visits to Sibelius, reports of Sibelius festivals or the Sibelius Violin Competition, or obituaries. Blum has already provided a guide to much of this kind of material in his *Bibliography*.

5) The *Guide* does not provide a catalogue of the compositions of Sibelius, either in manuscript or printed editions. These needs are soon to be filled by a thematic catalogue of the works of Jean Sibelius (described on pp. 7–8). Meanwhile, a preliminary work list (no. 13) is readily available on both sides of the Atlantic as well as a reasonably up-to-date chronological list of the works (see no. 18).

6) Language has helped to define the present parameters: the *Guide* contains studies published in English, Finnish, Swedish, Danish, Norwegian, German, French, Italian, and, in the case of monographs on Sibelius, in Czech, Hungarian, Portuguese, and Romanian. Excluded, however, are items in Russian, Estonian, and Japanese, in each of which is a growing body of Sibelius literature. Nevertheless, the user will find some of the best of East European and Estonian research, since many of these studies have been translated into one of the eight main languages within the scope of the *Guide*.

Every effort has been made to examine each item personally. However, despite the work having been carried on in five of the best libraries for Sibelius studies in the world and over a period of as many years, some items, dissertations in particular, have remained stubbornly elusive. Rather than omit a source that may be quite valuable for those who can find it, the bibliographical information is included with a note indicating that the annotation has been adapted from elsewhere.

Even with the exclusions, the *Guide* has swelled to more than 700 entries. Since a given entry often describes multiple editions of a book, different versions of an article, or revised translations, more than 1,000 sources are in fact represented. As anyone who has had the blind courage to compile this kind of bibliography will surely concede, sanity's touchstone is the search for the illuminating trends and clarifying features about a subject area. One of the first lessons to be learned from the Sibelius literature is that long before recycling became the watchword of environmentalists, the practice was widely used by those writing about Sibelius. Cecil Gray borrowed from Rosa Newmarch and Karl Ekman, Jr., who, in turn, had borrowed from Erik Furuhjelm and Karl Flodin, all of whom are used by Constant Lambert and Olin Downes. The recycling habit has been hard to break, infecting even the present scholarly climate, and in fact is a symptom of a deeper problem. As one author observed: "There is no lack of biographies, studies, and analytical notes [on Sibelius], but they are all as uncritical as were the pioneer books on Wagner. 'A scholarly counterblast' is an expression which has rung agreeably in my ears since I was a boy. Something of the kind is badly needed in the case of Sibelius" (entry no. 313). Although Robert Lorenz was writing in 1939 about England, his assessment described equally well the international situation at the time his article was published. While even then the Sibelius literature existed in great quantity, its quality was, and is, another matter. For indeed, the counterblast Lorenz called for did take place, but largely, and sadly, without the scholarly element.

Various explanations may be offered for the want of discrimination and the failure to include critical apparatus in research and writings about Sibelius. With any individual the passage of time allows a more balanced perspective, and Sibelius's astonishingly long life postponed measured evaluation for more than half the twentieth century. Meanwhile, the long "silence of Järvenpää," the thirty years seemingly devoid of creative achievement at the end of the composer's life, served to confound the critics and provoke reckless speculation. Within Finland, a land with a population of only some five million people, making disparaging remarks about a fellow countryman poses certain difficulties. Not only do such words come back to haunt the speaker (of the "people who live in glass houses should not cast stones" variety), worse, such pronouncements have sometimes been regarded as unpatriotic in a land whose identity and independence have come at an appallingly high price. Outside Finland the country's geographic isolation, poorly understood cultural differences, and barriers posed by not just one, but two difficult languages, neither of which is commonly taught in academic environments in the twentieth century, have contributed to the many imaginative interpretations and facile judgments of the composer and his music.

The tone of much of the Sibelius literature has also been influenced by Finland's political and economic history. The ravages of World War II (known in Finland as the Winter War and the Continuation War), which left thousands of Finns homeless, plunged the country into debt, and scarred far too many souls, prompted an entire generation to value, even revere, Sibelius with an overwhelming pride. His music was a bulwark against despair, an authentically Finnish constant for a people who, in the struggle to preserve the nation, had to endure great brutality and sorrow. Much, one is even tempted to say "all," of the early Finnish literature about Sibelius was thus invested with an attitude of worshipful respect toward a venerated figure. When, not long after the war, American professor Harold E. Johnson published a biography about the composer (no. 159) in which he not only refrained from calling Sibelius by the adulatory title "Master" but also found fault with him, Finns were shocked and outraged. It was as if the very essence of being Finnish were under attack.

It is only in the past decade that fresh and serious research has emerged on Sibelius. The landmarks, all by leading Finnish scholars, include the completion of a major biography (no. 175), the first to be fully researched and the first to portray Sibelius as a believable human being rather than a larger-than-life Nordic hero; the meticulously assembled catalogue of the large collection of Sibelius's music manuscripts now in the Helsinki University Library (no. 21); and the undertaking of a thematic catalogue. These tools form the basis for the tremendous tasks yet to be completed. Especially needed is an edition of the complete works in order to make available the many compositions no longer in print. Also deserving immediate attention is the inventory and publication of Sibelius's enormous correspondence and the location and consultation of essential archival records.

It has come as something of a personal revelation that, despite the widely held conception of the modern world as a global village, geographical distances, cultural divergences, and especially languages even today create serious obstacles to intellectual endeavor. Full knowledge and understanding of music and musicians, as in other human undertakings, are victories hard won. With a composer and a culture as complex as Sibelius's and Finland's, opportunities for disseminating misinformation are rife. All too often writers make errors in such basic matters as the composer's name (sometimes still mistakenly given in English-language publications as "Jan," never a correct form of Sibelius's first name), and problems compound from there.

Finland's linguistic history further muddles the situation. I am often asked, "What language is spoken in Finland?" To this obvious question, there was not always an obvious answer, since during the nineteenth century many educated Finns spoke Swedish, Sibelius's mother tongue. Today, however, the Swedish-speaking portion of Finland's population has declined to approximately six percent, and the majority of citizens speak Finnish. If both languages are necessary for the serious scholar, the music lover, too, needs to be aware of their implications. Many of the composer's works have titles in two or more languages: the tone poem known in English as *Oceanides* does not sound too different in Swedish, *Okeaniderna*, but its Finnish title is *Aallottaret*. And not everyone will recognize that *Tuonelan joutsen* is the famous *Swan of Tuonela*. Many important contemporaries who figured prominently in Sibelius's life and, thus, in the literature about him were also known by two, often very different-sounding, names. One example can stand for many: Sibelius's son-in-law, the conductor Jussi Jalas, who was born Blomstedt. The reason for this situation, often so confusing to the outsider, is that, in the late nineteenth and early twentieth centuries, many families converted their Swedish names to Finnish ones in the effort to establish an unambiguously Finnish national identity. Even today in Finland many cities and towns have names in both languages, some of which are translations, some adaptations from one language into the other, and some genuinely different. It is easy to recognize

Helsinki in Helsingfors, but it is less obvious that Åbo is Turku, Björneborg is Pori, or Träskända, Järvenpää.

The inconsistencies thus created are an American copy-editor's nightmare. More worrisome are the opportunities for misunderstanding a great composer. Nor is the condition eased by the difficulty, sometimes insuperable for anyone beyond the age of two, of learning the Finnish language, one of the most obscure and challenging in the world. In this book most of Sibelius's works are mentioned first by an accepted English title followed by the name, usually in Finnish or Swedish, that Sibelius assigned to the composition. Some works, however, are so well known by their generic titles (symphonies and quartets) or by their original names (*En saga*) that a translation would sound ridiculous. Cities in Finland are cited by their Finnish names in the text, but the bibliographic citation gives the city name as shown on the title page of the book or monograph. The table on p. xxiii gives both Finnish and Swedish names for the cities mentioned.

Alphabetization poses another kind of problem. The Swedish alphabet has the letters å, ä, and ö, with the latter two also appearing in Finnish; in both languages, these letters come at the end of the alphabet. In the present *Guide*, however, these letters have had to be integrated into the English alphabet as if they were ordinary a's and o's, with their differences to Scandinavian readers ignored. Capitalization of titles, however, follows the rules of the language in which the title appears. Library of Congress (LC) classification numbers and International Standard Book Numbers (ISBN) are cited when these are available.

For those unfamiliar with Finland's publishing houses, it should be mentioned that the publishing company known as Werner Söderström Osakeyhtiö, today sometimes abbreviated to WSOY, is a different enterprise from "Söderström & Co." Founded by Werner Söderström in Porvoo as one company, the firm split in 1891. Since that time, Werner Söderström Osakeyhtiö has mainly published books in Finnish, while Söderström & Co. chiefly publishes Swedish-language texts, and the bibliographic citation cannot be shortened to "Söderström" without creating a certain confusion.

An annotated bibliography is only a tool and surely belongs among a library's more prosaic items. Yet there is clearly a need to build a bridge across the gap that currently exists between Finland and elsewhere for the study and understanding of Sibelius both as a man and as a composer, for investigating his music, and for appreciating his country's rich cultural heritage. Such building is the ultimate construction to which library tools can be put, and to this end, somewhat more historical information about authors and context has been offered in some annotations than might otherwise be necessary.

Unfortunately, a scholar's homework is never done. Even as the *Guide* goes to press, I am haunted by the feeling that important sources may have been overlooked, excluded, or perhaps misrepresented. Yet if the greater tasks of research on Jean Sibelius are to be facilitated, a point of publication has to be reached. Perhaps those who use the *Guide* will contribute to these tasks by making suggestions for additions, corrections, and improvements. Meanwhile, the volume has already benefited from the help offered by many individuals on both sides of the Atlantic. The work has been conducted in several of the world's major research libraries: the Sibelius Museum in Turku, Helsinki University Library, the Sibelius Academy Library in Helsinki, and the British Museum in London as well as the less widely known but truly excellent library of the University of Georgia in Athens. The University of Georgia Research Foundation has provided support during various phases of this project as has the University's School of Music under the expert direction of Richard Graham. Support has also come from the Sibelius Academy in Helsinki.

It is a pleasure to acknowledge these institutions and the people in each, many of whom contributed ideas, conducted special searches, checked translations, and provided answers to countless questions. In Athens, Georgia, it has been music librarians Bill Coscarelli and Kevin Kelly who have borne the brunt of endless requests, always with good humor and stellar results. Susan Morris and Virginia Feher in the University of Georgia's Interlibrary Loan Department provided exemplary service and helped me to solve more than one bibliographical mystery. At the Sibelius Museum in Turku, Kitty von Wright suffered repeated interruptions, sent instant faxes on demand, and turned up piece after piece of valued information. Kitty, together with Ilpo Tolvas and Barbro Kvist, transformed the tedium of the work in the "dungeon," the tiny room filled with Sibeliana in the bowels of the archive, into some of my happiest experiences. Without the help of the large and good-natured staff at the Helsinki University Library, I would no doubt still be wandering round and round Carl Engel's glorious halls in utter confusion, but astonishingly, each and every one of the librarians there at one time or another has contributed to making the complicated byways of this historic institution steadily yield up its treasures. And the Sibelius Academy's librarian Irmeli Koskimies repeatedly took time to help, initiating me into the Academy's library system and locating sources I had nearly given up all hope of finding.

There are also the numerous individuals who, by being just a telephone call away, graciously gave of their time and knowledge. Helen Svensson at the publishing house today called Schildts (formerly Holger Schildt Förlag), Roger Lindberg of the venerable firm of Fazer (nowadays Warner/Chappell), and Marianne Bargum of Söderström & Co. kindly and informatively answered all my telephoned questions. Tuulikki Tammenaho at Werner Söderströms Osakeyhtiö unperturbedly endured an hour of surprise questioning about the history of her company when I burst into her office one wintry afternoon.

Some peerless souls have suffered my questioning, not once but repeatedly. George C. Schoolfield patiently set me straight time and again on matters ranging from history and literature to publishing and *koskenkorva*. Gitta and Carl Henning, Mårten Ringbom, and William Copeland contributed materials and ideas and discussed thorny issues with perfect frankness and equally perfect clarity. Maria Liisa Saarilammi corrected many of the Finnish translations and patiently nurtured my faltering Finnish-language skills. Carmen Tawaststjerna did the same for my Swedish while proving to be an inexhaustible source of inspiration, knowledge, and support. Over and over again Seija Lappalainen and Erkki Salmenhaara willingly provided materials, answered questions, and gave absolutely invaluable advice and instruction.

For the second time Geraldine Bergius has done yeoman's service in typesetting a manuscript of mine. Her superlative skills and charming Irish humor have made the production of the camera-ready copy, which for me would otherwise have been an onerous task, a real delight instead.

Erkki Salmenhaara together with Fabian Dahlström read the typed manuscript in its entirety; their keen criticisms and much-appreciated corrections have profited me personally and greatly improved the bibliography. And over all the years of research, it has been Fabian Dahlström and Kari Kilpeläinen who have freely shared their own findings, listened and guided through periods of frustration, and provided encouragement and belief in the worth of the endeavor. Such actions go beyond collegiality to deepest friendship and offer reassuring evidence that the building of the bridge is already well under way.

Glenda Dawn Goss
Helsinki, Fall, 1996

Cities in Finland Mentioned in the Guide

Finnish Name	*Swedish Name*
Helsinki	Helsingfors
Järvenpää	Träskända
Loviisa	Lovisa
Oulu	Uleåborg
Pori	Björneborg
Porvoo	Borgå
Turku	Åbo
Vaasa	Vasa

Jean Sibelius

I
Reference Works

In this section the reader will find the sources that provide the keys for entering into Sibelius's world: bibliographies of literature about the composer, lists of his compositions, ready reference entries in dictionaries and encyclopedias, and means of locating musical recordings.

In the realm of bibliographies, the field of Sibelius studies is rather well supplied, although the best remains Blum's quite irreplaceable 1965 list (no. 1). Most of the items given below are devoted specifically to Sibelius, and several are readily available in American libraries. The scholar, however, will want to know about some additional tools, which are not devoted to Sibelius alone, are not widely known outside Finland, and in some cases can be used only in that country. One is the bibliography compiled for the large project known as The Music History of Finland (Suomen Musiikin Historia) by Erkki Salmenhaara and Seija Lappalainen in 1993. In the form of an enormous database, the bibliography can be searched on computer but only in Helsinki at the Finnish Music Information Center. Another is Finland's national bibliography, *Suomen kirjallisuus/Finlands litteratur*, ongoing for more than a century. An essential verification and finding tool for books published in Finland, the national bibliography is presently available on CD-ROM as well as in monthly catalogues and annual volumes.

A special category within these bibliographies is occupied by guides to Sibelius materials in the United States. The great popularity of

Sibelius's music with American audiences, the immigration of many Finns to North America, and the dedicated efforts of certain Americans in Sibelius's behalf, from scholars like Harold E. Johnson to conductor Antonia Brico and music critic Olin Downes, are some of the factors that account for a rich array of Sibeliana in the United States. While these sources are listed in their own section below, articles that report on the state of Sibelius research are integrated into the general list of bibliographies.

* * *

A. Bibliographies of Literature on Sibelius

See also no. 201

1. Blum, Fred. *Jean Sibelius: An International Bibliography on the Occasion of the Centennial Celebrations, 1965*. Detroit Studies in Music Bibliography, no. 8. Detroit: Information Service, 1965. xxi, 114 p. ML134.S49B6

Compiled in honor of Sibelius's 100th birthday, Blum's bibliography—international in scope, partially annotated, and with an introductory essay—represents the state of Sibelius research in the 1960s. More than 1,400 sources are cited, including books devoted wholly or in part to the composer, analytical guides, phonorecords, dictionary and encyclopedia articles, and publishers' catalogues. Blum did not know Finnish, yet he created a tool that has remained indispensable. His bibliography is especially valuable for such special features as listing Sibelius articles within journals (music and non-music journals, scholarly and popular) and for including reviews of books, recordings, and concerts.

Rev.: *Sibelius-Mitteilungen* (February 1966): 10; *Die Musikforschung* 22 (1969): 100.

2. Dahlström, Fabian. "Sibelius Research." In *The Sibelius Companion*, 297–322. Edited by Glenda Dawn Goss. Westport, Conn.: Greenwood, 1996. ML410.S54S53 1996 ISBN 0-313-28393-1

The most extensive and up-to-date survey available of the field of Sibelius studies and an assessment of the state of research at the end of 1994. The chapter also includes the only English-language discussion of the history of music printing in Finland and a frank look at Sibelius's waffling in the matter of his opus numbers. Followed by a selected bibliography.

3. Hemming, Aarre. *Luettelo Jean Sibeliusta ja hänen teoksiaan käsittelevästä kirjallisuudesta* [Catalogue of Literature about Jean Sibelius and His Compositions]. Helsinki: Sibelius Society, 1958. 10 p. ML410.S54H5 1958

Commissioned by the Sibelius Society of Finland, this bibliography was intended primarily for foreigners; most articles in Finnish-language periodicals are therefore excluded. While the list of 165 items was greatly expanded by Fred Blum's bibliography (no. 1), Hemming's work is notable as an early attempt to impose some order upon the growing Sibelius literature.

4. Ringbom, Nils-Eric. "Litteraturen om Jean Sibelius" [The Literature About Jean Sibelius]. *Svensk tidskrift för musikforskning* 24 (1942): 122–25.

The first review of the Sibelius literature, originally published in 1940 in the newspaper *Svenska Pressen*. Ringbom's view is international in scope, although he concentrates on biographical and analytical books rather than articles. His survey remains interesting for the opinions expressed about those who wrote on Sibelius.

5. Ringbom, Nils-Eric. "Die Musikforschung in Finnland seit 1940" [Music Research in Finland Since 1940]. *Acta musicologica* 31 (1959): 17–24.

A short survey (pp. 20–21) of Sibelius literature from 1940 to 1958.

6. Suhonen, Maija. "Catalogue of Sibelius Monographs 1906–1989." *Finnish Music Quarterly*, 1990, nos. 3–4: 85–91.

The chronological order of this list of monographs, which includes both published works and dissertations, brings forward by nearly a quarter of a century the volumes listed in Blum's bibliography (no. 1) and vividly illustrates the growth of Sibelius scholarship during the twentieth century.

7. Väisänen, A. O. "Sibelius tutkimusongelmana" [Sibelius as a Research Problem]. *Valvoja* 71 (1951): 60–68.

Opining the shortage of new books about Sibelius, Väisänen gives a somewhat superficial review of the research existing in 1950 while taking to task Ilmari Krohn for his programmatic analyses of Sibelius's symphonies (see no. 575). Väisänen attributes the lack of new research to the failure of the Eighth Symphony to appear, suggesting that this is the research "problem" with Sibelius.

SIBELIUS MATERIALS IN THE UNITED STATES: FINDING TOOLS

8. Albrecht, Otto Edwin. *A Census of Autograph Music Manuscripts of European Composers in American Libraries.* Philadelphia: University of Pennsylvania Press, 1953. xvii, 331 p. ML135.A2A4

A description of three Sibelius autographs, *Oceanides* (*Aallottaret*), *Swanwhite* (*Svanevit*), and *Teodora*, preserved today in the libraries of Yale University, the Library of Congress, and Stanford University, respectively.

9. Krummel, Donald W. *Resources of American Music History: A Directory of Source Materials from Colonial Times to World War II.* Urbana: University of Illinois Press, 1981. 463 p. S.v. "Sibelius." ML120.U5R47 ISBN 0-252-00828-6

Through Krummel's valuable directory the various North American libraries with primary source materials relevant to Sibelius can easily be identified. Pertinent documents range from music manuscripts and correspondence to collections of newspaper clippings and contemporary accounts of the composer's visit to the United States. Although not every American resource is included (omitted, for example, is the Sibelius clippings file in the New York Public Library for the Performing Arts Research Collections,

Lincoln Center), Krummel's is nevertheless the best guide available to American resources for Sibelius.

10. Terrell, Gisela Schlüter. *The Harold E. Johnson Jean Sibelius Collection at Butler University: A Complete Catalogue*. Indianapolis: Butler University, 1993. xii, 101 p. ML136.I5I657 1993

A catalogue of the published scores, copies of manuscripts, books, articles, reviews, and photographs collected by Harold E. Johnson, whose archive has been described as the most important Sibelius collection outside Finland.

Rev.: *Music & Letters* 75 (1994): 484; *Die Musikforschung* 47 (1994): 205–6.

* * *

B. Work Lists and Related Studies

The first list of works ever published for Jean Sibelius appeared in the periodical *Euterpe* on September 13, 1902. Since that time scholars have attempted again and again to arrive at a complete inventory of the music but without success. Nearly every biography, from Karl Ekman, Jr.'s and Cecil Gray's to Harold E. Johnson's and Ferruccio Tammaro's, has included a list of compositions. Sibelius himself contributed to some of these lists, but he seems to have muddied the waters considerably by withholding works and even changing opus numbers (see nos. 2 and 22).

In 1982, the bibliographical circumstances began to change dramatically. The Sibelius family donated most of the composer's surviving music manuscripts to Helsinki University Library with the stipulation that the material be inventoried and classified. The resulting catalogue (no. 21), completed by Kari Kilpeläinen in 1991, provides the first comprehensive record of primary sources ever compiled for Sibelius. The task accomplished by Kilpeläinen has, in turn, advanced immeasurably the work on the first thematic catalogue for Sibelius, entitled *Jean Sibelius: Thematisches-Bibliographisches Verzeichnis seiner Werke*, being prepared by Fabian Dahlström and scheduled for publication before the end of the century by Breitkopf & Härtel. When this ambitious and sorely-needed volume is at last available, scholars will have another tool of paramount importance. The *Catalogue* will give not only thematic identifications and locations for Sibelius's music, including newly discovered works, it will also provide extensive bibliographical references and citations from such primary documents as the composer's letters to his publishers. The catalogue by Kilpeläinen and Dahlström's forthcoming work render all present work lists out of date. Nevertheless, older lists have been included here for the distinctive, and sometimes still worthwhile, perspectives they can provide. Work lists within biographies and lengthy articles are not annotated separately, but the reader will find them mentioned under "Selected Music Dictionaries and Encyclopedias" and "Biographies."

* * *

11. Andersson, Otto. "Jean Sibelius' verk: tabellarisk översikt" [Jean Sibelius's Work: Tabular Survey]. *Tidning för musik* 5 (1915): 184–90.

One of the first lists of Sibelius's works and the most complete available in 1915, although the compiler acknowledges that many early chamber compositions had to be omitted for lack of information. The table is organized chronologically, beginning in 1888. Within each year pieces are listed by genre, the categories being symphonic music (including marches and dances); choral music, melodramas, and dramatic works; solo songs with piano; *a cappella* choral works; and chamber, piano, and miscellaneous compositions.

12. Dahlström, Fabian. "Working toward the Thematic-bibliographical Catalogue of Jean Sibelius." *Fontes artis musicae* 40 (1993): 41–46.

The editor of the first Sibelius thematic catalogue explains the difficulties of the task, offers insight into the nature of the available primary sources, and assesses the state of Sibelius research.

13. Dahlström, Fabian. *The Works of Jean Sibelius*. Helsinki: Sibelius Society, 1987. 154 p. ML134.S49D3 1987 ISBN 951-99833-3-3

A preliminary work list compiled as part of the larger project of creating a thematic catalogue. Although by its author's own testimony the list is out of date, it has nevertheless provided an extremely useful reference tool, establishing a systematic means of classifying Sibelius's music, supplying instrumentation and first performance data, and furnishing such information as copyright holder, authors of texts, and titles by which works are known in various languages.

Rev.: *Finnish Music Quarterly*, 1987, nos. 3–4: 70–71.

14. De Lerma, Dominique-René. *A Register of Basic Conventional Titles and Publications Sources for Works of Jean Sibelius, 1865–1957.* Explorations in Music Librarianship, An Irregular Series of Occasional Papers for Members of the Midwest Chapter, Music Library Association. Kent, Ohio: M.L.A., 1967. 21 p. ML111.E9 no. 2

Compiled as a verification tool for classifying Sibelius's music at Indiana University School of Music, the *Register* long served a wider audience as a means of clarifying title translations from Swedish or Finnish, languages not widely known among scholars, librarians, or musicians. Today its usefulness has largely been supplanted by the more accurate indices in the Dahlström, Kilpeläinen, and Goss volumes (nos. 13, 21, and 18).

15. *Finsk biografisk handbok* [Finnish Biographical Handbook]. Edited by Tor Carpelan. Helsingfors: G. W. Edlunds Förlag, 1903. 2 vols. S.v. "Sibelius." CT1220.F5

The Sibelius entry, which includes a biographical summary and an evaluation of the composer's importance in Finland, is notable for publishing one of the earliest Sibelius work lists. Many compositions are assigned dates, although subsequent research has established a more accurate chronological picture.

16. "Förteckning öfver Jean Sibelius' kompositioner" [List of Jean Sibelius's Compositions]. *Euterpe*, September 13, 1902: 8–9.

Important for being the first inventory ever made of Sibelius's music. The works are organized by genre with dates provided for some, but not all, compositions.

17. "Giovanni Sibelius." *Bollettino bibliografico musicale* 7 (March 1932): 5–30.

A work list organized by genre and mentioning publisher, preceded by a biographical essay.

18. Goss, Glenda Dawn. "Chronology of the Works of Jean Sibelius." In *The Sibelius Companion*, 323–392. Edited by Glenda Dawn Goss. Westport, Conn.: Greenwood, 1996. ML410.S54S53 1996 ISBN 0-313-28393-1

Although most Sibelius work lists are arranged by genre, this inventory attempts to arrive at a chronological view of Sibelius's creativity. Certain to be revised as more precise datings come to light.

19. Hirsch, Ferdinand. "Das Werk Jean Sibelius' im Leipziger Musikverlag Breitkopf & Härtel" [Jean Sibelius's Work in the Leipzig Publishing House Breitkopf & Härtel]. *Musik und Gesellschaft* 15 (1965): 818–20.

List arranged by opus number of the Sibelius compositions published by Breitkopf & Härtel. Preceded by a short essay on the relationship of the composer to his publisher.

20. Johnson, Harold E. "Jean Sibelius." *La musica* 4 (1966): 365–80.

A short life and works account in Italian, primarily important for the extensive work list which represented the most complete and accurate compiled by any biographer at the time it was published.

21. Kilpeläinen, Kari. *The Jean Sibelius Musical Manuscripts at Helsinki University Library, A Complete Catalogue.* Wiesbaden: Breitkopf & Härtel, 1991. 487 p. ML134.S49H44 1991 ISBN 3-7651-0270-9

An inventory of the largest single collection of Sibelius music manuscripts in the world. Most of the materials came from Sibelius's home, Ainola, and include not only fair copies but also works at various stages of creation. The collection affords a unique opportunity to evaluate the composer's working methods, and the catalogue admirably reflects the nature and the importance of the materials. This book establishes the first reliable list of Sibelius autographs and contains a wealth of additional information, from performing forces and opus numbers to lists of juvenilia, student works, and sketches. Since its appearance in 1991, it has provided an essential tool for all subsequent work on the composer's music.

Rev.: *Musikrevy* 46 (1991): 319; *Die Musikforschung* 45 (1992): 432; *MLA Notes* 48 (1992): 1229–30.

22. Kilpeläinen, Kari. *Tutkielmia Jean Sibeliuksen käsikirjoituksista* [Research on Jean Sibelius's Manuscripts]. Studia Musicologica Universitatis Helsingiensis 3. Helsinki: Helsinki University, Department of Musicology, 1991. 303 p. ML410.S54K55 1991 ISBN 951-45-6138-4

The only source (pp. 160–66) to provide descriptions of the different work lists compiled at different times by Sibelius. In connection with these lists, the author considers the question of Sibelius's variable opus numbers. The full study is annotated as no. 418.

23. Layton, Robert. "Orders of Merit." *Books from Finland* 25 (1991): 234–35.

A short discussion of the confusion surrounding Sibelius's opus numbers based on the detailed and careful work of Kari Kilpeläinen (no. 21). For a fuller discussion of this matter in English, see no. 2.

24. Müller, Franz Karl. "Gesamtverzeichnis der Werke von Jean Sibelius" [Complete Catalogue of the Works of Jean Sibelius]. *Österreichische Musikzeitschrift* 12 (1957): 390–94.

A list of works by opus number to which date and publisher have been added. Compiled with Sibelius's assistance between 1952 and 1956 but not "complete."

25. Poroila, Heikki. *Yhtenäistetty Jean Sibelius: Teosten yhtenäistettyjen nimekkeiden ohjeluettelo* [Uniformity {for} Jean

Sibelius: Guide to Standard Names of the Works.] Suomen musiikkikirjastoyhdistyksen julkaisusarja 13. Helsinki: Suomen Musiikkikirjastoyhdistys, 1989. 93 p. 2d edition, 1996.

The various Finnish, Swedish, German, English, and occasionally Danish and Latin names by which Sibelius's works are known have long created confusion for non-Finns. One effort to provide clarity was made by Dominique-René de Lerma in 1967 (no. 14). Poroila provides a more recent checklist, organized by works with opus number, followed by works without opus numbers and lost works. The catalogue is illustrated, contains a short annotated bibliography, and has an index by title, in which, however, not all names are represented in all their languages.

26. Solanterä, Lauri. *The Works of Jean Sibelius*. Helsinki: R. E. Westerlund, 1955. 63 p. ML134.S49W5

Compiled in honor of Sibelius's ninetieth birthday as a commercial catalogue for Helsinki publisher R. E. Westerlund. Including both published and unpublished compositions and organized by opus number, the catalogue gives instrumentation, date, and publisher where appropriate. Subsequent research has made this catalogue largely obsolete.

27. Tanzberger, Ernst. *Jean Sibelius: Werkverzeichnis* [Jean Sibelius: Work Catalogue]. Wiesbaden: Breitkopf & Härtel, [1962]. 27 p. ML134.S49T4

A list with music examples and thus the closest to a thematic catalogue that currently exists. For full annotation, see no. 174.

* * *

C. Selected Music Dictionaries and Encyclopedias

For most people information about Sibelius will be readily accessible chiefly through dictionaries and encyclopedias. Because so many new facts about the composer's life and music have come to light just in the last decade, very few such entries will be completely accurate. Almost all, in fact, are adaptations of material found elsewhere. Nevertheless, these sources remain useful, not only because they supply ready reference but also for the bibliographies, work lists, facsimiles of music, and various kinds of illustrations they often contain. And entries in which Sibelius's achievement is evaluated or treated historically allow the reader to gauge the composer's wider reputation at a given point in time. Indeed, for those interested in *Rezeptionsgeschichte*, a survey of the composer's image through all the editions of a single music dictionary such as *Grove's* or *Riemann's Musik Lexikon* should prove instructive. Such a survey, however, is not the goal here, and only Sibelius's appearance in the most recent editions of selected music dictionaries and encyclopedias will be found below.

* * *

28. *Baker's Biographical Dictionary of Musicians*. 8th ed. Revised and edited by Nicolas Slonimsky. New York: Schirmer, 1992. S.v. "Sibelius." ML105.B16 1992 ISBN 0-02-872415-1

Summary of Sibelius's life and works based on previously published accounts and written in Slonimsky's inimitable style. Although certain "facts" need revising in light of current research, some first-performance dates are given as well as a bibliography of selected sources. An evaluation of the composer reveals little sympathy with his innovations: he is viewed primarily as one of the last representatives of nineteenth-century nationalistic romanticism.

29. Carpelan, Tor. *Finsk biografisk handbok*. Helsinki: G. W. Edlunds Förlag, 1903. S.v. "Sibelius." CT1220.F5

An early, detailed discussion of the composer's ancestry together with a list of works, the latter annotated as no. 15.

30. *Enciclopedia della musica*. Milan: Ricordi, 1963–1964. 4 vols. S.v. "Sibelius," by Vincenzo Terenzio. ML100.E45

A substantial entry that gives consideration to the oft-neglected stage music and emphasizes the North as Sibelius's source of inspiration. Illustrated with a half-page portrait and the composer's signature and supplied with a work list and an expansive bibliography of books in six languages.

31. *Great Soviet Encyclopedia.* New York: Macmillan; London: Collier, Macmillan, 1973–1983. 31 vols. Translation of 3d edition of *Bol'shaia sovetskaia entsiklopedia*. AE5.G68

An excellent source for a pre-Gorbachev, Soviet perspective on Sibelius and the music of Finland generally. For all relevant entries, the reader must consult the index. The main entry, in volume 23 (1976), written by M. A. Vachnadze, author of a Russian-language Sibelius biography, emphasizes the composer's patriotism and the local color of his music. The bibliography is short but useful for its Russian-language references.

32. Honegger, Marc. *Dictionnaire de la musique: Les hommes et leurs oeuvres.* New edition. Paris: Bordes, 1986. 2 vols. S.v. "Sibelius." ML100.D65 ISBN 2-04-016327-1. An edition published in 1993 was not available for examination.

Brief summary of the life, a selected list of works, and a bibliography together with a short, French-orientated discussion of the music (*Tapiola*, for instance, is described as "orchestral impressionism"). Although Honegger's entry is short, his is a great improvement over the treatment afforded Sibelius in another respected French dictionary, Fasquelle's *Encyclopédie de la musique*, in 1961. There the composer is given fewer than twenty lines, some containing factual errors, and only two bibliographical references, one of which is Leibowitz's odious pamphlet *Sibelius, le plus mauvais compositeur du monde* (no. 287).

33. *International Cyclopedia of Music and Musicians.* 11th ed. Edited by Bruce Bohle. New York: Dodd, Mead & Co., 1985. S.v. "Jean Sibelius," by Olin Downes. ML100.I57 1985 ISBN 0-396-08412-5

Sibelius's entry in the famous *Cyclopedia* originated by Oscar Thompson was written by Sibelius's most ardent champion in the United States. The same essay, beginning with the description of the composer as "a lonely and towering figure in the music of the early Twentieth Century . . . " and organized into "Background and Early Years," "The Nationalist," "The Symphonist," "Lesser Works," and "Evolution," has appeared in every one of the

Cyclopedia's editions since 1938. That nearly thirty years after his death in 1955 Downes was still regarded as a Sibelius authority is in part a testimony to how little research has been available on the composer in English. Downes provided a catalogue of works based, as he acknowledges, on the material found in the biographies by Cecil Gray and Karl Ekman, Jr.

34. Layton, Robert. "Jean Sibelius." In *The New Grove Turn of the Century Masters: Janáček, Mahler, Strauss, Sibelius*, 271–313. London: Macmillan, 1985; New York: Norton, 1985. 324 p. ML390.N467 1985 ISBN 0-393-01694-3

For annotation, see no. 36.

35. *Die Musik in Geschichte und Gegenwart.* Edited by Friedrich Blume. Kassel: Bärenreiter, 1949–1967. 17 vols. S.v. "Sibelius," by Nils-Eric Ringbom. ML100.M92

An article authoritatively written by one of Sibelius's biographers but, in the unfortunate MGG house style, with its long work list and extensive bibliography crammed into an astonishingly small space. There are facsimiles from Symphonies no. 1 and 6 (the latter presented as Tafel 33, a few pages beyond the article's end) and a photograph of Furtwängler visiting the composer at Ainola. The volume with the Sibelius entry in the new edition of this encyclopedia has not yet appeared.

36. *The New Grove Dictionary of Music and Musicians.* Edited by Stanley Sadie. London: Macmillan, 1980. 20 vols. S.v. "Jean Sibelius" by Robert Layton. ML100.N48 ISBN 0-333-23111-2

A useful overview of the main events in Sibelius's life and work in the familiar house style of *The New Grove*, including work list, bibliography, and illustrations, by an author well known for his many contributions to Sibelius studies. Corrections and additions to the essay may be found in the article of the same title in *The New Grove Turn of the Century Masters* (no. 34), in which Sibelius is grouped with Mahler, Strauss, and Janáček.

37. *The New Oxford Companion to Music.* Edited by Denis Arnold. Oxford: Oxford University Press, 1984. [Corrected edition.] 2 vols. S.v. "Sibelius," by Robert Layton. ML100.N5 1984 ISBN 0-19-311316-3

An expertly written summary, giving important activities in Sibelius's life and a fair and favorable evaluation of his achievement, which is described as consistently fresh in approach to form and innovative in orchestration.

38. *Otavan iso musiikki-tietosanakirja* [Otava's Large Music Encyclopedia]. Helsinki: Otava, 1979. 5 vols. S.v. "Sibelius," by Erik Tawaststjerna. ISBN 951-1-02380-2 (whole work); 951-1-05295-0 (vol. 5)

Similar to the same author's Sibelius article in *Sohlmans Musiklexikon* (no. 42), this essay by Sibelius's admired Finnish biographer is distinguished by its extensive discussion of the music and numerous music examples. Together with a work list and bibliography, there is a facsimile of a letter from Sibelius to Otava written in 1892 selling the rights to the seven Runeberg songs, op. 13.

39. Ranta, Sulho, ed. *Suomen säveltäjiä: Puolentoista vuosisadan ajalta* [Composers of Finland: From the Time of One and a Half Centuries Ago]. Helsinki: Werner Söderström Osakeyhtiö, 1945. S.v. "Sibelius." A later edition, edited by Einari Marvia, appeared in 2 vols., 1965. ML106.F6M4

Both editions were dedicated to Sibelius. In the earlier, the tone of the main entry (pp. 245–72) is set by the well-known quotation from Cecil Gray describing Sibelius as the greatest symphonist since Beethoven. Along with a biographical summary and general discussion of the works, the article includes many illustrations, both serious and humorous. The 1965 edition has even more iconographical material, and the discussion gives emphasis to the 1890s. A 1995 edition, which appeared after the time frame set by the *Guide*, includes a completely revised and authoritative entry on Sibelius written by the knowledgeable editor, Erkki Salmenhaara.

40. *Riemann Musik Lexikon.* 12th revised edition. Edited by Wilibald Gurlitt. Mainz: B. Schott's Söhne, 1959–1967. 3 vols. S.v. "Sibelius" in vol. 2 of *Personenteil* (1961) and vol. 2 of *Ergänzungsbande* (1975). ML100.R52 1959

Sibelius once complained in his diary that Hugo Riemann had attributed his *Kullervo* Symphony to Robert Kajanus. He may have been referring to the 9th edition (1919) of the famous *Lexikon*, revised and completed by Alfred Einstein the year after Riemann's death. There Kajanus is indeed (and correctly) said to have composed two symphonic poems, *Aino* and *Kullervo*, but no *Kullervo* is mentioned for Sibelius. These matters were rectified in the current edition, in which Sibelius receives both proper credit and a longer entry than his compatriot. The *Kullervo* Symphony is discussed, a lengthy if incomplete list of works appears, and a substantial bibliography is given. Additional bibliography may be found in the supplementary volume.

41. *Sävelten maailma 3* [Composers' World 3]. Edited by Jukka Isopuro. Helsinki: Werner Söderström Osakeyhtiö, 1992. S.v. "Jean Sibelius" by Veijo Murtomäki [in Finnish]. ISBN 951-0-15766-X

One of the most up-to-date encyclopedia articles available on Jean Sibelius, written by an authoritative author fully acquainted with Sibelius's music. The point of departure is that Sibelius is not merely a "national" composer any more than is Chopin or Verdi and, further, that Sibelius is the most significant symphonist of the century. Each symphony and each tone poem receives substantial, individual discussion. Consideration is even given to incidental music with songs and piano compositions briefly surveyed. Throughout are splendid, color illustrations, some full page, of Sibelius, his contemporaries, important biographical sites, and musical scores and programs.

42. *Sohlmans Musiklexikon* [Sohlman's Music Encyclopedia]. Stockholm: Sohlmans Förlag, 1975–1979. 5 vols. S.v. "Sibelius, Jean," by Erik Tawaststjerna. ML100.S66 1975 ISBN 91-7198-020-2

(complete work); ISBN 91-7198-025-3 (vol. 5, in which "Sibelius" is found)

A discussion of Sibelius's life in three periods (*Kalevala* romanticism, the 1890s; stylistic transition, 1900–1919; and synthesis, the 1920s) followed by a consideration of the works, organized by genre. There is a work list, a bibliography, and a short discussion of the Sibelius Society in Finland. Pages from Symphony no. 4 and *Pelléas och Mélisande* are reproduced in facsimile together with two photographs, one of the young and one of the old Sibelius.

43. *Suuri musiikkikirja: Musikkens verden teoksen mukaan suomeksi* [The Large Music Book: According to *The World of Music* in Finnish]. Edited by Tuomi Elmgren-Heinonen. Helsinki: Otava, [1960, c. 1957]. S.v. "Sibelius." ML100.E485S9 1957

An extensive article in a reference work that first appeared in Norwegian. The entry is distinguished by its many illustrations, including one of Finland's memorial Sibelius stamp, one captioned the "well-known hand with obligatory cigar," and the funeral procession from the great Church on Senate Square; a large number of quotations by writers from Erik Furuhjelm to Cecil Gray and Olin Downes; and a separate discussion of the symphonies and the Concerto for Violin, with a list of recordings for each and music examples. There is also a list of the best-known works.

44. *Suuri musiikki tietosanakirja* [Great Music Encyclopedia]. Keuruu: Weilin + Göös, 1989–1992. S.v. "Sibelius" by Erkki Salmenhaara. ML100.S844 1989 ISBN 951-35-4724-8 (complete work); 951-35-4730-2 (vol. 6)

In effect, a later edition of *Otava's Large Music Encyclopedia* (no. 38) but marketed by a different company. Because of the scope of the entire publication, the illustrated Sibelius entry has been much abbreviated by comparison. Nevertheless, it has the distinct advantage of having incorporated recent bibliographical sources, a consideration of the composer's influence, and a statement about current Sibelius research in Finland. There are also articles on the Sibelius Academy, the Sibelius Museum, the Sibelius Society, and the Sibelius Violin Competition.

45. Thompson, Kenneth. "Sibelius, Jean." In *A Dictionary of Twentieth-century Composers (1911–1971)*, 494–520. London: Faber & Faber; New York: St. Martin's Press, 1973. ML118.T5 ISBN 0-571-09002-8

Thompson reverses the usual procedure found in biographical dictionaries by concentrating on work lists and bibliography. The format is a refreshing and valuable contribution to the Sibelius literature in which musical compositions are organized chronologically and specific bibliography is cited for individual pieces. Even though recent research has altered some of the dating, the article retains its value for the bibliographic references to newspaper and popular articles not annotated in the present *Guide*.

* * *

D. Discographies

Most of the books and articles below contain discographies specifically devoted to Sibelius's music. The few exceptions have been included either because they shed light on the historical situation of Sibelius on record or because they are important sources that might otherwise go unnoticed. There are also a few studies that deal with aspects of recording the music. However, general discographic catalogues, such as the well-known *Schwann Catalog*, first issued in 1949, and its successors are not within the scope of this *Guide*.

Not surprisingly, some of the world's most important collections of recorded Sibelius exist in Finland, where technical aspects of recordings are of unsurpassed quality. The collection *Suomen äänitearkisto*, annotated as no. 60, comprises practically every Finnish recording made during the period 1901 to 1980. For those in Finland, it is possible to hear most of the numerous past performances recorded by the public radio station called Yleisradio on taped copies preserved at the Finnish Music Information Center in Helsinki. A card catalogue provides access to both old and new recordings.

Some books whose titles suggest discographies are not and they have been omitted. A case in point is Harvey Blanks's *The Golden Road: A Record-Collector's Guide to Music-Appreciation* (London: Angus & Robertson, 1968), which does not contain details of recordings but, unfortunately, does contain factual errors. To supplement the entries below, the reader is directed to pages 36–39 in Blum (no. 1) for "Representative Discographies and Indexes of Record Reviews." In this *Guide*, see also nos. 43, 149, 152, 158, 159, 177, 229, 284, 291, 296, 339, 367, 377, 528, 628, 659, 683, 687, 697.

* * *

46. Gorog, Lisa de, with the collaboration of Ralph de Gorog. *From Sibelius to Sallinen: Finnish Nationalism and the Music of Finland.* Contributions to the Study of Music and Dance, no. 16. Westport, Conn.: Greenwood, 1989. 252 p. ML269.5.D4 1989 ISBN 0-313-26740-5

> The volume's concluding discography (pp. 219–34) is useful for placing recordings of Sibelius's music in the context of other, mostly twentieth-century, Finnish composers. The full study is annotated as no. 476.

47. *The Gramophone Shop Encyclopedia of Recorded Music.* Compiled by R. D. Darrell, with a foreword by Lawrence Gilman. New York: The Gramophone Shop, 1936. xii, 574 p. ML156.G83 1936

> An early discography useful today for gauging which Sibelius recordings were available in the United States in the 1930s. Sibelius and Stravinsky, for instance, described as the "two towering musical giants of our day," are represented about equally. Available recordings for Richard Strauss, however, were more than double the number for either of these composers. Subsequent editions of the *Encyclopedia* appeared in 1942 and 1948 and provide one means of measuring Sibelius's place in the growth of the recording industry.

48. Haapakoski, Martti. "The Concerto That Holds a Record: The Sibelius Violin Concerto on Disc." *Finnish Music Quarterly*, 1990, nos. 3–4: 32–35.

The author lists 73 recordings, from the first in 1935 through the 1980s, and makes the point that Sibelius's Concerto for Violin seems to have been recorded more often than any other violin concerto in the twentieth century.

49. Hodgson, Anthony. *Scandinavian Music: Finland & Sweden.* London: Associated University Presses, 1984. 224 p. ML269.H6 1984 ISBN 0-8386-2346-8

Part II of this book is a selective discography organized by country and then by composer, with comments found in the main text. Useful for placing Sibelius recordings in a broad Scandinavian context. The historical portion of the book is annotated as no. 76.

50. "Jean Sibeliuksen sinfonialevytykset" [Recordings of Jean Sibelius's Symphonies]. *Rondo*, 1965, no. 6: 16–17.

Organized according to Symphonies no. 1–7, a list of over 50 recordings available in 1965, giving orchestra, conductor, record label, and number.

51. Johnson, Harold E. *Jean Sibelius: The Recorded Music/Musiikkia äänilevyillä/Grammofoninspelningar.* Helsinki: R. E. Westerlund, 1957. 31 p.

A preface in English, Finnish, and Swedish offers a brief history of Sibelius on record. The catalogue that follows, of recordings with their performers, is organized by opus number with preference given to American pressings.

52. Karttunen, Antero. "Tempokäsitysten muutoksista Jean Sibeliuksen sinfonioiden äänilevyesityksissä" [Concerning Tempo Changes in Recordings of Sibelius's Symphonies]. In *Juhlakirja Erik Tawaststjernalle 10.X.1976./Festskrift till Erik Tawaststjerna.* Edited by Erkki Salmenhaara, 93–100. Acta musicologica Fennica 9. Keuruu: Otava, 1976. ML55.T39 1976 ISBN 951-1-04106-1

A study demonstrating that in recordings of Sibelius symphonies from the 1930s until the mid 1970s, tempos generally tended to become slower. Some average times are given, by decade, for each movement of Symphonies no. 2 and 4.

53. Layton, Robert. "Sibelius, Germany and Karajan." *Finnish Music Quarterly*, 1994, no. 4: 22–26.

A discussion ranging well beyond the title as the author considers various Sibelius conductors, especially in Germany; elements that contributed to the composer's great popularity and to the equally great hostility shown him; the author's memories of historic Sibelius performances; and von Karajan's recordings and dedicated advocacy of Sibelius.

54. Layton, Robert. "Sibelius and the Gramophone." In *Suomen musiikin vuosikirja 1964–65*, 46–51. Helsinki: Otava, 1965. With Finnish summary.

A thoughtful comparison of some of the great interpreters of Sibelius's scores based on their recordings. Layton adroitly analyzes the qualities that make Kajanus's recordings in the 1930s so enduring, explains the role of recordings in establishing Sibelius in Britain, and observes that, in 1965 at least, Kajanus's recording of *Tapiola*, Beecham's of Symphony no. 6, and Koussevitzky's of Symphony no. 7 provided the yardsticks by which other interpretations could be measured.

55. Liliedahl, Karleric. *The Gramophone Co. Acoustic Recordings in Scandinavia and for the Scandinavian Market*. Helsinki: Finnish Institute of Recorded Sound, 1977. 567 p. ML156.2.L527G7 1977 ISBN 951-922208-1

A list of more than 14,000 Scandinavian recordings (750 of them Finnish) made by The Gramophone Company from 1899 until 1925 compiled from such sources as index cards, artists' contracts, and national recording archives. Indices by artists and titles of compositions provide the best access to the catalogue, but the lack of a composer index makes it difficult to extract all recordings of a given individual's works. Two notable Sibelius interpreters, Aino Ackté and Hanna Granfelt, appear only in an addendum, but there are numerous recordings of other important Sibelius performers such as Ida Ekman.

56. "Overview: Jean Sibelius." *American Record Guide*, November/December 1994: 55–59.

Selected, relatively recent recordings of the symphonies are recommended together with certain other works. There is also a discussion of various interpreters.

57. Pleijel, Bengt. "Sibelius på skiva" [Sibelius on Record]. *Musikrevy* 10 (1955): 311.

Short comparative discussion of selected available recordings, with much of the essay devoted to the symphonies as recorded by Sixten Ehrling and Anthony Collins. Other interpreters and works are briefly mentioned.

58. Salter, Lionel. *The Gramophone Guide to Classical Composers*. London: Salamander Books, 1978; re-issued by Peerage Books, 1984. 217 p. ISBN 0-907-40892-3

A popular guide to selected recordings available as of May 1978 of composers who interest the "majority of music lovers." A copiously illustrated volume organized alphabetically by composer and accompanied by biographical observations. Listed with recommended recordings are orchestra, conductor, and soloists together with the date of *Gramophone*'s review and both UK and US catalogue numbers and labels. Sibelius's entry (pp. 174–75) includes photographs of the composer.

59. Seppälä, Riitta. "Recording Sibelius." *Finnish Music Quarterly*, 1989, no. 4: 49–51.

A report on the project of Helsinki's Radio Symphony Orchestra to record a series of Sibelius's orchestral music conducted by Jukka-Pekka Saraste.

60. *Suomalaisten äänilevyjen luettelo/Catalogue of Finnish Records.* Compiled by Urpo Haapanen. Helsinki: Suomen Äänitearkiston Julkaisu, 1970–1982. 17 vols. ML156.4.N3F54 1970

A catalogue of items belonging to the Finnish Institute of Recorded Sound [*Suomen äänitearkisto*], a collection owned by a non-profit organization and stored at Broadcasting House, Yleisradio, Helsinki. The collection contains virtually every Finnish recording ever made, covering the period 1901–1980.

61. *Suomalaisten äänitteiden luettelo/Catalogue of Finnish Recordings.* Jyväskylä: Jyväskylän Yliopiston Kirjasto, 1985–. ML156.4.N3F57

Yearly catalogues of recordings produced in Finland, among which Sibelius is frequently represented.

62. Thomas, Guy. *The Symphonies of Jean Sibelius: A Discography and Discussion.* Bloomington, Department of Audio, Indiana University School of Music, 1990. 68 p. ML410.S54T4 1990

Thomas's chief purpose has been to provide a discography of the Sibelius symphonies, but he begins with a welcome essay that surveys the history of Sibelius on record and gives his personal evaluation of the best recordings. Although the discography makes no effort to be complete, it gives an admirable view of the variety and distinction of the recordings of these symphonies. An appendix lists side-breaks and timings of the 78 RPM sets studied.

Rev.: *Finnish Music Quarterly*, 1991, no. 3: 59.

63. Vidal, Pierre. "Jean Sibelius: Discographie critique établie par Pierre Vidal" [Jean Sibelius: Critical Discography Compiled by Pierre Vidal]. *Harmonie-Opéra Hi-Fi Conseil*, January 1982: 38–48.

An expansive, annotated discography by a French connoisseur of Sibelius, treating the reader at the outset to a portrait of Sibelius in both prose and pictures. Vidal offers his own selection of recordings, arranged by genre, together with insightful assessments of their value. Accompanied by illustrations of performers and conductors.

64. Worbs, Hans Christoph. "Eine Plattenschau zum 100. Geburtstag von Jean Sibelius" [A Record Show on the 100th Birthday of Jean Sibelius]. *Phono Prisma*, 1965: 158–59.

Brief discussion of performances during Sibelius's lifetime with attention given to Sir Adrian Boult's recording of ten symphonic poems and Tom Krause's recording of nine songs. Short discography.

II
Background

The isolation of Jean Sibelius, a feature of the composer's life consistently described in the literature, has been only superficially understood outside Finland. It is, of course, undeniable that the country's position on the fringe of northern Europe constitutes a geographical remoteness from the world. Studies show that people of nations on the periphery tend to develop self-sufficiency, closeness to nature, solid family ties, and individualism. Sibelius's geographical situation has thus accentuated the view of a lonely genius cut off from the mainstream of life.

Yet the full story of Sibelius is more complex—and more interesting. Here was a composer who sought balance in his life as in his art. Recent biographical study has shown that between 1889 and 1930, he alternated months of relative isolation in Finland with significant periods of time in one or another of the world's better-known music centers, often Berlin, sometimes London or Paris.

Within Finland, Sibelius could hardly be described as isolated, at least before he deliberately cut himself off from society by the move to Järvenpää in 1904. During Sibelius's lifetime, as today, Finland enjoyed a teeming cultural life in which writers, painters, composers, performers, historians, architects, philosophers, theater directors, actors, actresses, and critics socialized, exchanged ideas, and undertook collaborative projects. With many if not most of the leading artistic figures of his country, Sibelius had connections, often close ones. Moreover, the move north of Helsinki to what was then the small village of Järvenpää was not the move to total isolation often depicted.

Although it placed a healthy distance between the composer and such tempting "watering holes" as the Hotel Kämp, Ainola, as Sibelius named his new home, was located in an artist's colony in the county of Tuusula. The great Aleksis Kivi, known as the father of modern Finnish literature, had lived and died there; in Sibelius's time writer J. H. Erkko, artist Eero Järnefelt (Sibelius's brother-in-law), painter Pekka Halonen, writer Juhani Aho, and Aho's talented wife, artist Jenny Soldan-Brofeldt, all lived in close promixity to the Sibelius family. Indeed, one reason for the move was to insure that Aino and the children had nearby neighbors during the periods when Jean was abroad.

Thus, the present section lists important studies related to the backdrop against which Sibelius's life and music unfolded. The most important framework, illustrated clearly by the number and kinds of entries, was Finland, and, unfortunately for many, most of these sources are available only in Finnish or Swedish. The few English-language materials have tended to be general and superficial. One important exception appeared too late to be included in the *Guide*, but readers of English will want to consult George C. Schoolfield's splendid *Helsinki of the Czars: Finland's Capital, 1808–1918* (Columbia, S.C.: Camden House, 1996) for a better understanding of the rich tapestry against which Sibelius's activities unfolded in Helsinki. This volume aside, Sibelius has been better served in English by studies that portray him in the broader context of Scandinavia and the Baltic region. There will also be found a few items for establishing a framework for his music abroad.

* * *

A. Sibelius in Context

FINLAND

See also nos. 228, 240, 242

65. Aho, Antti J. *Juhani Aho: Elämä ja teokset* [Juhani Aho: Life and Works]. Helsinki: Werner Söderström Osakeyhtiö, 1951. 2 vols. Vol. I, 528 p.; vol. II, 478 p.

A biography of one of the leading writers connected with the newspaper *Päivälehti* and a man who later became Sibelius's neighbor at Järvenpää. There are scattered references to Sibelius throughout, most of an anecdotal nature. It is mentioned (II: 16–17) that the Sibelius family seldom had company at Ainola, the composer being devoted to his work, and that Aho and Sibelius discussed how music inspired poets and how poems inspired the composer. There is a brief account (II: 101) of *My Brothers in Foreign Lands (Veljeni vierailla mailla)*, the one Aho text that Sibelius set to music, and a discussion of Aho's *Juha* (II: 273ff), upon which it was once hoped that Sibelius would base an opera. Written by Aho's son, whose extensively consulted sources, letters, financial accounts, and newspaper records appear in the notes to each chapter.

66. Dahlström, Fabian. *Sibelius-Akademin 1882–1982* [The Sibelius Academy 1882–1982]. Translated into Finnish by Rauno Ekholm, *Sibelius-Akatemia 1882–1982*. Helsinki: Sibelius Academy Publications, 1982. 485 p. MT5.H4S538 1982 ISBN 951-859-162-8

A well-documented study that provides matriculation lists, recital programs, statistics of the student population, and other historical information about the institution where Sibelius studied in the 1880s, taught from the 1890s, and which eventually (from 1939) bore his name. Illustrated, including a photograph of Sibelius with his violin teacher Mitrofan Wasilieff.

67. Erickson, Runar. *Georg Schnéevoigts repertoar som dirigent och cellist* [Georg Schnéevoigt's Repertory as Conductor and Cellist]. Musikvetenskapliga institutionen vid Åbo Akademi, 4. Åbo: Åbo Akademi, 1984. 211 p.

A study of one of the most active Sibelius conductors who also occasionally performed Sibelius's chamber works as a cellist. Especially useful is the appendix that lists Schnéevoigt's conducting repertory by composer, giving year and performers.

68. Flodin, Karl. *Martin Wegelius: Levnadsteckning* [Martin Wegelius: Picture of a Life.] Svenska Litteratursällskapet i Finland, no. 161. Helsingfors: SLS, 1922. ix, 579 p. ML410.W42F5

Sympathetic, if boring, biography of Sibelius's first composition teacher, the man chiefly responsible for founding the institute today known as the Sibelius Academy. The author, for many years Helsinki's leading music critic, discusses the first performance of *The Watersprite* (*Näcken*, pp. 419–21), which Sibelius composed with his teacher, and quotes from Sibelius's early letters written abroad (pp. 464–69), thereby preserving some material that has since disappeared. No index, bibliography, notes, or music examples, although there is an annotated list of Wegelius's compositions.

69. Flodin, Karl, and Otto Ehrström. *Richard Faltin och hans samtid* [Richard Faltin and His Time]. Helsingfors: Holger Schildt Förlag, 1934. 366 p.

Danzig-born Faltin established himself in Finland in 1856 at the age of twenty-one, first in Viipuri and later in Helsinki, where he became a leading figure in the country's musical life. He conducted the Academic Orchestra at the University, where Sibelius played under his direction as early as 1885; he participated in the founding of the Helsinki Music Institute, where Sibelius studied; and he was active as composer, organist, and opera conductor. His life thus frequently intersected with Sibelius's, and this biography, begun by the eminent Helsinki critic Flodin and finished after his death by Otto Ehrström, portrays not only the intersections but also the nature of Helsinki's cultural life when Sibelius arrived in the city as a university student. Illustrated, with an index and list of compositions, although there is no bibliography or music examples.

70. Haapanen, Toivo. "Jean Sibelius." *Le nord* 4 (1941): 205–09.

Brief consideration in English of Sibelius's career against the background of Finland's musical history.

71. Haapanen, Toivo. *Suomen säveltaide* [Finland's Musical Art], 95–115. Helsinki: Otava, 1940. 178 p. ML304.H11s. Translated into

Swedish by Otto Ehrström as *Finlands musikhistoria* (Helsingfors: Söderström & Co., 1956).

A history of music in Finland, from the Middle Ages right up to the time of writing, that places Sibelius in the larger context of Finnish musical life. The chapter entitled "Spring Flood of Finnish Composition" ("Suomalaisten sävelten kevättulva," see esp. pp. 94–115) opens with Sibelius, who receives the lion's share of attention with a short biography followed by a survey of works. A few music examples and numerous illustrations.

72. Häkli, Pekka. *Arvid Järnefelt ja hänen lähimaailmansa* [Arvid Järnefelt and His World]. Helsinki: Werner Söderström Osakeyhtiö, 1955. 592 p.

A well-documented biography of Sibelius's famous brother-in-law for whose play *Death* (*Kuolema*) Sibelius composed *Valse triste*. There is an account of the birth of that famous work's melody and a number of incidents about the composer's relationship to different Järnefelt family members and literary personalities. A more objective book than Järnefelt's own *My Parents' Story* (no. 405), which is, after all, a novel, Häkli's biography, indexed and illustrated, provides an important introduction to the talented family into which Sibelius married.

73. Halonen, Antti. *Taiteen juhlaa ja arkea: Tuusulan taiteilijasiirtolan värikkäitä vaiheita Kivestä Sibeliukseen* [Art's Celebration and Everyday Life: The Colorful Stages of Tuusula's Artists' Colony from Kivi to Sibelius.] Helsinki: Tammi, 1952. 237 p.

The vibrant atmosphere of the artist's colony in which Sibelius's home, Ainola, was located, portrayed in prose and in pictures. Pages 218–24 contain a facsimile of a letter from Sibelius to Pekka Halonen (September 23, 1915); Eino Leino's birthday poem to Sibelius; and the composer's eight-measure musical greeting left in Emil Nestor Setälä's notebook in 1924.

74. Hannikainen, Ilmari. *Sibelius and the Development of Finnish Music.* With a Preface by Toivo Haapanen. Translated by Aulis Nopsanen. London: Hinrichsen Edition, 1948. 47 p. ML410.S54H3

A brief, affectionate introduction to Sibelius for readers of English. Against the background of Finland's musical history, the author, who taught piano at the Sibelius Academy, views Sibelius as the "climax of Finnish music." Abundantly illustrated, his book includes facsimiles from three manuscripts, portraits of Sibelius, and numerous photographs of Sibelius's musical predecessors and contemporaries.

75. Helasvuo, Veikko. *Sibelius and the Music of Finland.* Freely rendered into English and enlarged by Paul Sjöblom. Helsinki: Otava, 1952. 99 p. 2d revised edition, 1957; 3d revised edition, 1961. ML304.H4 1961

A useful introductory survey of musical life in Finland and more expansive than no. 74, although on the same order, this little volume presents Sibelius's life in the context of Finland's musical past on the one hand and the musical life of the 1950s on the other. Together with photographs of musically significant people and places, brief descriptions identify Finnish musicians and performing organizations and indicate aspects of the country's music education and scholarship. Illustrations differ among the editions, and in 1957 a section was added to provide a romantic picture of Sibelius at home.

76. Hodgson, Anthony. *Scandinavian Music: Finland & Sweden.* London: Associated University Presses, 1984. 224 p. ML269.H6 1984 ISBN 0-8386-2346-8

Part I of this book is concerned with the history of music in Finland and in Sweden; Part II is a selective discography (annotated as no. 49). Sibelius's music is discussed in several substantial passages in the pages on Finland, where he is placed in the larger context of his contemporaries. Several symphonies and tone poems are discussed with music examples, including *En saga*, which Hodgson attempts to demonstrate is indebted to the accentuation of spoken Finnish.

77. Karila, Tauno, ed. *Composers of Finland.* Helsinki: Suomen Säveltäjät, 1965. 108 p. ML390.K186S8 1965

A well-written, English-language reference source especially valuable for gathering into one place consequential Finnish composers and providing succinct summaries of their lives and works. Sibelius receives the longest entry (pp. 98–103), yet even more instructive are the many figures, from Erik Furuhjelm and Ilmari Krohn to Nils-Eric Ringbom and Heikki Klemetti, who are portrayed as composers in their own right and yet contributed to the performances of and writings about Sibelius's music. Each man is represented by a small photograph.

78. Klinge, Matti, and Rainer Knapas, Anto Leikola, John Strömberg. *Keisarillinen Aleksanterin Yliopisto 1808–1917* [Kaiser Alexander University 1808–1917]. Helsinki: Otava, 1989. 931 p. + indices. LF1705.H443 1987 ISBN 951-1-10228-1

With its scattered references to Jean Sibelius and to his brother Christian, who taught psychiatry at the University, this second in a two-volume history of what is today Helsinki University situates Sibelius and his music in the context of the University's life. Page 823 reproduces Albert Edelfelt's painting of the University's inaugural ceremonies of 1640 in which one of the figures is depicted with the face of Sibelius.

79. Lappalainen, Seija. *Tänä iltana yliopiston juhlasalissa: Musiikin tähtihetkiä Helsingissä 1832–1971* [Tonight in the University's Festival Hall: Music's Shining Moments in Helsinki 1832–1971]. Helsinki: Yliopistopaino, 1994. 382 p. + pictures. ISBN 951-570-222-4

A history of musical performances in the impressively beautiful Festival Hall of Helsinki University, where numerous Sibelius premieres and other presentations took place. Amply documented, including sizable quotations from contemporary reviews, reproductions of selected concert programs, and a chronological analysis of Festival Hall concerts by month and day together with principal performers or conductors. Sibelius's many associations with the Hall can easily be found through the well-constructed index. Some of the material concerning the Hall's structure, memorable performances, and fate during World War II can be read in English in the author's illustrated article "Star Moments at the Helsinki University Hall," *Finnish Music Quarterly*, 1994, no. 2: 2–10.

80. Mäkinen, Timo, and Seppo Nummi. *Musica Fennica*. Helsinki: Otava, 1965 [in English]. New enlarged edition, *Musica Fennica: An Outline of Music in Finland*. Helsinki: Otava, 1985. 191 p. ML309.F4M313 ISBN 951-1-08574-3. An even larger edition with an index appeared in German as *Musica Fennica* (Helsinki: Otava, 1989). ISBN 951-1-10233-8

Originally published for the Sibelius Centenary in 1965, *Musica Fennica* actually devotes few pages to Sibelius but rather surveys music in Finland from the Middle Ages to the present. It thus provides an introduction to the larger picture of Finland's music history for the general English- and German-language reader. A new edition appeared in 1996, under the able authorship of Erkki Salmenhaara, Kalevi Aho, Pekka Jalkanen, and Keijo Virtauro.

81. Marvia, Einari. *Oy Fazerin Musiikkikauppa 1897–1947* [Fazer's Music Company 1897–1947]. Helsinki: Fazer, 1947. 148 p. + unnumbered photographs. Translated into Swedish by Hans Rundt as *Ab Fazers Musikhandel: 1897–1947* (Helsingfors: Nordblad & Pettersson, 1948). Pages 46–49 of the Finnish version were published as "Fazer Sibeliuksen teosten kustantajana vuosisadan vaihteesa" [Fazer as Publisher of Sibelius's Works at the Turn of the Century], *Musiikkiviesti*, 1955, no. 11b: 4.

A history of the firm that evolved from Anna Melan's music shop in the 1880s through an association with R. E. Westerlund eventually to become the Fazer Music Company in 1919. The firm continues today as Warner/Chappell, but this history was written well before the business was purchased by Time Warner. There are scattered references to Sibelius throughout, although the lack of an index makes pertinent passages difficult to find. Pages 46–49 contain the most concentrated material, including photographs of some of the more elaborate sheet music covers published by the firm. No supporting notes or bibliography.

82. Marvia, Einari, and Matti Vainio. *Helsingin Kaupunginorkesteri 1882–1982* [Helsinki Philharmonic Orchestra 1882–1982]. Helsinki: Werner Söderström Osakeyhtiö, 1993. vii, 796 p. ML28.H37H4546 1993 ISBN 951-0-18312-1. Published in an abbreviated Swedish version as *Helsingfors stadsorkester 1882–1982* (Helsinki: Werner Söderström Osakeyhtiö, 1994). 168 p.

An exceedingly detailed history of the orchestra founded by Robert Kajanus, whose official name in English, Helsinki Philharmonic Orchestra, is not a literal translation from Finnish (which means Helsinki City Orchestra). Of interest to Sibelius enthusiasts is the chapter on the Orchestra School ("Orkesterikoulu 1885–1914," pp. 108–21), where Sibelius taught, and the appendix listing the orchestra's repertory from 1932 to 1982. Illustrated, with appendices of members, but no index nor citation of documents for Sibelius's tenure. The repertory list must be used in conjunction with Ringbom (no. 84), where programs from 1882–1932 are inventoried.

83. Okkonen, Onni. *A. Gallen-Kallela: elämä ja taide* [A{kseli} Gallen-Kallela: Life and Art]. Helsinki: Werner Söderström Osakeyhtiö, 1949. xvii, 944 p. Reprint. 1961.

An expansive life-and-works study of Sibelius's most famous Finnish artistic contemporary. The author deals with a great many personalities closely connected to Gallen-Kallela, including Sibelius, provides documentation from newspapers and correspondence, and reproduces 477 illustrations, mostly in black and white. Of particular importance to Sibelians are pp. 274–82, where Gallen's famous *Symposion* painting of Sibelius is discussed, and quotations are given from contemporary reviews. The 1961 printing includes a few additional plates.

84. Ringbom, Nils-Eric. *Helsingfors Orkesterföretag 1882–1932* [Helsinki Orchestra Companies 1882–1932]. Helsingfors: Frenckellin Kirjapaino Osakeyhtiö, 1932. 128 p. ML410.S54R51 1932. Translated into Finnish by Taneli Kuusisto as *Helsingin Orkesteri 1882–1932* (Helsinki: Frenckellin Kirjapaino Osakeyhtiö, 1932).

A history of the orchestra founded by Robert Kajanus, written by the violinist and musicologist who would later serve as the orchestra's librarian (1938–42) and *intendent* (1943–70). Useful sections can be found on Kajanus's Orchestra School and the Orchestra's trip to the World's Fair in Paris in 1900 together with facsimiles of programs of the Paris concerts, which, of course, included Sibelius's music. Most important are the chronological repertory lists, which show what music Sibelius may have heard as well as those of his works the orchestra played. These lists, however, are not complete. Popular concerts, student concerts, and concerts of light music have been omitted as has the repertory performed during Georg Schnéevoigt's tenure as conductor, 1912–1914. These omissions have unfortunately not been corrected in the more recent history of the Orchestra (no. 82).

85. Söderhjelm, Henning. *Werner Söderhjelm*. Helsingfors: Svenska Litteratursällskapet i Finland; Holger Schildt Förlag, 1960. 267 p. PB64.S68S6

This Swedish-language biography of philologist, literary critic, diplomat, and Helsinki University professor Söderhjelm (1859–1931) portrays an influential contemporary whose life often intersected with Sibelius's: from their voyage on the same ship to central Europe in 1889 to social contacts in the circle of Euterpists to the assistance Söderhjelm offered the composer in times of financial need. Abundant quotations from letters, diaries, and other documents, including a text of a letter from Sibelius in 1890, and illustrated, but unfortunately no source notes or bibliography.

86. Suomalainen, Yrjö. *Oskar Merikanto: Suomen kotien säveltäjä* [Oskar Merikanto: Finland's Home Composer]. Helsinki: Otava, 1950. 201 p. ML410.M538S9

An illustrated biography of the man widely believed to be the face-down figure in Gallen-Kallela's painting *Symposion*. Sibelius is mentioned here and there, most interestingly when the author quotes from his letter of 1917: the composer writes that he has been sick for quite some time (pp. 129–30). A more careful biography of this Merikanto, published in 1996 by Seppo Heikinheimo, appeared too late to be included here.

87. Suomalainen, Yrjö. *Robert Kajanus: Hänen elämänsä ja toimintansa* [Robert Kajanus: His Life and Work]. Helsinki: Otava, 1952. 284 p. ML410.S54S8 1952

Admiring biography of the conductor and composer who founded the Helsinki Philharmonic Orchestra and was the first to champion Sibelius's music abroad. Illustrated, but the limitation of the index to personal names and the lack of a table of contents make the book difficult to use (on the founding of the Orchestra, see chapter III; about the Orchestra School in which Sibelius taught, see pp. 104–107). A scholarly biography of this important figure is sorely needed.

88. *Suomen sana: Kansalliskirjallisuutemme valiolukemisto* [The Finnish Word: The Best Readings from Our National Literature]. Planned and edited by Yrjö A. Jäntti. Helsinki: Werner Söderström Osakeyhtiö, 1963–1967. 24 vols. PH341.J3

An enormous anthology of readings in the cultural history of Finland, all translated into Finnish. Entries range from Mikael Agricola's introduction to the New Testament (1548) to Alvar Aalto's lecture "Art and Technology" (1955). Quite a few texts concern Sibelius, including articles by performers, such as Ida and Karl Ekman, and by various critics. Although the items first appeared elsewhere, the anthology is a valuable resource for readers of Finnish, since it conveniently gathers into one place so many different texts. The key to using the volumes is the general index where under "Sibelius," "Sibeliana," and related terms the reader is referred to the appropriate authors, who appear in alphabetical order throughout the 24 volumes. A short biography of the author with a handsome color portrait precedes each reading.

89. Tarasti, Eero. "On the Roots of Finnish Music: Is Sibelius the Godfather?" *Scandinavian Review* 75 (1987): 91–97.

Written for a general audience, the article introduces readers of English to Sibelius's place in the broad context of Finnish musical life, both past and present.

90. Vainio, Matti. "Father of the Finnish Orchestra." *Finnish Music Quarterly*, 1989, no. 3: 26–33.

Robert Kajanus's life and work, which was inextricably entwined with Sibelius's, surveyed by an orchestra historian. Illustrated, including a poster of a Kajanus-led concert in Queen's Hall promising the premiere of Sibelius's Eighth Symphony.

91. Wennervirta, Ludvig. *Aino Ackté, Albert Edelfelt: Eräs taiteemme episodi* [Aino Ackté, Albert Edelfelt: A Certain Episode in Our Art]. Helsinki: Werner Söderström Osakeyhtiö, 1944. 99 p. ML420.A2W3 1944

This small book explores the relationship between the beautiful Finnish soprano to whom Sibelius dedicated such songs as *Autumn Evening* (*Höstkväll*) and *Jubal* and the composer's great friend Edelfelt who painted Ackté, conductor Kajanus, and others. Together with various paintings and black-and-white photographs of Ackté, the volume reproduces her correspondence with Edelfelt. Although Sibelius does not figure large in the book, there is some discussion of *Höstkväll*. See especially pp. 54–55, 94.

92. Wis, Roberto. "Ferruccio Busoni and Finland." *Acta musicologica* 49 (1977): 250–69.

A fascinating look at Helsinki in the years 1888–1890 through the eyes of Busoni, with references to his friendship with Sibelius.

Especially valuable for the extensive bibliographical documentation, the numerous quotations from letters, including one to Sibelius, and the list of the pianist's recitals in Helsinki during the period of his teaching there.

93. *Ylioppilaskunnan Soittajat 1926–1986: 60-vuotisjuhlakirja* [University Players 1926–1986: A 60th Year Festival Book]. Edited by Mika Ainola. Helsinki: Ylioppilaskunnan Soittajat, 1986. 188 p. ISBN 951-662-396-4

A history of instrumentalists connected with Helsinki University's Academic Orchestra with numerous references to Sibelius, from his solo performance of Beethoven's *Romance* in F major in 1889 to the awarding of his honorary membership in 1936. There is an alphabetical catalogue of players together with contents of concert programs given between 1926–1986, but no index.

SIBELIUS AROUND THE BALTIC

See also nos. 348, 358, 462, 587, 632

94. Fiala, Václav. *Trojzuk: Søren Kierkegaard, Edvard Grieg, Jean Sibelius* [Troika: Søren Kierkegaard, Edvard Grieg, Jean Sibelius]. Prague: Fr. Borový, 1945. 129 p.

Three separate essays, with the pages on Sibelius intended to portray the composer's musical personality to a Czech audience in celebration of the Finn's eightieth birthday. Its success may be measured by the fact that soon after its introduction in Czechoslovakia in November 1945, the book was quickly in short supply. The essay was a preliminary study for a more detailed monograph begun by the author but apparently never finished.

95. Leichter, K. "Sibeliuksen teosten esittämisestä Eestissä" [On Performances of Sibelius's Works in Estonia]. *Rondo*, 1965, no. 6: 14–15.

A brief survey of Sibelius's music in Estonia giving titles and dates of works performed as well as excerpts from various reviews.

96. Männik, Maris. "Finnish Music in Estonia in the Early 20th Century: Its Spread and Repercussions." In *The Baltic Countries 1900–1914*, 743–62. Studia Baltica Stockholmiensia 5:2. Acta Universitatis Stockholmiensis. Proceedings from the 9th Conference on Baltic Studies in Scandinavia, Stockholm, June 3–6, 1987. Edited by Aleksander Loit. Uppsala: [n.p.], 1990. DK502.6.C66 1987 ISBN 91-22-01391-1

Even though Jean Sibelius is not the author's main focus, the composer occupies an interesting place in this useful discussion of the musical ties between Finland and Estonia. Well supported with references to Estonian and Russian sources and illustrated with music examples.

97. Martinotti, Sergio. "Sibelius e Nielsen nel sinfonismo nordico" [Sibelius and Nielsen in Nordic Symphonism]. *Chigiana: rassegna annuale di studi musicologici* 22 (1965): 109–31.

A discussion of the background of two Nordic symphonists of first rank. The author mentions their meetings, the importance to them of Busoni's promotion of contemporary music, and cultural factors that shaped the musical development of each. Various Italian sources are cited, and there is a photograph of Sibelius and Nielsen at the Nordic Music Festival in 1919.

98. Miller, Mina F. *Carl Nielsen: A Guide to Research.* New York: Garland Publishing, 1987. xvi, 245 p. + unnumbered illustrations. ML134.N42M5 1987 ISBN 0-8240-8569-8

Although some of the same sources may be found in the present volume, Miller's excellent *Guide* leads the reader to discussions of Nielsen's music in which Sibelius figures too peripherally to be annotated here but which help to place the Finn in the larger context of Scandinavian music history.

99. Schjelderup-Ebbe, Dag. "Sibelius og Norge" [Sibelius and Norway]. In *Suomen musiikin vuosikirja 1964–65*, 80–90. Helsinki: Otava, 1965. With English summary.

The author traces the composer's connections to Norway, from his alleged reading of Norwegian literature in the original to his Norwegian visits. The sympathy between Sibelius and Edvard Grieg is explored with quotations from each composer's writings to or about the other. There are also numerous excerpts from Oslo newspaper reviews about Sibelius from the first half of the century.

100. Simpson, Robert. "Ianus Geminus: Music in Scandinavia." In *Twentieth Century Music*, 165–74. Edited by Rollo H. Myers. London: John Calder, 1960. 2d edition, New York: Orion Press, 1968. ML197.M95 1969

An essay largely devoted to Sibelius and Carl Nielsen, who are seen as representing the two faces of the Nordic Janus.

101. Söderström, Göran. "Strindberg och hans finska kontakter" [Strindberg and His Finnish Contacts]. *Strindbergiana: Sjunde Samlingen utgiven av Strindbergssällskapet.* Stockholm: Atlantis, 1992, 15–27. PT9816.S697

An instructive discussion of the connections between Swedish author August Strindberg and such Finns as Akseli Gallen-Kallela, Karl August Tavaststjerna, Albert Edelfelt, and others who were also members of Sibelius's circle. The composer figures here as well, especially in the matter of his incidental music composed for Strindberg's play *Swanwhite* (*Svanevit*), and the author quotes excerpts from the Sibelius-Strindberg correspondence.

102. Wallner, Bo. *Wilhelm Stenhammar och hans tid* [Wilhelm Stenhammar and His Time]. Stockholm: Norstedts Förlag, 1991. 3 vols. Vol. I: 682 p.; vol. II: 626 p.; vol. III: 589 p. ISBN 91-1-913232-8, vols. 1–3

The author's laudable scope and the care with which he has documented the life of the man to whom Sibelius dedicated his Sixth Symphony make this a work of particular importance. There is an entire chapter devoted to Sibelius in Volume II (pp. 551–69) and many references to the composer, often with musical examples and texts of his letters, throughout all the volumes.

SIBELIUS IN ANGLO-SAXON COUNTRIES

103. Elkin, Robert. *Queen's Hall 1893–1941*. With a Foreword by Dr. Malcolm Sargent. London: Rider & Co., n.d. [1944?]. 160 p. ML286.8.L5E45

The acoustically excellent if homely Queen's Hall, destroyed by enemy bombers on the night of May 10–11, 1941, was the place where Sibelius made his London debut. By chance, Sibelius was also represented on the very last Proms concert to be given in the same venue. These and other aspects of Sibelius's music in London's musical life emerge from Elkin's history. Of special interest is the Index of First Performances and the short history of the Philharmonic Gold Medal (pp. 61–62), which Sibelius received in 1935. The General Index, however, is incomplete where Sibelius is concerned.

104. Elkin, Robert. *Royal Philharmonic: The Annals of the Royal Philharmonic Society*. With a Foreword by Pau [sic] Casals. London: Rider & Co., n.d. [1946?]. 192 p. ML286.8.L52P53

Although barely mentioned in the historical essay, Sibelius's important connections to the Royal Philharmonic show up in the useful appendices. The first, which lists the most important works first performed in England at a Philharmonic concert, includes Sibelius's Symphonies no. 3 and 7. Appendix II names the Philharmonic Society's Gold Medallists, an award bestowed upon Sibelius in 1935. The most extensive appendix gives the Society's programs from 1912 to 1945, naming conductors and soloists. A word of caution: the index contains some but not all references to Sibelius.

105. Mueller, John H. *The American Symphony Orchestra: A Social History of Musical Taste*. Bloomington: Indiana University Press, 1951. A London edition was published by John Calder in 1958. Reprint. Westport, Conn.: Greenwood, 1976. ML200.M8 1976

In examining the history of American orchestras and the development of taste in the United States, Mueller establishes a valuable starting point for studying the dissemination of Sibelius's music in America. His clear and unemotional discussion of Sibelius's popularity in the United States is as refreshing in its tone as it is solid in its perceptions. Illustrations include popularity cycles for various composers, Sibelius among them. The statistical basis for his observations was provided in a later volume by his widow; see no. 106.

106. Mueller, Kate Hevner. *Twenty-Seven Major American Symphony Orchestras: A History and Analysis of Their Repertoires, Seasons 1842–43 through 1969–70*. Bloomington: Indiana University Press, 1973. 398 p. ML128.05M75 ISBN 0-253-36110-9

A two-part study that begins with analyses and commentary on the American symphonic repertory supported by statistics and charts. In part II the repertory itself is listed, proceeding by composer, with performance dates and timings provided. An indispensable tool for charting when and where the music of Sibelius as well as many other composers was played in the United States.

Rev.: *American Reference Books Annual*, 1974: 389.

107. Wood, Henry J. *My Life of Music*. With an Introduction by Sir Hugh Allen. London: V. Gollancz, 1938, 1946. Reprint of the 1946 edition. Freeport, N.Y.: Books for Libraries Press, 1971. 384 p. ML422.W86A2 1971 ISBN 0-8369-5820-9

A sometimes self-serving memoir by one of the first conductors to champion Sibelius in England. Wood mentions the composer only in passing, but he establishes an English context for the music and verifies the importance of such figures as Rosa Newmarch and Granville Bantock in promoting Sibelius and his works.

B. Contemporary Views of Jean Sibelius

Some of the most intriguing dimensions of a person are revealed in the descriptions, comments, and assessments made by contemporaries. Although shrewd observers of music history, those of the ilk of Charles

Burney, are rare, in critic Karl Flodin (1858–1925), Finland had a musically intelligent writer fully capable of compelling description. Flodin was like many in Finland, however, in that his "criticisms" often melted into embarrassingly fulsome praise of Sibelius, although he was also responsible for some unjustifiably harsh opinions. By the beginning of the twentieth century, the composer's tremendous importance to his nation meant that contemporaries all too often simply penned ecstatic paeans to their countryman. Yet despite some reservations, one cannot dismiss this kind of material out of hand. Some of it retains a certain value, if for no other reason than the vivid physical descriptions of a man whose image changed profoundly over the course of his life. And sometimes one finds dates, information about the genesis of compositions, and the occasional penetrating psychological insight.

Each author represented below knew Sibelius, and some were close friends. All observers, however, are not created equal under the best of circumstances, and Sibelius's extraordinarily long life exacerbated these inequalities. The responses to the young, still budding composer in the 1890s, a time when Finland was very much under the yoke of Russia, came from a far different world than those penned after the second decade of the twentieth century, when Sibelius was an unassailable, living symbol of an independent nation.

Until 1915 writings about Sibelius were almost all by Finns. In that year the celebration of the composer's fiftieth birthday as a national event signalled that Sibelius's reputation, at least within Finland, was not only secure but in danger of turning into idolatry. In the latter part of his life, the years from 1927 to 1957 known as "the silence of Järvenpää" during which Sibelius produced little for the world to see or hear, the nature of contemporary observation clearly changed. Finns tended to give accounts of a faultless master of the realm of tones rather than the truer-to-life recollections of a young man's gregarious, life-loving, and even boisterous spirit. Eyewitnesses from abroad were often sensation-seeking journalists or eager, young musicians wanting endorsements of their recordings or their compositions or just ordinary people simply wanting to be able to tell about having been in the presence of a great man. The composer effectively "held court," receiving numerous guests at his home, Ainola. Many visitors published accounts of these social calls, which invariably took the form of interviews.

In the past such reports have sometimes been cited as scholarly sources. Interviews with Sibelius, however, must be treated with circumspection. One often has the impression that the composer was so polite that he said what the visitor wanted to hear, to paraphrase his own words about the content of his letters. Bolstering this impression are the various contradictions that emerge, either between interviews on different occasions or between an interview and another account. The prudent will want to consider carefully who wrote each of the following narratives and will take note as well of the date of publication, for many of these memoirs were set down long after the events they purport to relate.

* * *

108. Amis, John. "Sibelius via Legge." *Gramophone* 67 (1989): 152.

An interview with Walter Legge, the man behind the Sibelius Society recordings in England, who recalls his conversations with the composer. Among other things, Legge reports finding a bridge where Sibelius got his inspiration for *Kyllikki*; alleges that Sibelius answered the question "Why, after the Fourth Symphony, did [you] not continue in the same vein?" with "Beyond that lies madness or chaos"; and tells an amusing story of Sir Thomas Beecham and Symphony no. 4.

109. Anderson, Marian. *My Lord, What a Morning*. London: Cresset Press, 1957. 240 p. ML420.A6A3 1957

An autobiography of the American contralto, Anderson's book includes a brief memoir of the day she and her accompanist, Finnish pianist Kosti Vehanen, performed for Sibelius at Ainola (pp. 118–19). Sibelius subsequently wrote to Olin Downes in Anderson's behalf; see no. 255, p. 199.

110. Askeli, Henry. "A Sketch of Sibelius the Man." *Musical Quarterly* 26 (1940): 1–7.

Despite its publication in a respected scholarly journal, this article simply presents an author's personal impressions of the composer's physical appearance, culinary habits, and domestic surroundings accompanied by photographs mostly borrowed from *Suomen Kuvalehti*.

111. Bantock, Granville. "Jean Sibelius." *Monthly Musical Record* 65 (1935): 217–19.

A birthday tribute in which Bantock, the composer responsible for Sibelius's first visit to England, eulogizes his friend whose works and accomplishments he romanticizes. He also relates some of his personal memories of Sibelius in England.

112. Bantock, Myrrha. *Granville Bantock: A Personal Portrait.* London: Dent, 1972. xii, 203 p. ML410.B21B3 ISBN 0-460-03971-7

Daughter of the British composer, Myrrha Bantock retained quite vivid memories of the Finnish guest who visited the Bantock home on several occasions. Scattered throughout her volume are references to such matters as Sibelius's baldness, his attraction to Aino Ackté, and his imposing physical presence.

113. Bantock, Raymond. Foreword to *The Music of Jean Sibelius* by Burnett James, 13–15. London: Associated University Presses, 1983. ISBN 0-8386-3070-7

The second son of Granville Bantock, Raymond met Sibelius as a child. He recounts humorous anecdotes about the composer and tells of visiting him at Ainola in the 1950s. The volume is more fully annotated as no. 158.

114. Bax, Arnold. *Farewell, My Youth.* London: 1943. Reprint. Westport, Conn.: Greenwood, 1970. 112 p. ML410.B275A3 1970 ISBN 0-8371-3246-0

One of England's leading twentieth-century composers gives an illuminating description (pp. 60–62) of the physical changes in Sibelius between 1909 and 1936 and recalls the regrettable evening when the Finn appeared before the Music Club in London (pp. 56–57).

115. Cohen, Harriet. *A Bundle of Time: The Memoirs of Harriet Cohen.* London: Faber & Faber, 1969. 330 p. ML417.C7A4 ISBN 0-571-08574-1

Cohen met Sibelius through his music: she learned *En saga* as a piano solo, a feat which won her Sibelius's eternal friendship. Here the pianist reminisces about her personal meetings with Sibelius, recalls his opinions about various composers, and renders him vivid in physical descriptions. She includes her own photograph of Sibelius in Helsinki, a brief letter from the composer (one of his stereotyped thank-you notes), and a rather withering epistle from Rosa Newmarch apropos the physical changes in the man.

116. Flodin, Karl. "Det första mötet" [The First Meeting]. *Musikliv och reseminnen.* Helsingfors: Söderström & Co., 1931, 262–63; first published in *Svenska Pressen*, November 1925; published in Finnish as "Ensimmäinen tapaaminen." *Aulos*, 1925: 13–14.

On the occasion of Sibelius's sixtieth birthday, critic Flodin recalls the first time he met the composer: at Forsström's Café in the late 1880s. This short, engagingly written memoir is the source of Flodin's famous description of Sibelius "juggling with colours and sounds as if they were bright glass balls . . . ". The full volume of Flodin's essays is annotated as no. 253.

117. Goossens, Eugene. *Overture and Beginners: A Musical Autobiography.* London: Methuen & Co., 1951. Reprint. Westport, Conn.: Greenwood, 1972. viii, 327 p. ML410.G643A3 1972 ISBN 0-8371-5597-5

Although most of the references to Sibelius are fleeting, there is one recollection (pp. 75–76) of the "gastronomic Sibelius of five-course meals and good wine." Included as well are brief quotations of the composer's charming English together with an assessment of his position in England and America.

118. Gray, Cecil. *Musical Chairs or Between Two Stools: Being the Life and Memoirs of Cecil Gray.* London: Home & Van Thal, 1948.

324 p. Reprinted with a new afterword by Pauline Gray, London: Hogarth, 1985. ML403.G7 ISBN 0-701-20642X (pbk)

Most of Gray's opinions about Sibelius and his music were expressed in his two books about the composer (see nos. 156 and 567), but in this account we have the candid recollections of personal encounters by one of the greatest Sibelius enthusiasts of the century. Gray describes (pp. 255–60 et passim) the composer's habits, his opinions, and aspects of his personality and enters into the written record one of those stories, widely circulated and infinitely varied, that grew out of Sibelius's legendary all-night dinner parties.

119. Ikonen, Lauri. "Jean Sibelius: Uusia Kalevala-teoksia" [Jean Sibelius: New Kalevala Works]. *Suomen musiikkilehti*, 1926: 93–94.

An interview for the Society for Culture and Education (*Kansanvalistusseura*) on the occasion of Sibelius's composition of the cantata *Song of Väinö* (*Väinon virsi*), whose text comes from canto 28 of the *Kalevala*. Sibelius seems to have replied chiefly in one-liners. Other works inspired by the Finnish epic, such as *Tapiola*, are discussed briefly together with *Oceanides* (*Aallottaret*), the composer's visits to Berlin and Italy, and music of young composers in Italy.

120. Jalas, Jussi. "Sibelius: 'Minulla ei koskaan ole ikävä, minulla on fantasiani'" [Sibelius: 'I am never bored, I have my fantasies']. In *Elämäni teemat* [Themes of My Life]. Edited by Olavi Lehmuksela, 53–75 et passim. Helsinki: Tammi, 1981. 251 p. ML422.J28A3 1981 ISBN 951-30-5328-8

Sibelius recalled by his son-in-law, conductor Jussi Jalas, who first met the composer in 1924. Especially useful for quoting the composer's musical observations and opinions and for sketching his relationship with various contemporaries.

121. Jordan, Sverre. *Fra et langt kunstnerliv* [From a Long Artistic Life]. Bergen: John Grieg, 1973. 196 p. See Chapter XIII (pp. 108–15) et passim. ML410.J786A3 ISBN 82-533-0152-9

These memoirs of Norwegian composer, critic, pianist, and conductor Sverre Jordan (1889–1972), who occupied a central place in the musical life of Bergen, include an engaging chapter on Sibelius whom Jordan first met in 1912. Bits of Sibelius's conversations are quoted; he is remembered as enthusiastically applauding after Schoenberg conducted his chamber symphony in Berlin; and he is portrayed in words and in photographs (opposite p. 51). Meanwhile, a Scandinavian context serves as the backdrop for remarks about Sibelius's music and his performances.

122. Kajanus, Robert. "Ristiäismatka" [Christening Journey]. *Kalevalaseuran vuosikirja* 12 (1932): 79–84.

Composer, conductor, and Sibelius promoter Kajanus affectionately recalls attending a Gallen-Kallela family christening at which Sibelius, who was also present, improvised chorale variations at the organ and sometimes seemed to forget the chorale tune being sung by the "choir," namely, the two bass voices of Kajanus and Mikko Slöör, brother-in-law of Gallen-Kallela.

123. Karttunen, Antero, ed. "'A Certain Kind of Look, All Blue.'" *Finnish Music Quarterly*, 1985, nos. 3–4: 86–91. The article appeared in Finnish as "Margareta Jalas muistelee isäänsä Jean Sibeliusta: 'Isällä oli sellainen sininen katse'" [Margareta Jalas Remembers Her Father Jean Sibelius: 'Father Had a Certain Kind of Blue Look'], in *Suomen Kuvalehti*, 1985, no. 49: 70–73.

A fond recollection of the composer by his last surviving daughter, vividly portraying aspects of the Sibelius family's home life. Margareta recalls certain details about the Eighth Symphony as well as childhood memories of her father playing Papageno's song from *Magic Flute* on the piano.

124. Kilpinen, Yrjö. *"Mahtava majakka säteilee maailmaan," Muistopuhe Kalevalaseuran kunniajäsenen Jean Sibeliuksen arkun ääressä Suurkirkossa 30.9.1957* ["A Powerful Beacon Radiates to the World," Commemorative Speech for Kalevala Society Honorary

Member Jean Sibelius in the Great Church, September 30, 1957]. Helsinki: Helsingin Liikekirjapaino Oy, 1958. 4 p.

Text of a funeral oration by a composer whose songs were extremely popular in Finland, England, and Germany. Kilpinen observes that while Sibelius and his music were loved around the world, the composer's music, which lives on, gave something tremendously valuable to Finland's people whom he, in turn, loved.

125. Konow, Walter von. "Muistoja Jean Sibeliuksen poikavuosilta" [Memories of Jean Sibelius's Boyhood]. *Aulos*, 1925: 28–30.

Walter von Konow, later historian and intendant of Turku Castle, first came to know Sibelius at the age of six. The charming portrait he paints of his best friend—the pranks, the theatricality, the imagination, the behavior in school—provides much of what we know today about the composer's childhood. Konow, however, seems to have been rather naïve, and his recollections may not be entirely reliable.

126. Krohn, Ilmari. *Sävelmuistoja elämäni varrelta* [Musical Memories During My Lifetime]. Helsinki: Werner Söderström Osakeyhtiö, 1951. 214 p.

Musicologist and composer Krohn, one of Sibelius's rivals for a position at Helsinki University in 1896, recalls such events as meeting the composer on board the ship bound for Germany in 1889 and attending the premiere of the Violin Concerto. He discusses in a nontechnical way his idiosyncratic interpretation of Sibelius's symphonies (annotated as nos. 574 and 575), which he believed had revealed the true emotional and programmatic meaning of these works. See especially pp. 128–39, with scattered quotes from Sibelius.

127. Lagus, Hugo. "Några musikminnen" [Some Music Memories]. *Finsk tidskrift* 118 (1935): 39–48.

A student at the Helsinki Music Institute in the 1880s, Lagus recalls Sibelius, Wegelius, Busoni, Armas Järnefelt, Alfred

Reisenauer, and others. Of Sibelius he provides a physical description and a commentary on his behavior.

128. Legge, Walter. "Conversations with Sibelius." *Musical Times*, March 1935: 218–20. Appeared in Swedish as "Samtal med Sibelius," *Nu*, March 22, 1935.

Surprisingly frank opinions from Sibelius on matters ranging from fellow composers to audience responses to his symphonies as reported by the indefatigable Walter Legge. As often happens, the composer's recollections are not infallible: His working method, he told Legge, involved "no sketches, no drafts, notes, or short scores: neither do I touch a piano." For a refutation of such claims, see, among other sources, no. 21.

129. Lipaev, Ivan. "Talvella ja keväällä Jean Sibeliuksen luona" [With Sibelius in Winter and in Spring]. *Musiikkitiede* 3 (1991): 3–11.

Recollections of two social calls paid to Sibelius in his first years at Järvenpää. Lipaev's report was originally published in 1913 in *Russkaia Muzykal'naia Gazeta* 30–31 (July 28–August 4, 1913) and is printed here in an unfortunately poor Finnish translation by Johanna Kiuru.

130. Marvia, Einari. "Kymmenen vuoden takainen käynti Ainolassa" [A Visit to Ainola Ten Years Ago]. *Pieni musiikkilehti*, 1965, no. 6: 33–36.

Marvia's visit to the ninety-year-old Sibelius is of interest for the old man's amusing recollections of his aunts and uncles and of his grandmother Borg, although there are few direct quotes. Two photographs show the old Sibelius at the piano and with Kirsten Flagstad.

131. Mezzadri, P. "Sibelius." *Musica d'oggi* 9 (February 1927): 37–39.

Short consideration of Sibelius against the background of Finland's musical history and an assessment of the works in two phases: one based in the nationalist tradition, the other more personal. The essay concludes with a report of Sibelius's comments made during an interview.

132. Newmarch, Rosa. *Jean Sibelius: A Short Story of a Long Friendship*. With a Foreword by Granville Bantock. Boston: C. C. Birchard, 1939; London: Goodwin & Tabb, 1945. 99 p. ML410.S54N22 1945c

Although her remarks on the music have been superseded, Newmarch provides a valuable human record of the Sibelius she first came to know in 1905. She uses letters and diary entries to furnish documentation for many of the composer's social and musical activities, relates an episode in the translating of Sibelius's songs, and perhaps most importantly, gives the texts of a number of letters from Sibelius. An appendix reproduces four additional letters to Granville Bantock in facsimile. Photographs include one taken by the author showing Sibelius on the shore of Lake Saimaa.

133. Paul, Adolf. "Mein Freund Sibelius, I–III" [My Friend Sibelius, I–III]. *Völkischer Beobachter* (January 22, 28, 29, 1938) [not paginated].

In this three-part article, author and pianist Paul, one of the composer's good friends from his Helsinki student days and throughout the remainder of his life, portrays an endearing Sibelius who was enchanted by E. T. A. Hoffman and pretty girls and who would as soon spend his last pocket money on a yellow rose as on a good cigar. He describes Sibelius's family, his hypochondria, and his social and musical activities in Berlin and concludes with an account of the composition of the *King Christian* music. A different illustration of Sibelius appears with each installment. The novelist in Paul colors much of his prose; hence, the trustworthiness of his account as historical fact remains questionable.

134. Paul, Adolf. *Profiler: Minnen av stora personligheter* [Profiles: Memories of Great Personalities]. Helsingfors: Söderström & Co.; Stockholm: Fahlcrantz & Co., 1937. 186 p.

Deftly sketched reminiscences, not only of Sibelius but also of other contemporaries who made the cultural world of Scandinavia so rich: Ibsen, Busoni, Georg Brandes, Albert Edelfelt, to name a few, illustrated with drawings by such artists as Edvard Munch. The chapter on Sibelius, "När Jean Sibelius dirigerade" [When Jean Sibelius Conducted], pp. 32–37, describes the composition and first performance of the music to Paul's play *King Christian II*. Originally published in the newspaper *Hufvudstadsbladet* (December 8, 1925), the article has been frequently reprinted in other newspapers and magazines, often in abbreviated form.

135. Paul, Adolf. "Zwei Fennonenhauptlinge: Sibelius/Gallén" [Two Finnish Leaders: Sibelius/Gallén]. *Deutsch-Nordisches Jahrbuch für Kulturaustausch und Volkskunde 1914*. Jena: Eugen Diederichs, 1914, 114–119, 121.

Paul recounts various colorful biographical incidents in the lives of Sibelius and their comrade, Axel Gallén, or as he later called himself, Akseli Gallen-Kallela. A drawing of the composer sketched by Gallén on a calling card accompanies the memoir. Paul, who had relocated to Berlin, also discusses Sibelius's difficulties in having his music performed in that city.

136. Pohjola, Johanna. "Kun pikku Helsinki kohisi" [When Little Helsinki Was Buzzing]. *Suomen Kuvalehti*, April 25, 1986: 69–73.

An interview with violinist Kai Kajanus, son of conductor and composer Robert Kajanus, who recalls various great figures from Sibelius to Eino Leino visiting his home during his boyhood.

137. Ranta, Sulho. "Jean Sibelius" [in Finnish]. *Suomalainen Suomi* (December 1935): 289–95. An English-language version appears as "Music, the Universal Language" in the *Cathay Cosmopolitan*, January 1936: 43–47.

Prompted by the celebration of Sibelius's seventieth birthday, Finnish composer and critic Ranta contributed this adulatory survey of Sibelius's work for a cultural and political periodical in Helsinki. He mentions compositions inspired by the *Kalevala* and by national and historical events as well as incidental music, songs, and symphonies. Ranta notes that Richard Strauss, Alexander Glazunov, and Sibelius had all turned seventy; of the three, only Sibelius, whom he rather cloyingly describes as never hypermodern but only himself, can really be called up-to-date.

138. Ranta, Sulho. *Musiikin valtateillä: Musiikkia ja muusikoita* [On the Highways of Music: Music and Musicians]. Helsinki: Werner Söderström Osakeyhtiö, 1942. 236 p.

Selected writings of Finnish composer Ranta. In a group of essays entitled "Sibeliana" (p. 9–39), he reflects on Sibelius's major works; offers several pages of sayings by Sibelius, remembered from a conversation in 1934; reminisces, sometimes ecstatically, about distinguished Sibelius conductors; and presents his ideas on the importance of Runeberg and Karelian song to Sibelius.

139. Ranta, Sulho. *Sävelten valoja ja varjoja: Toinen kirja musiikista ja muusikoista* [Lights and Shadows of Tone: Another Book about Music and Musicians]. Helsinki: Werner Söderström Osakeyhtiö, 1946. 302 p.

The three opening chapters (pp. 11–24) are devoted to Sibelius and include a birthday speech from 1945, a review of Sibelius's growth from nationalist composer to world figure, and a report of a visit to Ainola, also in 1945. The report includes various quotes from Sibelius on matters ranging from his American visit to encounters with such contemporaries as Robert Kajanus and Claude Debussy. Later in the volume Eero Järnefelt's portrait of the composer appears (between pp. 32–33), showing Sibelius in 1892.

140. Reuter, Jonatan. "Jean Sibelius i Tvärminne" [Jean Sibelius at Tvärminne]. In *Allehanda minnen*, 154–57. N.p.: Förlaget Bro, 1946. 293 p.

In his "Memories of All Kinds," poet Reuter describes Sibelius during the summer of 1902 when he visited the little seaside village of Tvärminne. Reuter suggests that the music of *At Sea (Till havs)*, his poem that Sibelius composed into a choral piece in 1917, contains impressions of this time. Reuter also remembers such contemporaries connected to Sibelius as Karl August Tavaststjerna, Carl Snoilsky, and Abraham Ojanperä.

141. Similä, Martti. *Sibeliana*. Helsinki: Otava, 1945. 55 p. ML410.S54S7 1945

In honor of Sibelius's eightieth birthday, Similä, Finnish pianist, composer and orchestral conductor who often performed Sibelius's compositions, assembled his memoirs of a friend and his music. Divided into four parts, "Introduction," "Theme," "Music," and "Intimacies," this little book relates conversations by and about Sibelius, tells about certain Sibelius performances, and describes encounters with distinguished contemporaries. Illustrated with music examples and delicate drawings by Aarne Nopsanen.

142. Söderjhelm, Werner. *Skrifter* [Writings]. Vol. 3, *Profiler* [Profiles]. Helsingfors: Holger Schildt Förlag, 1923. 301 p.

The *Profiles* of this professor and critic portray Sibelius in the context of Finland's cultural community, beginning as they do with essays about Sibelius's friend, artist Albert Edelfelt. About Sibelius there is the speech Söderjhelm made on the occasion of the composer's fiftieth birthday ("Jean Sibelius: Tal vid femtioårsfesten," pp. 173–81), in which Söderhjelm admiringly places his compatriot in the company of Finland's shining artists, from Akseli Gallen-Kallela and Juhani Aho to Ida Aalberg and Karl August Tavaststjerna.

143. Tawaststjerna, Erik. "Ainola 1956." In *Scènes historiques: Kirjoituksia vuosilta 1945–58* [Historic Scenes: Writings from the Years 1945–58], 225-28. Helsinki: Otava, 1992. ML60.T2955 1992 ISBN 951-1-12113-8

A visit with the aged Sibelius, interesting for the composer's views on certain contemporaries such as Bartók, remarks on tempo, and self-perception.

144. Tawaststjerna, Erik. *Voces intimae: muistikuvia lapsuudesta* [Intimate Voices: Pictures Remembered from Childhood]. Helsinki: Otava, 1990. 142 p. Appeared in Swedish as *Voces intimae: minnesbilder från barndomen* (Helsingfors: Söderström & Co., 1990). ML423.T19A3 1990 ISBN 951-52-1328-2

A memoir about growing up in Finland that includes references to Sibelius, the seldom-reproduced Antti Favén picture of the composer (from 1925, p. 86), and the opening measures of the melodrama *The Lonely Ski Trail* (*Ett ensamt skidspår*, p. 93). Tawaststjerna recalls hearing Robert Kajanus conduct Sibelius's Symphony no. 4 in the Festival Hall of Helsinki University in 1930 (pp. 127–31). The most valuable contribution here is surely Tawaststjerna's recollection that the composer, on leaving this concert, paused on seeing the glistening night sky and recited the words of the poet Karl August Tavaststjerna, "Slowly as the evening clouds their purple lose—." This anecdote has been translated into English by David McDuff as "An Early Encounter with Sibelius," *Books from Finland* 27 (1993): 134–36.

145. Turunen, Martti. "Kaksi tuntia mestarin puheilla" [Two Hours Speaking with the Master]. *Suomen musiikkilehti*, 1931: 2.

Sibelius's impressions and opinions of jazz are recorded in several quotations. The composer admits that he was not particularly sympathetic to jazz, although characteristically he gives most of his views in analogies that admit of various interpretations.

146. Väisänen, A. O. "Jean Sibelius vaikutelmistaan" [Jean Sibelius Gives His Impressions]. *Kalevalaseuran vuosikirja* 1 (1921): 77–81.

An interview intended to coincide with the publication of the first yearbook of the Kalevala Society. Sibelius purports to remember his early impressions of the *Kalevala*, tells about hearing the famed rune singer Petri Shemeikka, and discusses various *Kalevala*-inspired works, including *Swan of Tuonela* and *En saga*, which elsewhere he described as originating from a world other than that of the *Kalevala*. Here he asserts that *En saga* was originally composed as a nonette, which he was advised to arrange for the organ in Porvoo (!). There is also an important statement about program music: Sibelius mentions a planned but never excecuted composition on the *Kalevala* story of forging the Sampo and explains that music should not sound literal; rather, he says, the forging should sound *ppp*, as though coming from far away. A page from the manuscript of *Kullervo* is reproduced.

147. Vehanen, Kosti. *Marian Anderson: A Portrait.* New York: Whittlesey House, McGraw-Hill, 1941. 270 p. Reprint. Westport, Conn.: Greenwood, 1970. ML420.A6V4 1970. ISBN 0-8371-4051-X. Appeared in Finnish as *Vuosikymmenen Marian Andersonin säestäjänä* [A Decade as Marian Anderson's Accompanist] (Helsinki: Werner Söderström Osakeyhtiö, 1941). 198 p.

A memoir by the Finnish pianist who was accompanist to Marian Anderson. Of interest for the Sibelius anecdotes and remarks quoted, including (p. 25–29) a description of Anderson singing for Sibelius at Ainola and (p. 153) the composer's prediction that the twenty-first century will be for Handel what the twentieth has been for Bach. One photograph of Aino and Jean Sibelius, looking rather grim in his large hat, with the author. No index to either edition.

148. Wasenius, K. F. "Elegi av Jean Sibelius (Några personliga minnen)" [Elegy by Jean Sibelius (Some Personal Memories)]. *Tidning för musik* 6 (1916): 17–19.

The versatile Wasenius played viola in the Music Institute quartet with Sibelius, engaged in music publishing from 1888 until 1907, and eventually became known as the music critic "Bis." In this memoir he recalls visiting Sibelius in the winter of 1898. According to Wasenius, the composer sat at the piano for an hour playing the newly composed music to Adolf Paul's play *King Christian II*, one of several clear indications of Sibelius's vital relationship to the keyboard. The "Elegy" of the title refers to one of the numbers from this music in which Wasenius found his "life's song" and which he believed resonated with the Finnish spirit.

III
The Life

A. Biographies

Biographies began to be written about Jean Sibelius during the composer's lifetime. The very first was Erik Furuhjelm's *Jean Sibelius* (no. 155) published in 1916. Nearly twenty years later, Karl Ekman, Jr., brought out a more expansive life and works account in honor of Sibelius's seventieth birthday (no. 154). Both volumes contain material that seems to have come directly from the composer. Yet despite the cooperation of the composer and his family, or perhaps partly because of it, establishing a fair and accurate biographical picture of Sibelius has not been an easy task.

Within Finland, the great reverence still accorded Sibelius renders it difficult to portray him with the human frailties that make all men kin. Most of the early Finnish biographies were written in tones of awe, and few of them contain any kind of critical apparatus such as source notes or bibliography. Only with Erik Tawaststjerna's *Jean Sibelius* (no. 175), published in five volumes over a twenty-year period, and the one-volume *Jean Sibelius* by Erkki Salmenhaara (no. 170) has the balance of the adulatory Finnish biographies begun to be redressed by studies that are thoroughly researched and carefully documented. Unfortunately, the publication of the English translation of Tawaststjerna's volumes without the author's extensive documentation and the existence of the Salmenhaara biography only in Finnish have meant that much information is still denied the wider community of scholars and music lovers.

Abroad, the picture is also complicated. Early foreign biographers, men like the American novelist Elliot Arnold (no. 149), so romanticized the subject that it might be questioned whether their work even belongs in a scholarly bibliography. At best, such books tend to show an image of Sibelius that was fostered at a given time and place in history. The first attempt to put Sibelius scholarship on an objective and solid footing was made by Harold E. Johnson. During two years in Finland during the 1950s, Johnson sought out primary sources in libraries and archives and led a campaign for the location and preservation of this material. When his biography (no. 159) appeared, however, its critical tone sharply divided the community of Sibelius lovers. Enthusiastically welcomed in the United States as an antidote to what many viewed as the sensational myth-making surrounding the composer, Johnson's book was execrated in Finland and England. The first full-scale biography to steer successfully between the shoals of adulation on the one side and condemnation on the other was Robert Layton's (no. 160), published in 1965, and subsequent updated editions still prove their worth. Most of the volumes listed below discuss Sibelius's music as well as his life. And many have special features, such as work lists, quotations from letters, and illustrations, that give them a certain value even when some of their "facts" are known to be inaccurate.

* * *

149. Arnold, Elliot. *Finlandia, The Story of Sibelius*. Illustrated by Lolita Graham. New York: Henry Holt, 1941; revised, 1950. 247 p. ML410.S54A7 1950

The first full-length biography of Sibelius published in the United States, written in the novelistic style employed by its author in his children's stories and in his war fiction, *First Comes Courage* and *Commandos* (Arnold was a captain in the U.S. Army Air Force who was awarded the Bronze Star during World War II). The typeface and illustrations in his Sibelius book are those typically found in books written for children, for whom the volume was originally intended. Arnold incorporated a number of myths in his narrative, and even though Sibelius himself provided some corrections for the revised edition, all too many of the "facts" are not supported by current evidence. The volume, which includes a list of recordings, reached a wide audience; by 1945 there had been five printings.

150. Balogh, Pál, almási. *Jean Sibelius.* Kis zenei könyvtár, 18. Budapest: Gondolat, 1961. 153 p. ML410.S54B3

Balogh's little book provides an introduction to Sibelius for Hungarian readers. It contains a biographical calendar, a work list organized by opus numbers, a short bibliography as well as photographs and music examples.

151. Brüll, Erich. *Jean Sibelius: für Sie porträtiert* [Jean Sibelius: Portrayed for You]. Leipzig: VEB Deutscher Verlag für Musik, 1986. 82 p. ML410.S54B78 1986 ISBN 3-370-00152-7

Short biography for readers of German based on published sources and including a chronology and summary of works. Among the illustrations is a facsimile of the famous letter to Busoni in which Sibelius says that without Busoni, he (Sibelius) would have remained "eine Erscheinung aus dem Wäldern" ["an apparition out of the woods"].

Rev.: *Musik und Gesellschaft*, July 1987: 386.

152. Dernoncourt, Sylvie. *Sibelius.* Translated from French by María de la Paz Díaz González. Madrid: Espasa-Calpe, S.A., 1985. 103 p. ML410.S5D318 ISBN 84-239-5383-1 (pbk)

Although based on secondary sources, this biography, apparently published only in Spanish, begins somewhat differently from most by providing a chronology in which important dates in the life and work of Sibelius are aligned with notable musical, artistic, and historical events around the world. A catalogue lists 18 "principal" compositions plus songs; there is also a discography.

153. Downes, Olin. *Sibelius the Symphonist.* New York: The Philharmonic-Symphony Society of New York, 1956. 48 p. ML410.S54D7

Written in the last year of Downes's life (the proofs were corrected on his death bed and published posthumously), this little book presents Sibelius as viewed by his most enthusiastic champion in the United States. It begins with a biographical portrait and then discusses the symphonies, the major tone poems, and the Concerto for Violin. Most of the opinions had been expressed before, repeatedly, in lectures, reviews, and newspaper articles. The biographical portion had appeared separately the previous year under the title "Sibelius, Today and Tomorrow," in *The Saturday Review*, December 10, 1955: 30–31, 34, 36.

154. Ekman, Karl, Jr. *Jean Sibelius: en konstnärs liv och personlighet.* Helsingfors: Holger Schildt Förlag; Stockholm: Bokforlaget Natur och Kultur, 1935. 271 p.; 2d edition, 1935; 3d edition, 1936; 4th revised and enlarged edition, entitled *Jean Sibelius och hans verk* ([Helsingfors]: Holger Schildt Förlag, [Stockholm]: Forum, 1956). ML410.S54E43 1935

Translated into Finnish as *Jean Sibelius: taiteilijan elämä ja persoonallisuus* (Helsinki: Otava, 1935); 2d edition, 1935; 3d edition, 1935; 4th revised and enlarged edition: *Jean Sibelius ja hänen elämäntyönsä* (Helsinki: Otava, 1956).

Translated into English by Edward Birse as *Jean Sibelius: The Life and Personality of an Artist* (Helsingfors: Holger Schildt Förlag, 1935). Another edition was entitled *Jean Sibelius: His Life and Personality.* With a Foreword by Ernest Newman (London: Alan Wilmer, 1936; New York: Alfred A. Knopf, 1938; 2d edition, 1946. Reprint. Westport, Conn.: Greenwood, 1976). ISBN 0-8371-6027-8

Translated into Danish by Bodil Bech as *Jean Sibelius: en kunstners Liv og Personlighed* (Copenhagen: Martins Forlag, 1941).

Karl Ekman, Jr., was the son of soprano Ida Ekman, the first singer to perform Sibelius's songs in central Europe, and Karl Ekman, a conductor and pianist who had studied with Busoni and was a personal friend of Sibelius. These background influences set the tone of a sympathetic if sometimes sophomoric biography ("Intimate contact with nature enabled him to devote himself with undiminished power to producing fresh beauties") published to coincide with the composer's seventieth birthday. The book was written with the help of Sibelius, whose views are frequently quoted or paraphrased. Later, however, the composer complained in his diary that Ekman, Jr., had attributed to him phrases he did not say. Yet the author also interviewed Sibelius's friends and sought out his correspondence, particularly letters to Baron Axel Carpelan, and the illustrations include some of these sources in facsimile. The revised 1956 version, which exists only in Finnish and Swedish, contains additional material and is considered Sibelius's "authorized" biography. Containing a work list, the volume attracted widespread attention as is indicated by the numerous editions and translations.

Rev.: For the literally dozens of reviews, see no. 1, pp. 2–3.

155. Furuhjelm, Erik. *Jean Sibelius: hans tondiktning och drag ur hans liv* [Jean Sibelius: His Musical Compositions and Features of His Life]. Borgå: Holger Schildt Förlag, 1916; Stockholm: Albert Bonniers Förlag, 1917. 229 p. ML410.S56F99

Translated into Finnish by Leevi Madetoja as *Jean Sibelius: hänen sävelrunoutensa ja piirteitä hänen elämästään* (Helsinki: Werner Söderström Osakeyhtiö, 1916).

Furuhjelm was a Finnish composer whose volume is the first book-length biography of Sibelius. Intended for Sibelius's fiftieth birthday, the book was not published until the following year; its appearance was delayed to enable Furuhjelm to locate the score of the *Kullervo* Symphony, on which he particularly wanted to comment. One of Furuhjelm's central themes was Sibelius's empathy with nature, a characteristic which is traced from the composer's childhood. The author gives especially sensitive treatment to the early works, providing numerous music examples from the chamber compositions written prior to 1885 and sketching a rich panorama of potentially influential musical events in Sibelius's hometown. Along with abundant quotations of music examples up through Symphony no. 5, there are many illustrations of the composer and his family.

156. Gray, Cecil. *Sibelius*. London: Oxford University Press, 1931. ix, 224 p. 2d edition, 1934. Reprint. Westport, Conn.: Hyperion, 1979. Translated into Spanish by Daniel Martini as *Sibelius* (Buenos Aires: Editorial Sudamericana, 1954). ML410.S54G7

Gray's rhapsodic *Sibelius* hailed the composer as the greatest master of the symphony since Beethoven and completely uninfluenced by Wagner. These observations and other sharp criticisms and omissions of Germans in their self-proclaimed supremacy in symphonic music reflected the xenophobic attitudes prevalent in Great Britain in the 1930s, while the unfortunate mixing of fact with fictional hyperbole (he argued that Sibelius was more Swedish than Finnish) engendered an outcry against both the book and its subject. Yet Gray has a perceptive discussion of nationality in music, insight into the "problem" of Sibelius's fecundity, and a deep sympathy with the music, which he surveys and catalogues at the book's end, thereby providing a work list that has served many a scholar. The frontispiece is Ivar Helander's photograph of the composer, and the book is dedicated "To the Finnish People in sympathy and admiration."

157. Hauch, Gunnar. *Jean Sibelius*. Copenhagen: Skandinavisk Musikforlag, 1915. 17 p.

An ingratiating biographical essay that welcomes the end of German hegemony in music and hails the rise of Northern composers, among whom Sibelius is foremost. No music examples or bibliography.

158. James, Burnett. *The Music of Jean Sibelius*. With a Foreword by Raymond Bantock. East Brunswick, N.J.: Associated University Presses; Rutherford, N.J.: Fairleigh Dickinson University Press, 1983. 174 p. ML410.S54J33 1983 ISBN 0-8386-3070-7

James's book appears in a series intended "to clarify each composer's sound" for the general listener. To that end, he offers a summary of life events followed by a survey of Sibelius's works by category, often making adroit comparisons to contemporary English music. This fine volume, with its music examples, illustrations, bibliography, and annotated appendix of "Recommended Recordings," affords an excellent introduction to the man and his music.

Rev.: *Music & Letters* 66 (1985): 147–49; *Musical Times*, December 1984: 705.

159. Johnson, Harold Edgar. *Jean Sibelius*. New York: Alfred Knopf, 1959. xi, 287 p.; London: Faber & Faber, 1960. Reprint. Westport, Conn.: Greenwood, 1978. ML410.S54J6. Translated into Finnish by Yrjö Kivimies (Helsinki: Otava, 1960); translated into Swedish by Olof Hoffsten (Helsingfors: Holger Schildt Förlag; Stockholm: Rabén & Sjögren, 1961), with added discography.

Published just two years after the composer's death, Johnson's monograph caused consternation in Finland. It portrayed Sibelius as obscuring his musical debts to Finnish folk music, to his friend the conductor Robert Kajanus, and to Wagner, depicted him as ungrateful to the Finnish Government for his lifelong pension, and showed him as unsympathetic to the struggles of younger composers. As he put it, Johnson attempted to reduce the composer to "mortal stature." In America the book was praised for its "objectivity." In retrospect the attitude appears symptomatic of the American backlash against Sibelius in the years immediately following his death. To his credit, however, Johnson made important discoveries of music lost or forgotten (the original score of *The Lizard*, for instance); he created the most complete work list of the time, which he later revised and published separately (see no. 20); and above all, he drew attention to the importance of the primary sources.

Rev.: In addition to the numerous reviews listed in Blum, no. 1, pp. 5–6, see no. 191.

160. Layton, Robert. *Sibelius*. London: J. M. Dent; New York: Farrar, Straus, and Giroux, 1965; revised, 1978, 1992. Reprint. 1971, 1983, 1984; 4th edition, New York: Schirmer Books, 1993. 247 p. Translated into Swedish by Stig Jacobsson (Borås: Norma, 1987). ML410.S54L35 1992 ISBN 0-460-8606-4X

Using the Master Musicians series familiar "Life and Works" format, Robert Layton's *Sibelius* was first published in 1965 when the author, with respectful but never adulatory tone, endeavored to rectify the negative critical reactions fostered by the wildly enthusiastic volumes of Cecil Gray and Constant Lambert (nos. 156 and 349) and the judgments considered too harsh of Harold E. Johnson (no. 159). Well written and useful, the current edition benefits from a great deal of recent research, adding such things as a discussion of the complications of cataloguing Sibelius's works. The volume is illustrated with numerous music examples and photographs and contains a calendar, a systematic catalogue of works, and a convenient appendix of personalia that identifies some of the lesser-known figures in Sibelius's life.

Rev.: *Music Review* 45 (1984): 310.

161. Levas, Santeri. *Jean Sibelius: muistelma suuresta ihmisestä* [Jean Sibelius: Memories of a Great Man]. Helsinki: Werner Söderström Osakeyhtiö, 1957–1960. 2 vols. Vol. I: *Nuori Sibelius* [The Young Sibelius], 260 p.; Vol. II: *Järvenpään Mestari* [Master of Järvenpää], 370 p. ML410.S54L45. New combined edition under the original title (Helsinki: Werner Söderström Osakeyhtiö, 1986). ISBN 951-0-13306-X. Translated into Estonian by S. Liiberg as *Jean Sibelius* (Tallinn: 1971). 384 p.

A shortened version, translated into English by Percy M. Young, was entitled *Sibelius: A Personal Portrait* (London: J. M. Dent, 1972; Lewisburg, [Pa.]: Bucknell University Press, 1973); 2d edition (with color photographs) (Helsinki: Werner Söderström Osakeyhtiö, 1986). 158 p.

Santeri Levas, who worked as Sibelius's personal secretary for over two decades, first published this Finnish-language biography not long after the composer's death. Not a musician himself, Levas dwelt less upon technical aspects of the music and more upon events. He was an especially keen observer of the last two decades of the composer's life, during which he recorded anecdotes, aphorisms, and eccentricities. His biography includes a list of works and, in the Finnish editions, a bibliography valuable for references to selected newspaper and periodical articles as well as to books. The one-volume Finnish edition and the second English one contain beautiful color illustrations, many of them seldom seen in the context of Sibelius biography. Some depict Sibelius in contemporary artworks, and their selection and arrangement give graphic testimony to the vibrancy of Finland's cultural life.

162. Levas, Santeri. *Sibelius: A Personal Portrait.* Translated by Percy M. Young. London: J. M. Dent, 1972; Lewisburg, Pa.: Bucknell University Press, 1973; 2d edition, Helsinki: Werner Söderström Osakeyhtiö, 1986. ML410.S54L4513 1986 ISBN 951-0-13608-5

Annotated as no. 161.

163. Machado, Walter. *Jean Sibelius, o gênio das sinfonias cósmicas* [Jean Sibelius: A Genius of the Cosmic Symphonies]. Rio de Janeiro: Belo Horizonte, 1961. 99 p.

In a most individual book, the author presents in ecstatic prose and in his own imaginative drawings his personal impressions of the sublime and cosmic power of Sibelius's music. He dwells particularly on *Swanwhite* (*Svanevit*), *Tapiola*, and Symphonies no. 2 and 7 and identifies the latter with the celestial ambience of the universe. There is a short biographical chapter, a list of selected works, and a brief bibliography, including several Brazilian sources.

164. Newmarch, Rosa. *Jean Sibelius: A Finnish Composer*. Leipzig and London: Breitkopf & Härtel, [1906], 24 p. Translated into German by Ludmille Kirschbaum as *Jean Sibelius: ein finnländischer Komponist* (Leipzig: Breitkopf & Härtel, 1906). ML410.S54N2

Rosa Newmarch's booklet is a published version of a paper first read at a soirée of the Concert Goers' Club in London, February 22, 1906. An enthusiast of Russian and Czech nationalism, Newmarch emphasized Sibelius's Finnish background and temperament, especially evident in the early *Kalevala*-inspired works. Briefly discussing the symphonic, piano, and vocal works up through Symphony no. 2, she correctly predicted a popular future for the then little-known *Finlandia* and foresaw distinction for the composer as a symphonist rather than as a Finnish Wagner. Newmarch's book was the first publication devoted entirely to Sibelius and helped to popularize the composer in both England and America.

165. Niemann, Walter. *Jean Sibelius*. Leipzig: Breikopf & Härtel, 1917. 70 p. ML410.S54N24

Sibelius's most vociferous advocate in Germany, Niemann repeatedly emphasized Sibelius's roots in Finnish folk song and Northern melancholy, often to the composer's detriment. In this volume, he points out Sibelius's debts to Wagner and Debussy and includes a work list compiled from Breitkopf & Härtel's catalogue. Niemann's little book, the first Sibelius biography in German, is of interest today chiefly for its depiction of Sibelius as viewed in Germany around the time of World War I.

For a response to the nationalist image propounded here, see Toivo Haapanen, "Uusi Sibelius-tutkielma ja kysymys Sibeliuksen musiikin suomalaisuudesta" [The Newest Sibelius Research and the Question of the Finnishness of the Music of Jean Sibelius], *Säveletär*, 1918, no. 9: 109–14.

166. Ottaway, Hugh. *Sibelius*. Novello Short Biographies. London: Novello, 1968. 18 p. ML410.S54O9

Although brief, Ottaway's *Sibelius* is a calm and measured introduction that includes thoughtful comments on the symphonies, *Kullervo*, and *Tapiola* and a list of principal works.

167. Pickenhayn, Jorge Oscar. *Sibelius*. Buenos Aires: Editorial Julio Korn, 1960. 44 p.

A review of the high points of Sibelius's life and music for Spanish readers. The author concludes with a summary of contemporary opinions about the works, adroitly drawing parallels to prevailing opinions about Stravinsky and Schoenberg. No bibliography or music examples.

168. Pirsch, Georges A. *Jean Sibélius*. Gilly: Éditions de la Nouvelle Revue Belgique, 1944. 88 p. ML410.S54P578

An introduction for the general French-language reader, Pirsch's *Sibélius* derives much of its information from Karl Ekman, Jr.'s biography (duly acknowledged). The volume is perhaps most interesting for the perspective provided on Sibelius from the French-speaking world, especially as Pirsch includes citations from French and Belgian critics. A stern portrait of Sibelius and a brief bibliography of sources, mostly French, help to round out a Gallic view of the composer.

169. Ringbom, Nils-Eric. *Sibelius*. Helsingfors: Holger Schildt Förlag; Stockholm: Albert Bonniers Förlag, 1948. 165 p. ML410.S54R5. Translated into Finnish by Margareta Jalas (Helsinki: Otava, 1948). 126 p.

Translated into English by G. I. C. de Courcy as *Jean Sibelius: A Master and His Work* (Norman, Oklahoma: University of Oklahoma Press, 1954). 196 p. Reprint. Westport, Conn.: Greenwood Press, 1977.

Translated into German by Edzard Schaper as *Jean Sibelius: Ein Meister und sein Werk* (Olten, Switzerland: Verlag Otto Walter AG, [c. 1950]). 207 p. Translated into Danish by Johan Kock as *Sibelius* (Copenhagen: Nyt Nordisk Forlag Arnold Busck, 1950). 162 p.

Ringbom's biographical material is drawn from the work of earlier biographers, Ekman and Furuhjelm, its blandishing tone evident from the subtitle of the English translation. The author, the respected intendant of the Helsinki Philharmonic Orchestra, provides interpretations of the music, of which he gives numerous examples, and quotations from personal conversations with the composer. List of works.

170. Salmenhaara, Erkki. *Jean Sibelius*. Helsinki: Tammi, 1984. 470 p. ML410.S54S18 1984 ISBN 951-30-549O-X

The most detailed one-volume biography of Sibelius available, although its Finnish-language text limits its wider use. Based in part on material found also in no. 175. The author, a Finnish scholar and composer, provides insightful discussions of the music. He has also reproduced many excellent period photographs and concert programs, provided a Sibelius family genealogical chart, and, perhaps best of all and accessible even to those who do not read Finnish, compiled a detailed chronology that clarifies events in Sibelius's peripatetic life. Brief bibliography and well-produced music examples.

Rev.: *Synkooppi* 7 (1984): 32.

171. Sbârcea, George. *Jean Sibelius, Viaţa şi opera* [Jean Sibelius, Life and Works]. [Editura Muzicala a Uniunii Compozitorilor din Republica Socialista Romania]: Bucarest: Editora Musicalâ, 1965. 280 p. Picture essay and music examples not paginated.

Although Sbârcea's book appeared as part of the Sibelius centennial celebrations, it is not just an appreciative essay but a considered study based on existing scholarship and on an interview with the composer in 1943. An extensive picture essay, work list, and music examples make this a substantial introduction to Sibelius in Romanian.

172. Schouwman, Hans. *Sibelius.* Haarlem: Gottmer, 1949. 222 p. ML410.S56S37

A pianist and singer, Schouwman wrote his book to make Sibelius's compositions, especially the orchestral works, better understood in Holland, where even in 1950 Sibelius's music was not regular concert fare. Examples of principal themes and a list of main works by genre.

173. Tammaro, Ferruccio. *Jean Sibelius.* Torino: Eri/Edizioni Rai, 1984. 508 p. ML410.S54T2 1984

An extremely informative Italian-language biography that ought to be more widely known. While the author acknowledges some debt to the work of Erik Tawaststjerna (no. 175), he quotes from letters cited nowhere else, contributes a fresh discussion of the music vis-à-vis historical currents (illustrated with substantial excerpts from the scores), and generously supplies useful and often little-known details about Sibelius's contemporaries (where else does one find mention of William Grant Still's *Threnody* for the composer? See p. 465). An expansive bibliography, photographs, facsimiles, and work list.

Rev.: *Nuova rivista musicale italiana* 23 (1989): 151–52.

174. Tanzberger, Ernst. *Jean Sibelius: Eine Monographie, Mit einem Werkverzeichnis* [Jean Sibelius: A Monograph, With a Catalogue of Works]. Wiesbaden: Breitkopf & Härtel, 1962. 296 p. ML410.S54T25

The catalogue of works was also published separately as *Jean Sibelius: Werkverzeichnis* (Wiesbaden: Breitkopf & Härtel, [1962]). 27 p. Annotated as no. 27.

Tanzberger was one of the few German scholars in the first part of the century to undertake serious research on Sibelius. Like his countryman Walter Niemann before him, Tanzberger was strongly disposed toward the nationalist-romantic view of Sibelius. Although the work relies on Ekman, Jr. (no. 154) for some facts, it also incorporates a discussion of Sibelius's reputation in Germany through the 1950s, culminating with a transcription of the debate between the author and René Leibowitz, one of Sibelius's most caustic critics (see no. 287). The lion's share of attention, however, goes to the music, for which Tanzberger has supplied numerous motivic examples. His analyses are marked by a tendency to see the music as either strophic form or bar form, ideas developed at length in no. 533. Bibliography, illustrations.

Rev.: *Suomen musiikin vuosikirja 1962–63* (Helsinki: Otava, 1963), 58–60.

175. Tawaststjerna, Erik. *Jean Sibelius*. Helsinki: Otava, 1965–1988. 5 vols. Vol. I, translated by Tuomas Anhava, 1965; revised 1989. 357 p. Vol. II, translated by Tuomas Anhava, 1967. 329 p. Vol. III, translated by Erkki Salmenhaara, 1972. 403 p. Vol. IV, translated by Erkki Salmenhaara, 1978. 414 p. Vol. V, 1988. 439 p. A luxury edition of the five volumes was published by Otava in 1989. ML410.S54T294

Translated into English by Robert Layton as *Sibelius* (London: Faber & Faber, 1976–1986). Vol. I, 1865–1905. 316 p. ISBN 0-571-08832-5; Vol. II, 1904–1914. 302 p. ISBN 0-571-08833-3

Appeared in Swedish as *Jean Sibelius: Åren 1865–1893*, edited by Gitta Henning (Helsingfors: Söderström & Co., 1992). 296 p. ISBN 951-52-1445-9. *Jean Sibelius: Åren 1893–1904*, edited by Gitta Henning (Helsingfors: Söderström & Co., 1993). 255 p. ISBN 951-52-1468-8. *Jean Sibelius: Åren 1904–1914*, edited by Fabian Dahlström and Gitta Henning (Helsingfors: Söderström & Co., 1991). 384 p. ML410.S54T29 1991 ISBN 951-52-1337-1

The most extensive biography ever written about Sibelius. The work is the first to portray Sibelius's weaknesses as well as his strengths and the first to draw extensively on family correspondence as well as the composer's diary, which has since been restricted from scholarly use. For Finns, Tawaststjerna's sophisticated literary style, his thorough knowledge of the country's cultural and historical life (this enormously cultivated man was a pianist, a mathematician, a diplomat, a music critic, and eventually the professor of musicology at Helsinki University), and his love of his subject, to which he devoted some thirty years of his life, make his biography a literary and cultural achievement as much as a biographical one.

Partly because of the manner in which the volumes appeared—volumes I–IV were originally written in Swedish, then translated into Finnish for publication in Helsinki, subsequently translated into an abridged English edition, and only, in the 1990s, finally beginning to appear (although not in chronological order) in the original Swedish—the translations effectively represent quite different editions. The English translation, which also involves considerable rewriting, compresses the first three volumes into two, with a concomitant loss of material, including virtually all of the scholarly documentation. The reader is advised to see the very detailed review by George C. Schoolfield in *Scandinavian Studies* 50 (1978): 242–47 for some of the other significant abridgements of volume I. The English edition does, however, have the great advantage of an index with each of its two volumes. No index appeared in the Finnish edition until volume V, and the revisions that had meanwhile taken place in volume I mean that the index is valid only for the revised text. The appearance of the Swedish editions, from the author's original manuscripts in volumes I–IV, being edited by Tawaststjerna's able assistant Gitta Henning, is an especially welcome event, because these volumes provide the only source in which excerpts from Sibelius's diary can be read in the original language.

Rev.: Aho, Kalevi, "A Biography Akin to the Life of Its Subject: Erik Tawaststjerna's Monumental Biography of Sibelius Completed" in *Finnish Music Quarterly*, 1990: 76–92. The same review appeared under its Finnish title, "Elämäkerta joka on kuin kohteensa" in *Kanava* 17 (1990): 136–48, and has been reprinted in *Taiteilijan tehtävät postmodernissa yhteiskunnassa*, 280–300 (Jyväskylä: Gaudeamus, 1992).

For a discussion of Tawaststjerna's method, see no. 612, and the two reviews in *Musikrevy* 47 (1992): 182–83, 181.

Rev. of vol. V: *Parnasso* 39 (1989): 229–32; *Rondo*, March 7, 1989: 47; in English: *Books from Finland* 23 (1989): 102–03; *Finnish Music Quarterly*, 1989, no. 1: 50–51.

Rev. of English editions: of vol. I, in *Books from Finland* 11 (1977): 112–15; *Music & Letters* 58 (1977): 462–63; *Scandinavian Studies* 50 (1978): 242–47; of vol. II: in *Music & Letters* 68 (1987): 281; *Scandinavian Studies* 61 (1989): 279–80; *Times Literary Supplement* 1986: 1194.

Rev. of Swedish edition: vol. III, *Jean Sibelius: Åren 1904–1914*, in *Horisont* 39 (1992): 109–10.

176. Törne, Bengt de. *Sibelius: A Close-Up*. London: Faber & Faber; Boston: Houghton Mifflin, 1937. 117 p. In subsequent editions, the author's name appears as Bengt von Törne. ML410.S54T64 1937

Translated into Finnish by Margareta Jalas as *Sibelius: lähikuvia ja keskusteluja* (Helsinki: Otava, 1945). 110 p. 2d enlarged edition (Helsinki: Otava, 1965). 121 p.

Translated into Swedish as *Sibelius: i närbild och samtal* (Helsingfors: Söderström & Co.; Stockholm: Fahlcrantz & Gumaelius, 1945). 115 p.; revised 1955.

Translated into Italian by Vittoria Guerrini as *Conversazioni con Sibelius* (Firenze: Casa Editrice Monsalvato, 1943). 103 p.

Parts of the volume have also appeared frequently as articles in English, German, Finnish, and Swedish. The most substantial of these is entitled "Sibelius as a Teacher," *The Criterion* 16 (1937): 220–34; reprinted in *The Criterion 1922–1939 in Eighteen Volumes*, vol. 16. Edited by T. S. Eliot. London: Faber & Faber, 1967, 220–34.

Perhaps Sibelius's best-known pupil as a result of this endlessly promoted book, Bengt Axel de (von) Törne (1891–1967), Finnish composer and writer, preserved the fruits of his composition lessons with Sibelius during 1916–1917 in memories abundantly spiced with observations that are supposedly the great man's own. Here is Sibelius's famous remark about Wagner, his identification of the orchestra's greatest geniuses as Mozart and Mendelssohn, and many comments about orchestration. The Swedish edition of 1945 has a new chapter entitled "Sibelius inför sitt tionde decennium" [Sibelius on the Eve of his Tenth Decade]. It was this book, irksomely publicized by its author (the success of which is evident from the numerous translations), that aroused the rage of Theodor Adorno and René Leibowitz and prompted their vindictive ripostes; see nos. 287 and 292.

177. Vignal, Marc. *Jean Sibelius: l'homme et son oeuvre* [Jean Sibelius: The Man and His Work]. Paris: Éditions Seghers, 1965. 192 p. ML410.S54V5

Coming from a country whose citizens have often maligned Sibelius, Vignal's book is notable among other things as the first Sibelius biography in French. In a sympathetic and capable discussion, Vignal weaves the historical background to the composer's life around his narration of the biographical events and then considers the major orchestral works. This volume, although small, includes music examples, handsome photographs, a work list, a discography, and a short bibliography.

B. Biographical Articles

The changing frontiers of any discipline are usually first reflected in articles. Some of the most fascinating aspects of Sibelius and his music thus exist in this form. While articles devoted to the composer's style and specific musical compositions will be found in the music portion of this *Guide* (see the section Stylistic Studies as well as specific titles of compositions), those dealing chiefly with biographical matters appear below. Generally speaking, the most recent references and those addressing specific and well-defined topics are the best. However, some of the older material retains its value as will be indicated.

* * *

GENERAL

178. Andersson, Otto. "Jean Sibelius: Biografisk tabell" [Jean Sibelius: Biographical Table]. *Tidning för musik* 5 (1915): 175–82.

> An annotated biographical calendar that begins with the birth of "Hindrik Mattsson Sibbe" on October 3, 1709 and ends with the "completion" of Symphony no. 5 on December 4, 1915 (Andersson could not have known in 1915 that the work would be revised twice). Based on contemporary sources and probably on Andersson's own conversations with the composer, this table, largely forgotten today, supplies many useful and still accurate details (the correct year, for example, that Sibelius began to study violin with Gustaf Levander).

179. Andersson, Otto. "Jean Sibelius et la musique finlandaise" [Jean Sibelius and Finnish Music]. In *Finlande et Finlandais*, 175–96. Published under the direction of Werner Söderhjelm. Paris: Librairie Armand Colin, 1913. DK449.S7. The same article appears as "Jean Sibelius" in *La revue scandinave*, 1911: 366–76.

> This essay is far more interesting today for the context in which it appears than for its intrinsic merit, containing as it does a few errors and being necessarily incomplete. The volume, devoted entirely to aspects of Finland but published in French under the direction of a Helsinki University professor and a friend of the composer, had the stated goal of demonstrating the value of Finland's national culture and consequently Finland's right to

remain an independent and separate entity at a time when Russia was steadily threatening the dreaded "Russification." Intellectuals and especially the French had shown deep sympathy for Finland in 1900 when Sibelius, Kajanus, and the Helsinki Philharmonic Orchestra made appearances at the World's Fair in Paris. It is this sympathy to which the book makes a clear bid. Among the essays is a review of the history of Finland in French literature, articles on Finnish feminism and sport, and a discussion of French and Finnish art.

180. Furuhjelm, Erik. "Jean Sibelius." *Ord och bild* 23 (1914): 213–27.

Ord och bild (Word and Picture) was a liberally illustrated Swedish-language monthly devoted to art, literature, and music. In this biographical article, which contains material that appeared in Furuhjelm's fuller biography in 1916 (no. 155), the author places the composer in cultural history, emphasizing literature and art and including various reproductions of Sibelius as the subject of photographs and paintings.

181. Hall, David. "Jean Sibelius." *American-Scandinavian Review* 53 (1965): 378–87.

A short survey of Sibelius's life, although no longer completely accurate in light of current research. Illustrations include a facsimile of the opening measures of the piano miniature *Granen*, op. 75, no. 5.

182. Hill, Ralph. "Sibelius the Man." In *The Music of Sibelius*, 9–13. Edited by Gerald Abraham. London: Lindsay Drummond, New York: Norton, 1947. ML410.S54A5

Brief character sketch based on second-hand information, chiefly the testimonies of Walter Legge, Arnold Bax, and Bengt de Törne.

183. Kuusisto, Taneli. "Jean Sibelius." *Oma maa* 12 (1962): 106–30.

Illustrated survey of the composer's life written for a Finnish audience, appearing as it does in a nationalistic reference work (*Oma maa* means "Own Land" and its first edition appeared in 1907–1912). The musical discussion is integrated into the biographical events with a few music examples.

184. Molinari, Guido. "Jean Sibelius: un compositore saggio" [Jean Sibelius: A Wise Composer]. *Rassegna musicale Curci* 44 (1991): 13–18.

A late twentieth-century Italian view of Sibelius that briefly surveys the composer's life and works. The author views Sibelius as having avoided the polemics as well as the challenges of musical modernism.

185. [Unsigned]. *Miniature Essays: Jean Sibelius*. London: J. & W. Chester, 1924. 13 p.

An admiring piece, in both English and French, put out by one of Sibelius's publishers. It seeks to meet such criticisms of the music as its concentration and the abrupt switches from one idea to another. The opening measures of *Pohjola's Daughter* are reproduced in facsimile.

CHILDHOOD, YOUTH, AND FAMILY BACKGROUND

See also no. 389

186. Andersson, Otto. "Ett särdrag hos Sibelius och hans släkt" [A Characteristic of Sibelius and His Family]. *Tidning för musik* 5 (1915): 191–94.

Andersson, who was preparing a Sibelius biography that was never finished, wrote a series of articles about the early life and family background. In the article above he discusses "wanderlust" as a feature inherited by Sibelius from both lines of ancestors, and he mentions the composer's own peripatetic wanderings.

187. Andersson, Otto. "Sibeliussomrar i Korpo" [Sibelius Summers in Korpo]. In *Studier i musik och folklore* II, 92–101. Svenska Litteratursällskapet i Finland, no. 432. Åbo: Svenska

Litteratursällskapet i Finland, 1969. ML304.A53. First appeared in *Hufvudstadsbladet*, December 11 and 14, 1965.

An account of the Sibelius family visits to an island in the Baltic archipelago during the summers of 1886 and 1887. Andersson bases his narrative on interviews with Sibelius and Ina Wilenius, the pianist who joined the Sibelius brothers to play trios, including Jean's newly composed ones, during those summers. The author discusses the two compositions Sibelius dedicated to Mrs. Wilenius, *To Longing* (*Till trånaden*) and *In the Twilight* (*Au crépuscule*), as well as *Andante cantabile*, a work dedicated to Mrs. Wilenius's niece Ruth Ringbom. Ruth was a violinist who seems to have developed a brief romantic relationship with Christian Sibelius. Although the speculation about the *Korpo Trio* has been updated by the identification of the manuscript (see no. 21), much of the other information retains its usefulness.

188. G[rani]t-Ilm[oniemi], E[eli]. "Jean Sibelius förfäder" [Jean Sibelius's Ancestors]. *Tidning för musik* 6 (1916): 102–03.

Five genealogical tables trace Sibelius's ancestry back to Mårten Olofsson, born in the 1680s. Reprinted here from the *Helsingin Sanomat*, which published the tables on May 23, 1916, the text is accompanied by a note from the *Tidning*'s editor, Otto Andersson, excusing the lapses in his own biographical table (no. 178) and calling this outline "definitive." The whole enterprise, however, caused Sibelius consternation, and he registered his dismay in his diary.

189. Karttunen, Antero. "Roots: Sibelius, Finland, and the Town of Hämeenlinna." *Finnish Music Quarterly*, 1990, nos. 3–4: 6–9.

A brief review of Finnish history precedes a description of the composer's childhood hometown, Hämeenlinna. Illustrations include a map of the town and a drawing of a parade by the young composer.

190. Koskimies, Yrjö S. "Nuori Sibelius ja Hämeenlinna" [Young Sibelius and Hämeenlinna]. *Arx Tavastica* 7 (1987): 43–51.

A consideration of how the city of Sibelius's childhood shaped his life and outlook by a resident of present-day Hämeenlinna, who was among the first to consult the town's records for what they reveal about its favorite son. The piece is especially useful for citation of little-known archival sources, although some of the locations have changed since publication. English- and Swedish-language versions of the essay were published together with the Finnish text in an iconography; see no. 246. N.B.: Source notes there are given only in the Finnish portion.

191. Layton, Robert. "Sibelius: The Early Years." *Proceedings of the Royal Musical Association* 91 (1964–65): 73–84.

A well-written essay that encapsulates the state of research on Sibelius in the 1960s, cites a number of the sources, and considers the influence of various Russian composers on the young composer. The essay also serves as a kind of review of Johnson's biography *Jean Sibelius* (no. 159). Two music examples from early quartets.

192. Marvia, Einari. "Jean Sibeliuksen musikaalinen sukuperintö" [Jean Sibelius's Musical Family Background]. *Uusi musiikkilehti*, 1955, no. 9: 47–81. A summary of this study appears under the same title in *Kirkko ja musiikki*, 1965, no. 5: 4–6.

The most detailed genealogical study available of the composer's family, illustrated with photographs of relatives and extensive genealogical charts. For anyone wishing to know such matters as how opera singer Kim Borg is related to Jean Sibelius, this is the place to look (p. 63).

193. Setälä, Helmi. "Jean Sibelius." In *Kun suuret olivat pieniä* [When the Great Were Small], 78–88. Helsinki: Otava, 1911. Setälä published a later edition, in 1949, under her maiden name, Helmi Krohn.

Aspects of Sibelius's youth summarized in a volume written by a member of the distinguished Krohn family. Helmi's father was Julius Krohn, professor of Finnish and comparative folklore at Helsinki University; her brother was the Ilmari Krohn known to

Sibelius enthusiasts as one of the composer's rivals for a position at Helsinki University in 1896 (both lost to Robert Kajanus). Their sister Aino was a prolific writer of short stories and poems, one of which, *In the Moonlight* (*Kuutamolla*), Sibelius set to music. Helmi (1871–1967) was also a writer and married Emil Nestor Setälä (see no. 282). Along with Sibelius, her book deals with other contemporaries whom she knew, including Ida Ekman, Akseli Gallen-Kallela, and Eliel Saarinen. The first edition was dedicated to Juhani Aho. Illustrated.

194. Tawaststjerna, Erik. "Der junge Sibelius: von der Dur-Moll-Tonalität zu einer Synthese von modalen und dur-moll-tonalen Elementen" [The Young Sibelius: From Major-Minor Tonality to a Synthesis of Elements from Modality and Major-Minor Tonality]. In *Das musikalische Kunstwerk: Geschichte, Ästhetik, Theorie. Festschrift Carl Dahlhaus zum 60. Geburtstag*, 639–50. Edited by H. Danuser, Helga de la Motte-Haber, Silke Leopold and Norbert Miller. Laaber: Laaber Verlag, 1988. ML55.D185 1988 ISBN 3-890-07144-9

An examination of the Finnish folk melodies of such singers as Larin Paraske from whose "reservoir of ideas" Sibelius seems to have worked. Parallels are drawn to Bartók who differed from Sibelius in the scholarly direction his interests took. Tawaststjerna suggests that the young composer's confrontation with modality enriched his musical language, an enrichment evident in *Kullervo* (1892), in his University lecture in 1896, and, ultimately, in Symphony no. 6. Music examples and supporting notes, although, unfortunately, there are errors in the note numbers.

SIBELIUS THE CONDUCTOR

See also no. 227

195. Havu, Ilmari. "Sibeliuksen johtajavierailu Oslossa 1910" [Sibelius as Guest Conductor in Oslo 1910]. *Kalevalaseuran vuosikirja* 44 (1964): 229–39.

The background to Sibelius's second visit to Oslo (Christiania) as revealed in the composer's letters to Iver Holter, director of Christiania's Music Association, in 1909–1910. The letters, in which Sibelius discusses the program, sets his fee, and inquires about different instrumentalists in Swedish, are given in Finnish translation. Facsimile of a part of one document is shown together with portraits of Sibelius and Holter, excerpts from concert reviews, and an interview.

196. Pajanne, Martti. "Muusikkojen muistelmia mestarista orkesterinjohtajana" [Musicians' Memories of the Master as Orchestra Conductor]. *Uusi musiikkilehti*, 1955, no. 9: 15–16.

Recollections of Sibelius conducting by various orchestra players. A reproduction of Sigurd Wettenhovi-Aspa's painting depicts Sibelius on the podium, baton in hand. The author's opinion is that Sibelius's last appearance as a conductor, in 1939 when he led *Andante festivo* in a recorded performance broadcast over the radio, showed clearly how the spirit of a work and its overall meaning were the vital aspects of his interpretations. For recent discussion about the authenticity of that historic recording, see *Finnish Music Quarterly*, 1995, no. 4: 57–58.

197. Paul, Adolf. "När Jean Sibelius dirigerade" [When Jean Sibelius Conducted]. In *Profiler: Minnen av stora personlighter*, 32–37. Helsingfors: Söderström & Co., 1937.

Annotated as no. 134.

198. Tawaststjerna, Erik. "Sibelius sena dirigentdebut i Stockholm" [Sibelius's Late Conducting Debut in Stockholm]. *Musikrevy* 39 (1984): 72–77.

A discussion of events surrounding Sibelius's appearance in Stockholm conducting Symphony no. 6 on March 1, 1923, with citations of the composer's diary entries and responses from contemporary critics. Although the same discussion is available in the author's Sibelius biography (no. 175, vol. V), the diary entries appear here in their original Swedish as do extracts from newspaper reviews.

199. Wuolijoki, Sulo. "Jean Sibelius johtajana" [Jean Sibelius as Conductor]. In *Hämettä ja hämäläisiä*, 43–47. Helsinki: Oy Suomen Kirja, 1945.

In this memoir by citizens from the Finnish province of Häme, where Sibelius's hometown Hämeenlinna is situated, the author recalls singing in the 350-member chorus that gave the premiere of *Origin of Fire* (*Tulen synty)* in 1902. With tongue in cheek, he first describes the attitude of choral conductor Heikki Klemetti, who led the rehearsals, and then the moment when Sibelius ascended the podium to conduct the performance.

STUDIES IN HELSINKI

200. Joensuu, Väinö. "Mestari oppipoikana" [The Master as a Student]. *Suomen musiikkilehti*, December 1925: 153–54; January 1926: 4–5.

The author recalls Sibelius during the composer's student years at the Helsinki Music Institute (1885–1889). The works Sibelius performed on his violin are listed together with performers who assisted him, and excerpts from some of the first reviews of the early compositions are reproduced. It is instructive to discover that as early as the 1880s the composer was being hailed as an authentic Finnish voice in music.

201. Salmenhaara, Erkki. "Jean Sibelius ja Helsingin Yliopisto" [Jean Sibelius and Helsinki University]. *Musiikki* 20 (1990): 23–38.

Sibelius's connections to Helsinki University began when he matriculated in the department of physics and mathematics in the spring of 1885 and continued in various ways throughout his life, from an application for a position to composing cantatas for the University's graduation ceremonies. Salmenhaara reviews the many ties in an essay delivered as a lecture in English at the First International Sibelius Conference in 1990. Especially valuable in the printed Finnish version is the bibliography of Sibelius research at Helsinki University ("Sibelius-tutkimusta Helsingin Yliopistossa"), including a list of published and unpublished theses and dissertations. The English text will appear in the forthcoming *Proceedings of the Second International Sibelius Conference*, since it was inadvertently omitted (along with several other presentations) from the first *Proceedings*. Meanwhile, a short summary in English may be read in the jubilee exhibition publication entitled *In Search of Knowledge, September 7–October 27, 1990: Porthania* (Helsinki: Helsinki University, 1990), 27–29.

SIBELIUS AND THE 1890S

202. Salmenhaara, Erkki. "Nuori Sibelius ja 1890-luku: Suomalaisen sävelkielen synty" [Young Sibelius and the 1890s: The Birth of Finland's Musical Language]. *Rondo*, 1982, no. 4: 11–17.

Salmenhaara's purpose is to demonstrate that the young Sibelius created a national musical language while simultaneously defining his own style, one that was also stimulated by modern trends. He thus reviews Sibelius's activities during the crucial decade of the 1890s, the experiences and stimulae of which ultimately enabled him to create a work such as Symphony no. 6, which is clearly Finnish, yet not "national romantic."

203. Tawaststjerna, Erik. "Sibeliuksen Kullervo-sinfonian syntytaustaa: Wienin vuosi 1890–91" [The Background to the Birth of Sibelius's *Kullervo* Symphony: The Year 1890–1891 in Vienna]. *Kalevalaseuran vuosikirja* 45 (1965): 35–44. The article appears in both English and German in *Jean Sibelius*, 6–10. Helsinki: Published for the Sibelius Centenary Year by the Sibelius Centenary Committee, 1965. Edited by Timo Mäkinen and Riitta Björklund. The centenary volume is annotated as no. 239.

A look at Sibelius's study year in Vienna, 1890–1891, and its importance to the *Kullervo* Symphony. Substantiated with quotes from the composer's letters to his fiancée Aino Järnefelt and Martin Wegelius, a consideration of his teacher Karl Goldmark's advice, and music examples.

204. Tawaststjerna, Erik. "Sibelius Wagnerkris" [Sibelius's Wagner Crisis]. *Musikrevy* 21 (1966): 186–191.

A discussion of Sibelius's trip to Bayreuth in the summer of 1894 and the powerful responses on hearing Wagner that the young

Sibelius revealed in his letters written at the time; taken from the author's biography (no. 175), where it can also be read in English and Finnish. Illustrated here with pictures of Sibelius and also of Tawaststjerna.

SIBELIUS THE TEACHER

See also no. 176

205. Kotilainen, Otto. "Mestarin muokattavana" [The Master at Work]. *Aulos*, 1925: 23–24.

A student of music theory and composition at the Helsinki Music Institute in 1892 describes the striking differences between Wegelius's and Sibelius's approaches to teaching: the former a strict disciplinarian, the latter, his polar opposite. Here is the account of the composer dismissing the female students so that they might go shopping. Kotilainen recalls studying with Sibelius for a year or more, sometimes having his lessons in the composer's home, at that time in Kerävä. Perhaps Sibelius's teaching had some effect, since Kotilainen himself later became a teacher at the Helsinki Music Institute.

206. Madetoja, Leevi. "Jean Sibelius opettajana" [Jean Sibelius as a Teacher]. *Musiikki* 17 (1987): 92–94.

A short memoir, originally published in 1925 in the periodical *Aulos*, that includes pithy quotes from lessons with Sibelius ("There should be no dead notes! Every note should live!" and "You should throw yourself into the water, so that you will learn to swim!"). Madetoja (1887–1847), together with Toivo Kuula who is also mentioned, were among the composer's few pupils in the years after Sibelius left full-time teaching.

SIBELIUS AND HIS FRIENDS

207. Andersson, Otto. "Sibelius och Kajanus" [Sibelius and Kajanus]. In *Studier i musik och folklore I*, 78–86. Skrifter utgivna av Svenska Litteratursällskapet i Finland, no. 408. Åbo: Svenska Litteratursällskapet, 1964. ML304.A53

A two-part article that originally appeared in the Swedish-language newspaper *Hufvudstadsbladet* on December 8, 1956, and January 3, 1957. Andersson discusses the circumstances surrounding the appointment to Helsinki University for which Sibelius and Kajanus competed in 1896 and the yearly stipend awarded Sibelius after Kajanus was chosen for the position.

208. Layton, Robert. "Jean Sibelius and the Real Axel Carpelan." *Books from Finland* 20 (1986): 161–62.

Layton summarizes for English readers what is known about Axel Carpelan based on Erik Tawaststjerna's biographical research. A paradoxical figure who played an extraordinary role in Sibelius's life, Carpelan was a frustrated musician who nevertheless revealed great insight in his musical advice to Sibelius and, though leading a penurious existence himself, raised money again and again to assist Sibelius.

209. Tawaststjerna, Erik. "The Two Leskovites." *Finnish Music Quarterly*, 1986, no. 3: 2–9.

Tawaststjerna traces the friendship of Busoni and Sibelius from the time of Busoni's arrival in Helsinki in 1888. The term "Leskovite" was used to designate the pianist's social circle, a group named after the pianist's Newfoundland hound, Lesko. Busoni's various efforts in Sibelius's behalf are mentioned as is their meeting in London in 1921 and critical responses to Sibelius's music. No source notes but there are quotations from different letters and illustrations, including a facsimile of Busoni's letter of August 25, 1903, in which he tells Sibelius that he needs "good weapons" in the struggle against the Berlin critics.

SIBELIUS AND ITALY

210. Berri, Pietro. "Jean Sibelius a Rapallo" [Jean Sibelius in Rapallo]. *Rapallo, rivista bimestrale di vita cittadina* 8 (1965): 2–13.

A review of the composer's sojourn in Rapallo during the winter of 1901 when Symphony no. 2 was in progress. Berri provides a capsule biography, mentioning Sibelius's later connections to Italy, and considers the composer's position in that country. Among the many illustrations are photographs of Sibelius's pension in Rapallo, the program conducted by Sibelius at the Augusteo in Rome in 1923, and a photograph of Kim Borg giving a recital in Rapallo in 1958.

211. Gummerus, E. R. "Sibelius och Italien" [Sibelius and Italy]. *Musikkultur*, 1965, no. 6: 8–9. Reprinted in *Hufvudstadsbladet*, May 18, 1965.

A discussion of some of the composer's connections to Italy, beginning with his friendship with Italian pianist and composer Ferruccio Busoni and continuing through Sibelius's 1923 concert in the Augusteo, about which the author, who was present, adds personal recollections. Illustrated with a copy of Albert Edelfelt's portrait of the composer.

SIBELIUS IN TURKU

212. Saarilahti, Päivö. "Jean Sibelius Turussa" [Jean Sibelius in Turku]. *Turun soitannollinen seura 1790–1965*, 153–68. Edited by Marianne Ringbom. Turku: Turun Soitannollinen Seura, 1965. Translated into Swedish as "Jean Sibelius i Åbo." In *Musikaliska sällskapet i Åbo 1790–1965*, 151–66. Edited by Marianne Ringbom. Åbo: Musikaliska Sällskapet i Åbo, 1965. ML55.M9878A

Although Sibelius is more readily associated with Helsinki and Järvenpää than with the southwestern coastal town of Turku, his personal and professional ties to that important and historic city were many. This illustrated article provides a revealing discussion of these connections. Especially valuable are the various responses to his concerts quoted from different local newspapers.

SIBELIUS IN THE UNITED STATES

See also no. 380

213. Andersson, Otto. *Jean Sibelius i Amerika* [Jean Sibelius in America]. Åbo: Förlaget Bro., [1955]. 167 p. Finnish edition: *Jean Sibelius Amerikassa* (Helsinki: Otava, [1960]). 141, [2] p. ML410.S54A6

Although a book rather than an article, this work has been included in this section because of its special biographical nature. On two trips to the United States in 1950 and 1954, Andersson, founder and director of the archive known as the Sibelius Museum, collected materials for the archive and interviewed individuals with connections to Sibelius, including some who recalled the composer's visit in 1914. Andersson surveys the American performances, the critics' responses, and the personal bonds but treats his subject reverentially and glosses over the anti-Sibelian forces evident in the United States by the 1950s.

214. Stoeckel, Carl. "Some Recollections of the Visit of Jean Sibelius to America in 1914." *Scandinavian Studies* 43 (1971): 53–88.

The memoirs of Carl Stoeckel, the American patron who with his wife Ellen commissioned *Oceanides* (*Aallottaret*) and was Sibelius's host during the composer's one visit to the United States, were originally deposited as a manuscript in the library of Yale University. These memoirs provide the most detailed, first-hand account in existence of the three weeks in 1914 when Sibelius was in America. To Stoeckel's account, published here for the first time, George C. Schoolfield has added excellent annotations, a biographical note about Stoeckel, and a transcription of some of Sibelius's correspondence pertaining to the visit.

SIBELIUS AND VIENNA

See also no. 372

215. Revers, Peter. "Jean Sibelius and Vienna." In *The Sibelius Companion*, 13–34. Edited by Glenda Dawn Goss. Westport, Conn.: Greenwood, 1996. ML410.S54S53 1996 ISBN 0-313-28393-1

The most accurate and thorough investigation available of Sibelius's study year in Vienna, from his composition lessons with Robert Fuchs and Karl Goldmark to the music that he heard. There is an enlightening discussion of how the music of Goldmark and of Bruckner affected Sibelius; music examples from both earlier composers suggest affinities with such works as *En saga* and Symphony no. 4. The author also demonstrates what Anton

Webern called *Fasslichkeit* (the law of comprehensibility) in the scores of Sibelius, with analogies to composers of the Second Viennese school.

THE SILENCE OF JÄRVENPÄÄ

216. Dahlström, Fabian. "Tystnaden i Järvenpää: Några randanmärkningar" [The Silence of Järvenpää: Some Remarks]. *Musikrevy* 47 (1992): 179–81.

The so-called "silence of Järvenpää," the time when Sibelius lapsed into inactivity, is examined in light of Kari Kilpeläinen's dating of the composer's manuscripts (see no. 418) and the author's own preparation of a thematic catalogue. Substantial compositional activity, here set forth chronologically, emerges from this examination of the composer's late years.

C. Letters

During his lifetime Sibelius wrote and received hundreds, if not thousands, of letters. The value of these documents has only begun to be appreciated. As with any correspondence, the fresh and unstudied response, the accurate recording of dates and places, and the descriptions of people, times, and events are often unsullied in Sibelius's letters. There are also, however, the contrived epistles and the self-serving accounts. Sibelius's own revealing comment, that he often wrote in his letters what he thought the recipient wanted to hear, registers a note of caution against blithe trust in these primary sources.

Most of Sibelius's correspondence is preserved today in Finland. The National Archives (Kansallisarkisto, formerly Valtionarkisto) in Helsinki conserve a large fond of family letters. Another important Helsinki collection belongs to the Helsinki University Library. Laila Koukku's exemplary catalogue, *Jean Sibelius: Yksityisarkisto* [Jean Sibelius: Personal Archive] (Helsinki: Helsinki University Library, 1993), in which identifications of Sibelius's correspondents and their dates have been provided, is available in the library in typescript. (The catalogue is also essential for locating the Library's concert programs from the years 1888 to 1967.) The Sibelius Museum in Turku is a third important repository of Sibelius correspondence. In addition, countless letters are scattered throughout the world in collections both public and private.

At present there is no inventory of Sibelius's letters, much less any comprehensive edition such as exists for Mozart, Liszt, or other major composers. The most extensive editions of Sibelius's correspondence are currently found in no. 218, which includes the composer's letter exchange with Olin Downes, and in the forthcoming *Jean Sibelius: The Hämeenlinna Letters, Scenes from a Musical Life 1874–1895*. This volume contains annotated transcriptions and translations of seventy-eight documents discovered in the Spring of 1995 by the present author, who is preparing them for publication at Schildts Förlag in Helsinki. Elisabeth Järnefelt's recently published correspondence, *Elisabeth Järnefeltin kirjeitä: 1881–1929*, edited by Suvisirkku Talas (Helsinki: Suomalaisen Kirjallisuuden Seura, 1996), also contains some epistles from Sibelius.

Given the dearth of published material, the facsimiles, transcriptions, and quotations from letters that can be found throughout the Sibelius literature take on great value. Some of these published sources appear below together with significant editions of family correspondence. Facsimiles and quotations from letters also appear in many biographies (see especially nos. 154 and 175), and the soon-to-be-published thematic catalogue will contain a great deal of epistolary matter. Many contemporaries who were not relatives mention Sibelius in their correspondence (Virgil Thomson writing to Theodor Adorno, for instance), but these hundreds of additional letters are outside the scope of the present bibliography. In this *Guide*, one should also see nos. 68, 73, 85, 86, 92, 99, 101, 102, 115, 132, 203, 209, 235, 239, 241, 246, 261, 370, 378, 382, 420, 496, 545, 551, 582, 589, 659, 665.

* * *

217. "Eräs Akseli Gallen-Kallelan kirje Jean Sibeliukselle" [A Certain Letter from Akseli Gallen-Kallela to Jean Sibelius]. *Kalevalaseuran vuosikirja* 12 (1932): 39–40.

Translation into Finnish of the artist's original Swedish-language letter to Sibelius in the year both turned fifty. By invoking the image of Cervantes' Man of La Mancha, Gallen-Kallela reminds his friend of their shared interests in the heady days of the 1890s.

218. Goss, Glenda Dawn. *Jean Sibelius and Olin Downes: Music, Friendship, Criticism.* Boston: Northeastern University Press, 1994, Appendix A, 179–234. ML385.G7 1995 ISBN 1-55553-200-4

An annotated transcription of seventy-six letters and telegrams exchanged between Sibelius and music critic Downes during the period 1927–1955 and preserved in the Hargrett Library at the University of Georgia. The full study appears as no. 255.

219. Havu, Ilmari. "Sibeliuksen johtajavierailu Oslossa 1910" [Sibelius as Guest Conductor in Oslo 1910]. *Kalevalaseuran vuosikirja* 44 (1964): 229–39.

Five letters, preserved in the Oslo University Library and written by Sibelius to Iver Holter in the years 1909–1910, are reproduced. The article is annotated more fully as no. 195.

220. "Jean Sibelius." In *Letters of Composers: An Anthology 1603–1945*, 324–25. Compiled and edited by Gertrude Norman and Miriam Lubell Shrifte. New York: Alfred A. Knopf, 1946. xviii, 422 p., xx index pages. ML90.N67

Two letters of Sibelius, the first of which, dated May 20, 1918, had already appeared in Ekman's biography (no. 154); the second, dated March 10, 1930, is addressed to Rosa Newmarch. Here the composer states that he is continuing to compose but despairs of "so much in the music of the present day that I cannot accept." Both letters are given in English.

221. Leino, Eino. *Kirjeet taiteilijatovereille, arvostelijoille ja tutkijoille* [Letters to Artistic Friends, Critics, and Scholars], vol. 3. Edited by Aarre M. Peltonen. Helsinki: Otava, 1961. 379 p.

Six, mostly short, communications to Jean and Aino Sibelius in Finnish, French, German, and Latin, dating from the years 1906–

1924, written by the man usually considered to be Finland's leading literary figure of the early twentieth century.

222. Newmarch, Rosa. *Jean Sibelius: A Short Story of a Long Friendship*. With a Foreword by Granville Bantock. Boston: C. C. Birchard, 1939. London: Goodwin & Tabb, 1945. 39 p.

Texts of Sibelius letters, including four in facsimile; for full annotation, see no. 132.

223. Nettel, Reginald. *Music in the Five Towns 1840–1914: A Study of the Social Influence of Music in an Industrial District*. London: Oxford University Press, 1944. 120 p. ML286.N48

A social history of music in the region in England known as the Potteries, this short volume includes a facsimile of a letter from Sibelius (p. 85, no date shown) agreeing to become a patron of the North Staffordshire Orchestral Society. There is also a brief account (p. 83) of his music being performed in the Potteries.

224. "Olin Downesin kirjeitä Sibeliukselle" [Olin Downes's Letters to Sibelius]. *Uusi musiikkilehti*, 1955, no. 9: 20–23.

Three letters from the American critic to the composer, dated December 15, 1948, November 9, 1950, and November 2, 1951, translated into Finnish. Two of the letters may be read in their original in no. 218.

225. Söderbäck, Peter. "Nyförvärv 1978 och bestånd i arkiv, bibliotek och museer" [New Acquisitions 1978 and Holdings in Archives, Libraries, and Museums]. *Svenskt musikhistoriskt arkiv, Bulletin* 16 (1980): 11–19.

A list compiled from institutional reports of materials acquired by Swedish archives, libraries, and museums during the year 1978 in which it is announced that Uppsala University Library has obtained 180 letters written by Sibelius to Adolf Paul (1889–1954).

226. Stoeckel, Carl. "Some Recollections of the Visit of Jean Sibelius to America in 1914." *Scandinavian Studies* 43 (1971): 53–88.

Transcriptions of six letters pertaining to Sibelius's visit to the United States. Five were written by the composer to various Americans and one was written to Sibelius by a Yale official announcing Yale's decision to confer upon the composer the honorary degree of Doctor of Music (pp. 84–88). The full article is annotated as no. 214.

227. *Yhdeksän mustaa joutsenta, Swanin sisarusten kirjeitä: kokemuksia, elämyksiä ja ajatuksia autonomian ajan Suomessa* [Nine Black Swans, The Swan Sisters' Letters: Experiences, Life, and Thoughts in the Time of Autonomy in Finland]. Edited by Antero Manninen. Suomalaisen Kirjallisuuden Seura, no. 579. Helsinki: SKS, 1993. 374 p. DL1065.Y47 1993 ISBN 951-717-742-9

The nine dark-haired daughters born to C. G. and Emilia Swan between 1863 and 1878 were destined to have close ties to the Sibelius family. The youngest, Nelma, married Sibelius's brother Christian; her sister Saimi married Aino Sibelius's brother Eero Järnefelt. Not surprisingly then, this collection of family letters portrays the dynamics of the extended family, establishes connections among leading figures in Finland, furnishes useful dates, and discusses such things as Jean's conducting and the death of his little daughter Kirsti in 1900. The letters, in Finnish, date from 1884 to 1917; there are brief annotations and an exemplary index enabling the reader to identify persons at a glance by profession and dates.

D. Iconographies

By its very nature, iconography is a part of the biographical record. The Sibelius iconography is particularly rich. Where images of the composer himself are concerned, there are beautiful and revealing paintings and powerful sculptures by contemporaries who knew him well, both socially and artistically. These works began to appear as early as the 1880s. Photographs, some taken by friends like Rosa

Newmarch and Harriet Cohen, others, by professionals of the artistic calibre of Yousuf Karsh, survive from nearly every stage of his life. Such materials have hardly begun to be mined for the treasures they can yield about the man, his music, and his changing image, both public and private. A promising beginning, however, has been made by the studies annotated as nos. 230 and 231.

As for other kinds of evidence considered iconographical, a gratifying quantity of letters, pages of musical manuscripts, photographs of friends and places, maps, and other documents have been reproduced in books and articles. A comprehensive catalogue of all these materials would constitute a volume of its own. At the present time, among the few means for finding iconographical sources are the files of photographs in the Sibelius Museum in Turku.

The entries in this section represent only a selection and only items that can mainly be classified as iconographies. It has sometimes been difficult to decide whether to categorize a book as a biography or an iconography, and several of the titles below clearly serve both purposes. No attempt has been made to provide cross-references to the thousands of pieces of iconographical evidence in books, articles, and especially Finnish periodicals. The volumes of *Euterpe*, *Säveletär*, *Suomen Kuvalehti*, *Lucifer* (the Christmas publication of Finland's Federation of Swedish Journalists), and more recently, *Finnish Music Quarterly* are lavishly illustrated, sometimes in color. For those with access to these volumes and time to spare, a dip into their pages will be as entertaining as it will be rewarding.

* * *

See also no. 78

228. Aho, Antti J., ed. *Juhani Aho ja hänen aikansa* [Juhani Aho and His Time]. Helsinki: Werner Söderström Osakeyhtiö, 1948. 183 p.

> Although devoted to Sibelius's contemporary, writer Juhani Aho, the many reproductions of pictures and documents and quotations from contemporaries and their writings help to establish a literary and artistic context for the composer. Included are a facsimile of Aho's homage to Sibelius, Eero Järnefelt's sketch of the composer, and a description of Sibelius in the newspaper *Päivälehti*.

229. Burnett-James, David. *Sibelius: The Illustrated Lives of the Great Composers.* London, New York: Omnibus Press, 1989. 128 p. ML410.S54B87 1989 ISBN 0-7119-1061-8. Paperback edition: ISBN 0-7119-1683-7

A readable biography (whose author is not the Burnett James who also wrote a Sibelius biography, no. 158) woven around assorted pictures and programs across the composer's long life and directed to a general audience. The book has few reference notes and contains a list of the works the "average listener is likely to encounter." The numerous photographs, however, and the sections "Sibelius on Record" and "The Sibelius Museum" furnish material not readily available elsewhere.

230. Donner, Philip. "Unohdettu Sibelius: Säveltäjä ja idoli valokuvina" [The Forgotten Sibelius: The Composer and Idol in Photographs]. In *Suomen musiikin koko kuva*, 40–43. Helsinki: Suomen Etnomusikologinen Seura, 1983.

A thought-provoking, illustrated examination of Sibelius in pictures accompanied by a discussion of how the iconography has contributed to the composer's "idolization." The author considers such matters as the retouching of the photograph of young Sibelius on his mother Maria's lap: by eliminating Linda, the sister who was also in the original photo, a "Madonna and child" portrait was created. Consideration is also given to the frequent photographs of the composer with severe countenance in the midst of nature. Donner observes that pictures contradicting the prevailing image, such as the laughing Sibelius or the composer attending the Lapua peasant march with Aino, are rarely published.

231. Donner, Philip, and Juhani Similä. "Jean Sibelius: Teollistumisajan musiikkimurroksen idolihahmo" [Jean Sibelius: The Idol Figure in the Music Crisis of Industrial Times]. In *Musiikkikulttuurin murros teollistumisajan Suomessa*, 33–49. Edited by Vesa Kurkela and Riitta Valkeila. Jyväskylä: Jyväskylän Yliopiston Musiikkitieteen Laitos, 1982.

Numerous satirical drawings, paintings, and a photograph of Sibelius are used in the authors' investigation of Sibelius as a Finnish idol. The full study is annotated as no. 267.

232. Ehrström, Eric E. O. "Gallenin kahden maalauksen syntyvaiheesta" [The Stages of Birth of Gallén's Two Paintings]. *Kalevalaseuran vuosikirja* 12 (1932): 95–99.

A discussion of the background to Gallen-Kallela's paintings *Väinämöinen's Departure* and *Symposion*, the latter well known to Sibelians for depicting the composer with Robert Kajanus, Gallen-Kallela himself, and the face-down figure thought to be Oskar Merikanto. Both paintings underwent significant revision before attaining final form, and some of the changes are explored here with black-and-white illustrations. No discussion, however, of either work's rich symbolism.

233. Jalas, Margareta, ed. *Jean Sibelius.* With an introduction [in Finnish, Swedish, and English] by Veikko Helasvuo and picture captions by Sirkka Rapola. Helsinki: Otava, 1952, 1958. 79 p. ML410.S56J21 1958

The fifth Sibelius daughter edited these photographs of her father and family members. Paintings by contemporary artists are shown together with landscapes and objects considered significant in the composer's life (such as cigars and a violin), and even a view from the prow of a ship, allegedly the one bearing Sibelius to America. Each photograph has a brief caption in three languages. The short introduction, in which Sibelius is portrayed as a lonely, exalted genius, preserves the tone of adulation prevalent in Finland in Sibelius's last years.

234. Karsh, Yousuf. *Portraits of Greatness.* Toronto: University of Toronto Press, 1959; London: Thomas Nelson, 1960. Reprint. 1961. 207 p. TR680.K3 1961

Karsh of Ottawa, as this eminent photographer is known, endeavored "not merely to produce a likeness but to reveal the mind and the soul behind the human face." In 1949 Karsh created one of the best-known photographs of the old Sibelius. The context in which the composer appears in this volume, among superb portraits of other great twentieth-century figures, from Pablo Picasso, Igor Stravinsky, and Frank Lloyd Wright to Carl Jung, Sir Laurence Olivier, and Eleanor Roosevelt, adds a striking historical dimension to the iconographical statement. A personal account of the portrait sitting accompanies each photograph.

235. Lampila, Hannu-Ilari. *Sibelius.* Jyväskylä: Gummerus, 1984. 127 p. With English summary. ML410.S54L3 1983 ISBN 951-20-2505-1. Translated into Czech by Pavol Tvarožek (Bratislava: Opus, 1989).

Basing his text primarily on Erik Tawaststjerna's research, Lampila provides a summary biography in Finnish interspersed with selected iconography. Although most of the photographs are of family, friends, and colleagues, there is one facsimile from the Scherzo of Symphony no. 6 and another of a letter to Robert Kajanus concerning *Snöfrid* (1915). There is a short list of important works. Photographs differ in the Czech edition.

Rev.: *Synkooppi* 7 (1984): 36.

236. Layton, Robert. *Sibelius and His World.* London: Thames and Hudson; New York: Viking Press, 1970. 120 p. ML410.S54L352 1970b ISBN 0-500-13026-4

For annotation, see no. 241.

237. Levas, Santeri. *Jean Sibelius ja hänen Ainolansa* [Jean Sibelius and His Ainola]. Helsinki: Otava, 1945. 137 p. Translated into Swedish as *Jean Sibelius och hans hem* (Helsingfors: Holger Schildt Förlag, 1945). ML410.S54L488

A fond personal memoir in words and pictures, Levas's volume shows Sibelius in old age in black-and-white photographs that will not be familiar to most readers. There are also views of Ainola and its surroundings, pictures of Sibelius's family, reproductions of artworks depicting the composer, and photographs of memorabilia, including the honorary degree awarded by Yale

University and the certificate of membership in the Royal Academy of Music.

238. Levas, Santeri. *Jean Sibelius ja hänen Ainolansa* [Jean Sibelius and His Ainola]. Helsinki: Otava, 1955. 128 p. ML410.S54L43 1955

A different edition from no. 237, this version has text summaries in Swedish, English, and German. It contains additional iconographical material (although not as nicely reproduced), including a page in facsimile from Symphony no. 5, and concludes with a chronology of important events.

239. Mäkinen, Timo, and Riitta Björklund, eds. *Jean Sibelius.* Helsinki: Published for the Sibelius Centenary Year by the Sibelius Centenary Committee, 1965. 53 p. [In Finnish and Swedish]. Translated into English by Kingsley Hart and Philip Binham. Translated into German by Dietrich Assmann, Friedrich Ege, and C. A. von Willebrandt.

An anniversary volume published for the Sibelius Jubilee Year with excellently reproduced black-and-white photographs of the composer, his family, some of his leading interpreters, and portions of scores and letters. The text consists of reminiscences and congratulatory notes from leading musical figures together with several essays, most of which have been printed elsewhere, such as Tawaststjerna on the birth of the *Kullervo* Symphony (annotated as no. 203), de Törne on Sibelius as a teacher (see the annotation to no. 176), and Parmet on Sibelius as a symphonist.

240. Martin, Timo, and Douglas Sivén. *Akseli Gallen-Kallela: Elämäkerrallinen rapsodia* [Akseli Gallen-Kallela: Biographical Rhapsody]. Sulkava: Watti-Kustannus, 1984. 256 p. ND955.F53G3435 1984 ISBN 951-99488-4-8. An English adaptation by Keith Bosley and Satu Salo appeared as *Akseli Gallen-Kallela: National Artist of Finland* (Sulkava: Watti-Kustannus, 1985). 255 p. ND955.F53G3436 1985 ISBN 951-95945-0-7

A welcome find in a desert sparsely populated with English-language texts about Sibelius's most important artistic contemporary in Finland. Beautiful color plates represent "the heart of Akseli Gallen-Kallela's output." Also reproduced are sketches and paintings of Sibelius and many of his friends, while the biographical text quotes from the artist's letters and notes. The volume thus provides vivid entrée into the creative world of Finland during Sibelius's lifetime.

241. Oramo, Ilkka. *Jean Sibelius: Kuvaelämäkerta* [Jean Sibelius: A Life in Pictures]. Helsinki: Otava, 1965. 99 p. Translated into Swedish by Bertel and Karin Kihlman as *Jean Sibelius: en bildbiografi* (Helsingfors: Söderström & Co., 1967). 99 p.

A pictorial biography in black and white, the book also features running commentary. There are portraits of family and contemporaries, geographical scenes important in the life of Sibelius, drawings by and about the composer, and facsimiles of selected letters and music manuscripts. The same pictures are reproduced in *Sibelius and His World* (London: Thames and Hudson, 1970. 120 p.) with an English text by Robert Layton. To the English-language edition has been added a chronology of significant events in the composer's life.

Rev. of English edition: *Music & Letters* 52 (1971): 77–78; *American Record Guide*, June 1971: 735.

242. Palola, Eino. *Runoja, värejä, säveleitä: Taitelijaelämää Tuusulassa* [Poems, Colors, Music: Artistic Life at Tuusula]. Helsinki: Otava, 1935. 133 p.

An account of the artists' colony at Tuusula, the county where Sibelius's home, Ainola, was located. Illustrated with black-and-white photographs of the most famous residents (Sibelius, Eero Järnefelt, Pekka Halonen, J. H. Erkko, Juhani Aho, and Emil Nestor Setälä) and their families, friends, and homes. No critical apparatus but the book supplies iconographical evidence about Sibelius's artistic environment. Also reproduced is Frans Emil Sillanpää's memoir of his encounter with Sibelius (pp. 66–67).

243. Paul, Adolf. "Zwei Fennonenhauptlinge: Sibelius/Gallén" [Two Finnish Leaders: Sibelius/Gallén]. *Deutsch-Nordisches Jahrbuch für*

Kulturaustausch und Volkskunde 1914. Jena: Eugen Diederichs, 1914, facing p. 121.

Reproduces a seldom-seen sketch of Sibelius drawn by Akseli Gallen-Kallela on a calling card. For a complete annotation of this source, see no. 135.

244. Salmenhaara, Erkki, and Hertta Tirranen. *Sibeliuksen Ainola/ Sibelius and Ainola*. English text by Hertta Tirranen. Helsinki: Werner Söderström Osakeyhtiö, 1976. 42 p. text + 21 unnumbered p. of pictures. ML410.S54S2 ISBN 951-0-07533-7

Commemorating the country home at Järvenpää where Sibelius lived from 1904 until his death, the authors have compiled a black-and-white photographic record of the house and surroundings that were so important to Sibelius's later creativity. The Finnish text emphasizes highlights of the composer's life and is organized around the major orchestral works, while the brief English introduction focuses on the reception of the symphonic compositions.

245. Sandberg, Börje, ed. *Jean Sibelius*. Helsinki: Otava, 1940. 62 p. ML410.S54J4 1940

Strictly an iconography, as the only text is a preface by Toivo Haapanen. The volume contains black-and-white photographs, most from after 1910. Several are characteristic of the romanticized Sibelius (a hand with a smoking cigar and a top hat with a cane), although there is also a facsimile of a page from Symphony no. 3.

246. *Sibeliuksen Hämeenlinna/Sibelius och hans Tavastehus/Sibelius and His Home Town*. Text by Yrjö S. Koskimies. Edited with an Introduction by Eino Örlund. Hämeenlinna: Karisto, 1990. 88 p. ISBN 951-23-2923-9

Photographs, drawings, and facsimiles of Sibelius letters relating to the composer's life in Hämeenlinna, the town of his birth. The useful essay, printed in three languages, is annotated as no. 190.

IV
Rezeptionsgeschichte

Rezeptionsgeschichte, or "reception history," means different things to different people. Because it has to do with the impact made by a work of art on listeners, viewers, or readers, collecting opinions about artworks is usually considered an essential part of its study together with evaluating these opinions. Reception historians, however, must necessarily make subjective choices and formulate interpretations of their own, thereby adding their personal philosophies, and hence, another dimension, to the historical record.

Raw material for studying Sibelius *Rezeptionsgeschichte* can be found, literally by the ton, in newspapers and journals in dozens of languages. Every collection of newspaper clippings in the world is a potential resource. Finland undoubtedly has the largest accumulations. During Sibelius's lifetime Finnish newspapers and periodicals not only published the writings of national critics about Sibelius, they also printed foreign reviews in translation. Thus the scope of Finland's collections is unusually broad. The Sibelius Museum in Turku has the most comprehensive material: early reviews written by Karl Flodin, by the critic known as Bis (K. F. Wasenius), and by many others are preserved together with writings that go right up to the present time.

Other important repositories are in Helsinki. The University Library preserves a Sibelius clippings file (MS 206.76–81) with material mostly from the years 1920 to 1960. The Finnish Music Information Center, founded in 1971, maintains files with recent reviews, articles, and programs. And in Helsinki's Swedish newspaper archive, Föreningens Brages Urklipsverk, founded by Otto Andersson in 1906, there are four Sibelius scrapbooks with articles taken from Swedish-language newspapers. The great bulk of these clippings comes from 1906 and later, but a few date as far back as 1890.

Every collection of newspaper cuttings is likely to have its own organization. However, it is possible to gain direct access to much of the vast amount of newspaper and magazine material through various indices. While such well-known tools as *The New York Times Personal Names Index*, the various *Reader's Guides*, and many special music indices are beyond the scope of this volume, three little-known tools that should help the serious Sibelius scholar should be mentioned. The first is Riitta Heino's much-appreciated index to Finnish music periodicals, *Suomen musiikkilehtien artikkeleita: Hakemisto vuosilta 1887–1977* [Finnish Music Periodicals: Index for the Years 1887–1977] (Helsinki: Kirjastopalvelu Oy, 1985. 312 p.). This is a finding tool to the contents of sixteen music periodicals of Finland, organized by subject and personal names, and the author has had the great good sense to index reviews as well as scholarly contributions. For those wishing to locate article-length studies or contemporary responses to Sibelius in Finland, whether in Finnish-language publications like *Säveleitä* and *Säveletär* or in such Swedish-language journals as *Euterpe* and *Finsk musikrevy*, Heino's index is an essential starting point.

There is also an index to Finnish newspapers in the Helsinki University Library, where most of the newspapers can be read on microfilm. Entitled *Suomen Sanomalehtihakemisto 1771–1890*, these 90 volumes, the keys to newspaper articles through 1890, are in several series, including Biographica, Topographica, and different subject headings. The researcher must seek under personal names, applicable city names, and subjects in order to get the full benefit of the index. And for those interested in the coverage given Sibelius in the current-events magazine *Suomen Kuvalehti*, founded in 1916, the magazine from time to time publishes a cumulative index, in which authors and subjects are analyzed.

The present section is organized into four parts. The first, "Sibelius and the Critics," contains published collections of reviews originating in newspapers and magazines that have substantial material about Sibelius together with books and articles about the critics. The second,

"Reputation: Perception and Evaluation," lists assessments of Sibelius's historical position and achievement and is organized by country. The third, "Influence," includes studies of the effect of Sibelius's music on other composers, while the fourth is "Sibelius in Music Histories." Some might question whether music histories belong with *Rezeptionsgeschichte.* Authors of music histories, however, inevitably provide assessments of composers and their works by the context in which each composer is placed and by the extent and type of coverage given. The author of a twentieth-century music history who includes Sibelius, or who excludes him, weaves new threads into the tapestry illustrating the history of the composer's music. One history famous for its slighting of Sibelius is Martin Wegelius's *Huvuddragen av den västerländska musikens historia* [Principal Forms of Western Music History], 3 vols. (Helsingfors: 1891–1893]. Despite an apparent pride in his most outstanding pupil, Wegelius nevertheless dismissed Sibelius and Finnish music generally in this first edition of his music history. That slight has been more than rectified by Erkki Salmenhaara, who was responsible for volumes 2 and 3 of the jointly written *Suomen musiikin historia* [History of Finnish Music], 4 vols. (Helsinki: Werner Söderström Osakeyhtiö, 1996). Although the publication date puts the history outside the scope of the *Guide*, it should be noted that Salmenhaara's fine discussions of Sibelius form the most extensive and up-to-date in any history of music.

Where English-language music histories are concerned, Paul Henry Lang gave Sibelius only passing mention in the more than 1,000 pages of his *Music in Western Civilization* (New York: Norton, 1941, see pp. 927 and 941), the standard midcentury music history (in which the composer is misnamed "Jan" in the index). More recently, Glenn Watkins's history of twentieth-century music, *Soundings* (New York: Schirmer, 1988), simply bypasses the composer altogether. Yet six Sibelius symphonies and such great tone poems as *Tapiola* belong among the twentieth-century's masterpieces. Fortunately, there are some important music histories in which Sibelius's life and works do have an interesting place, and these will be found below.

The "categories," of course, sometimes overlap. Moreover, in a fundamental sense, every biography, periodical article, or newspaper piece ever written about Sibelius and his music is a document of its time and thus a contribution to *Rezeptionsgeschichte*. The many periodical issues devoted entirely or in substantial part to Sibelius, for instance, contain a wealth of evidence for the reception historian. These periodicals, however, have been placed in a different section, Special Categories. Other choices had to be made, especially with regard to critics who knew the composer personally, for their writings can legitimately be placed in one of several categories. Under "Sibelius and the Critics" readers will find *collected* reprints of newspaper and magazine articles, including those by such Finnish writers as Karl Flodin and Leevi Madetoja; individually published essays evaluating the music have been placed under "Reputation: Perception and Evaluation." When these same writers turn to personal descriptions of the composer, their narratives have been categorized as "Contemporary Views of Jean Sibelius." What is lost in consistency of citing all authors in a single place will perhaps be compensated for by the perspective on Sibelius that emerges; meanwhile, readers can retrieve all entries for a given author through the index. Those interested in the topic of *Rezeptionsgeschichte* will want to consult each of these sections as well as the evaluations found in such sources as music dictionaries and encyclopedias. See also nos. 99, 105, 106, 498, and p. 144.

* * *

A. Sibelius and the Critics

247. Baker, Frank. "Couple the Tubas: Notes upon Sibelius." *Chesterian* 16 (1935): 64–69.

A criticism of the critics for having bundled Sibelius into a neat package labelled "Finland." Baker finds in such glorious works as Symphonies no. 3 and 5 something far more than can be expressed in journalistic labels.

248. Cardus, Neville. *Cardus on Music: A Centenary Collection.* Selected and edited by Donald Wright. London: Hamish Hamilton, 1988. ML60.C179 1988 ISBN 0-241-12285-6

Three reviews (pp. 217–25), from 1929, 1931, and 1962, of Symphonies no. 5, 7, and 2 respectively, echo a persistent theme: the manliness of the Sibelius symphonies. Even though a steadfast champion, in 1931 Cardus found Symphony no. 7 too sparse and austere for his taste.

249. Diktonius, Elmer. *Opus 12: Musik.* Helsingfors: Holger Schildt Förlag, 1933. 174 p.

Diktonius (1896–1961) was a Helsinki-born writer and composer who ran afoul of conservative musical tastes with his very first compositions. He consequently found an outlet for his creative urges in poetry (in such collections as *Hårda sånger* [Hard Songs], a parody of the title of Karl August Tavaststjerna's novel *Hard Times*) and in criticism. He eventually became one of the most important music critics in Finland. This little volume is a collection of his critical writings reprinted from *Arbetarbladet* and *Nya Argus* in which various composers, past and present, make an appearance. Cecil Gray's Sibelius book provides the impetus for Diktonius's longest essay on the composer, but excerpts from other reviews appear as well. See especially pp. 35–49, 123.

250. Downes, Edward. *Adventures in Symphonic Music.* Decorations by John O'Hara Cosgrave II. New York, Toronto: Farrar & Rinehart, 1944; London: Frederick Muller and Ascherberg, Hopwood & Crew, 194–?. Reprint. Port Washington, N.Y.: Kennikat Press, 1972. xii, 323 p. MT6.D745 1972 ISBN 0-8046-1500-4

Comments (pp. 64–66, 101–02, 276–86, et passim) on several of the symphonies and tone poems and the Concerto for Violin by the son of Sibelius's champion, Olin Downes. Most of the material originated either as commentary for CBS's Symphonic Hour or for the pages of the *Boston Transcript*.

251. Downes, Irene, ed. *Olin Downes on Music: A Selection from His Writings During the Half-Century 1906 to 1955.* New York: Simon and Schuster, 1957. Reprint. New York: Greenwood, 1968. xxxi, 473 p. ML60.D73 1968

Among the reviews reprinted here from the *Boston Post* and the *New York Times*, some half dozen concern Sibelius. Although some are abbreviated and most are given new titles that differ from their newspaper originals, the selection nevertheless affords an excellent idea of how Downes championed his hero. It also places Sibelius's music in the context of the many other works heard in Boston and New York during the first half of the twentieth century. For a list of this critic's Sibelius reviews in these two newspapers, see no. 255.

252. Downes, Olin. *Sibelius*. Translated by Paul Sjöblom. Helsinki: Otava, 1945. 186 p. ML410.S54D6 1945

Published in Finland just after World War II, Olin Downes's *Sibelius* is an anthology of articles selected from the *New York Times*, *Musical America*, and other American journals, although the exact issues are not identified, and translated into Finnish. The only parts of the volume not previously published in English are the introductory essay on Downes, "Sibeliuksen apostoli" ("Sibelius's Apostle"), by Sjöblom's father Yrjö, and Downes's preface, "Ave atque laudatio" (also printed separately in *Suomen Kuvalehti* [1945/49]: 1251). Here Downes relates his earliest reactions to Sibelius and compares the composer to Walt Whitman. A translation of this preface back into English (the original has been lost) may be found in the Olin Downes Collection at the University of Georgia, MSS 688, Correspondence File "Sjöblom."

253. Flodin, Karl. *Musikliv och reseminnen* [Music Life and Travel Memories]. Helsingfors: Söderström & Co., 1931. 304 p.

Some of Helsinki critic Karl Flodin's (1858–1925) most influential and revealing writings, the product of a career that began in the 1880s and continued until his death. His candid and incisive opinions were feared and respected in Finland, particularly as he was a Swedish-language critic, widely travelled, and a knowledgeable composer. The volume begins, significantly, with a group of writings labelled "Wagneriana," disclosing something of the impact of Wagner's influence at the end of the nineteenth century, and continues with commentaries on Willy Burmester, Busoni, Strauss, Mahler, and Hans von Bülow as well as Sibelius. The Sibelius reviews come from such journals as *Ateneum* and

Euterpe, and the source for each is blessedly identified within the Table of Contents at the end of the book.

254. Frankel, Benjamin. "Sibelius and His Critics." *The Listener*, June 29, 1961: 1130–1131.

A consideration of Sibelius's reputation, why he is criticized, and criticism of the critics. From a talk in the Third Programme.

255. Goss, Glenda Dawn. *Jean Sibelius and Olin Downes: Music, Friendship, Criticism*. Boston: Northeastern University Press, 1994. xi, 274 p. ML385.G7 1995 ISBN 1-55553-200-4

An exploration of the relationship between Sibelius and his most enthusiastic American critic against the background of American life in the first half of the twentieth century. Such matters as New York's Stravinsky fervor are taken into consideration as is the role played by both Downes and Serge Koussevitzky in the Eighth Symphony and the anti-Sibelian campaign led by Virgil Thomson in the 1940s. An appendix contains the annotated correspondence between Downes and Sibelius. There is also a list of Downes's writings and lectures about the composer and a separate bibliography.

256. *Great Concert Music: Philip Hale's Boston Symphony Programme Notes*. Edited by John N. Burk. With an Introduction by Lawrence Gilman. New York: Garden City Publishing Co., 1939. xix, 400 p. MT125.H34 1939

The descriptive, largely dispassionate program notes of Philip Hale (1854–1934), the Boston critic said to have elevated the writing of program notes to an art, are assembled here alongside Hale's trenchant newspaper criticisms of the same works. The writings about Sibelius (pp. 292–307) deal with Symphonies no. 1, 2, 4, 5, and 7 and the tone poems *Finlandia* and *Swan of Tuonela*.

257. Hylton Edwards, Stewart. *Critics and Composers: Selected Articles, Lectures, and Radio Talks*, 63–66 et passim. New York:

Vantage, 1984. xi, 100 p. + unnumbered appendix. ML60.H985 1984 ISBN 0-533-06022-7

Essays on topics ranging from Benjamin Britten and Henry Purcell to African, Portuguese, and folk music by the "Royal Philharmonic Society Prizeman and Wainwright Memorial Scholar," as the author is identified. Sibelius is mentioned in passing and in the short "Tribute to Jean Sibelius" (pp. 63–66), one page of which is a photograph. The tribute consists of reflections that are entirely personal in nature.

258. Madetoja, Leevi. "Jean Sibelius ja hänen musiikkinsa" [Jean Sibelius and His Music]. *Musiikki* 17 (1987): 68–101.

Reprints of various writings about Sibelius by one of his best-known pupils under a title supplied by the editor of the texts, Erkki Salmenhaara. The articles originally appeared between the years 1913 and 1935 in *Uusi Suometar*, *Helsingin Sanomat*, *Karjala*, *Aulos*, and *Musiikkitieto*. Of particular importance is Madetoja's description of Sibelius as a teacher, one of the few such accounts (annotated separately as no. 206), and the essay on the fiftieth anniversary, the only portion that remains of an intended biography.

259. Newman, Ernest. *More Essays from the World of Music: Essays from 'The Sunday Times.'* Selected by Felix Aprahamian. London: John Calder, 1958; New York: Coward-McCann, 1958. 260 p. Reprint. New York: Da Capo Press, 1978. ML60.N493 1978 ISBN 0-306-77520-4

Once described as the "Sainte-Beuve of his calling," Ernest Newman was also one of Britain's earliest and most devoted Sibelius champions. In this collection appear four of his most lucid and engaging essays on Sibelius written between March 1920 and September 1957: "Sibelius: Two Symphonies," "Sibelius: Most Personal of Great Composers," "Sibelius on Composition," and an obituary notice (pp. 113–28).

260. Newman, Ernest. "Sibelius no. 4: Its English History." In *Essays from the World of Music: Essays from 'The Sunday Times,'* 127–32.

Selected by Felix Aprahamian. London: 1956. Reprint. New York: Da Capo Press, 1978. 190 p. ML60.N49 1978 ISBN 0-306-77519-0

This essay was originally published August 29, 1937. Newman's perceptive and witty piece on the Fourth Symphony offers a valuable synopsis of Sibelius's fortunes in Britain and an explanation, by one of the composer's most knowledgeable music critics, of the public's difficulty in understanding this particular work.

261. Parmet, Simon. *Con amore: Essäer om musik och mästare* [Con amore: Essays on Music and Masters]. Helsingfors: Söderström & Co., 1960. 253 p. ML60.P2. Translated into Finnish by Clara Snellman-Borenius as *Sävelestä sanaan: esseitä* (Helsinki: Werner Söderström Osakeyhtiö, 1962).

A collection of writings by conductor and Sibelius admirer Parmet (né Pergament) who also wrote a book about the symphonies. The articles here, which originally appeared in various newspapers and journals between 1930 and 1960, include a substantial group in a special section called "Sibeliana" (pp. 74–142) in which are reprinted Parmet's reviews of books about Sibelius, his consideration of the fate of the Eighth Symphony (an article annotated as no. 643), and his remarks about a letter written by the composer in 1936, reproduced in facsimile on p. 138. Original sources are given for the pieces (on p. 253).

262. Rands, Bernard. "Sibelius and his Critics." *Music Review* 19 (1958): 105–11.

Observing the neglect of Sibelius as a serious composer except in the English-speaking world, the author suggests that the composer's problem with his critics had to do with his treatment of form. With the "germ-motive" theory, popular among British critics, Rands finds a way to demonstrate the unity of the composer's works, illustrated with several music examples.

263. Scholes, Percy A. *The Mirror of Music 1844–1944: A Century of Musical Life in Britain as Reflected in the Pages of the Musical Times.*

London: Novello & Co. jointly with Oxford University Press, 1947, 2 vols. Reprint. Freeport, N.Y.: Books for Libraries Press, 1970. xix, 964 p. ML285.S35 1970 ISBN 0-8369-5443-2

A brief survey (Vol. I, pp. 448–49) of performances of Sibelius's music in Britain with quotations from the *Musical Times* and annotations that correct misinformation purveyed there.

264. Slonimsky, Nicolas. *Lexicon of Musical Invective: Critical Assaults on Composers Since Beethoven's Time*. 2d edition. New York: Coleman-Ross, 1965. 325 p. ML3785.S5 1965

Slonimsky's well-known, often hilarious compendium includes two pages (pp. 178–79) of excerpts from some of the worst Sibelius reviews ever written in New York and Boston newspapers and journals, most of them concerning Symphony no. 4. The earliest date from 1913 and the last comes from Virgil Thomson's 1940 piece (see no. 265).

265. Thomson, Virgil. *The Musical Scene*. New York: Alfred A. Knopf, 1945. xiv, 301 p. + xv index pages. Reprint. New York: Greenwood, 1968. ML60.T5 1968

A selection of reviews, virtually all from the *New York Herald Tribune* during the period October 9, 1940, to July 23, 1944, by an articulate American composer who was also one of Sibelius's most vituperative assailants. The numerous references to Sibelius, easily found through the index, steadfastly reiterate the sentiments expressed in Thomson's debut piece at the *Tribune*: that Sibelius's music is "vulgar, self-indulgent, and provincial beyond all description."

B. Reputation: Perception and Evaluation

See also nos. 195, 579, 666, 707, 709, 710, 724

FINLAND

266. Borg, Kim. "Jean Sibelius und die Finnen" [Jean Sibelius and the Finns]. *Österreichische Musikzeitschrift* 12 (1957): 386–89.

The gifted Finnish singer and Sibelius relative Kim Borg explains why Sibelius is so important to Finns, both the musical professional and the "man in the street." Sibelius died after the essay was written but before it was published, making the article the singer's epitaph to his countryman. Illustrated with a photograph of a very grave-looking Sibelius.

267. Donner, Philip, and Juhani Similä. "Jean Sibelius: Teollistumisajan musiikkimurroksen idolihahmo" [Jean Sibelius: The Idol Figure in the Music Crisis of Industrial Times]. In *Musiikkikulttuurin murros teollistumisajan Suomessa*, 33–49. Edited by Vesa Kurkela and Riitta Valkeila. Jyväskylä: Jyväskylän Yliopiston Musiikkitieteen Laitos, 1982.

A rare and refreshing study that deals with how Sibelius became an idol in Finland. The authors, whose point of departure is ethnomusicological and cultural, examine different manifestations of the Sibelius "cult," its perpetrators, and its changes. Their sources range from music literature and iconography to newspapers, recordings, and radio interviews and their extensively documented article is filled with fascinating information, including a variety of entertaining illustrations, a portion of a revealing 1948 radio interview with Sibelius, and the controversial two measures of *Flickan kom ifrån sin älsklings möte* improvised by Ralf Gothóni in a 1981 recording with Jorma Hynninen. If not an exhaustive study of the topic, it is an interesting (if less than objective) beginning by two figures who have contrived to make Harold E. Johnson (no. 159) appear saintly by comparison.

268. Donner, Philip, and Juhani Similä. "Jean Sibelius: The Idol." *Idols and Myths in Music*, 66–79. Edited by Philip Donner. *Musiikin suunta*, vol. 7. Helsinki: Suomen Etnomusikologinen Seura, 1985.

A look at how myths grew around Sibelius in Finnish culture, with a survey of visual images, recorded interviews, and personal relics. Treating their subject humorously, the authors nevertheless provide extensive documentation, illustrations, and music examples.

269. Flodin, Karl. "Die Erweckung des nationalen Tones in der Finnischen Musik" [The Awakening of the National Tone in Finnish Music]. *Die Musik* 3 (1903–1904): 287–89.

Critic Flodin places Sibelius briefly against the background of Finland's music history. Calling him the *Dolmetscher* (the interpreter) of Finland, he asserts that Sibelius has a "school," since a number of younger Finnish composers are already following in his footsteps.

270. Flodin, Karl. *Finska musiker och andra uppsatser i musik* [Finnish Musicians and Other Essays in Music], 29–34. Helsingfors: Söderström & Co., 1900. 170 p.

A book dedicated to Richard Faltin, which combines essays on Finland's then-leading composers, including Faltin, Martin Wegelius, Robert Kajanus, Oskar Merikanto, Armas Järnefelt, and Sibelius, with chapters on Europe's recognized greats from Bach to Wagner. The chapter on Sibelius (pp. 29–34) bears Liszt's epigram (*Génie oblige*) and begins with an essay on genius. Flodin's message is that Sibelius's music will eventually be understood well beyond Finland's borders because the world inevitably pays attention to a genius.

271. Flodin, Karl. "Jean Sibelius." *Norden*, 1902: 123–30.

A decidedly partisan essay that describes Sibelius as lighting up the northern landscape like the blossoming at midsummer and calling him the greatest, most productive and original composer in Finland. Although not yet forty, Sibelius, in Flodin's view, had left his storm-and-stress years behind. With great prescience Flodin predicts a third period for Sibelius in which the ethnographic Finnish element would again play an important role.

272. Flodin, Karl. "Jean Sibelius, fosterlandets tonsättare" [Jean Sibelius, Composer for the Fatherland]. *Finsk musikrevy* 1 (1905): 423–36.

Flodin waxes poetic about Sibelius, whom he believes is giving voice to the nation, and describes him as richer, more powerfully inspired than any other composer in Finland.

273. Flodin, Karl. *La musique en Finlande* [Music in Finland]. Paris: Typographie Morris Père & Fils, 1900. 23 p. A German translation appeared as *Die Musik in Finnland* (Helsingfors: F. Tilgmann, 1900). ML304.F5

On the occasion of the Helsinki Philharmonic Orchestra's European tour of 1900 which culminated with their participation in the World's Fair in Paris, Flodin prepared this booklet to be distributed to audiences. His introduction ("the land of 1,000 lakes, the silent forests, the solitary countryside . . . the songs inspired by sadness and reaching back to antiquity") and the cover depicting a bard in flowing robe, with a swan and a bear reclining humbly at his feet, helped to romanticize Finland. Principal figures in Finland's musical life are identified, and among the photographs is one of a notably Napoleonic-looking Sibelius with right hand in his breast pocket and hair in disarray.

274. Frosterus, Sigurd. "Sibelius' Koordinater" [Sibelius's Coordinates]. *Nya Argus* 15 (1932): 79–84, 95–99. Reprinted in *Stålålderns Janusansikte och andra essäer*, 191–228. Helsingfors: Söderström & Co., 1935.

Frosterus (1876–1956), critic, theorist, author, and architect, views Finland's cultural heritage as supplying points of reference for Sibelius's creativity. No music examples, although major works are discussed and comparisons made to the broader European musical tradition.

275. Heikinheimo, Seppo. "Sibelius: A Sacred Oak." *Nordic Sounds*, 1982, no. 2: 3–4.

An evaluation of Sibelius's historic position, daring for its highly critical tone from a fellow Finn, who observes that an objective assessment of Sibelius's music and personality is still a risky undertaking in Finland. The author, who was the controversial music critic for the *Helsingin Sanomat*, acknowledges the mastery of Symphonies no. 4 and 5 but hears "fairly banal passages" in the first two symphonies, calls Symphony no. 3 weak and boring, and finds Symphonies no. 6 and 7 "clearly senile." He offers his own theory as to why Sibelius's diaries have been withheld from scholarly scrutiny: The composer's constant contemplation of his own misery is painfully characteristic of the pseudo-genius, as opposed to the real genius, described by Wolfgang Hildesheimer in his book *Mozart*. Few in Finland, however, subscribe to this explanation.

276. Kokkonen, Joonas. *Ihminen ja musiikki: Valittuja kirjoituksia, esitelmiä, puheita ja arvosteluja* [Man and Music: Selected Writings, Lectures, Speeches, and Criticisms]. Edited by Kalevi Aho. Helsinki: Gaudeamus, 1992. 503 p. ML160.K77 1992 ISBN 951-662-554-1

Along with many passing references, three articles are devoted to Sibelius in this anthology by one of Finland's recent leading composers (d. 1996): "The Master's Way" (pp. 49–51), "Sibelius's Fourth Symphony" (pp. 52–60), and a speech given during the intermission of the composer's 100th birthday concert (pp. 61–64). The most substantial of these, the remarks on Symphony no. 4, indicate composer Kokkonen's close acquaintance with the work.

277. Kokkonen, Joonas. "The National and International Sibelius." *Finnish Music Quarterly*, 1990, nos. 3–4: 14–17.

Consideration of Sibelius's stature at different times during the twentieth century. Among the explanations offered for the composer's changing fortunes are the importance of Finnish nature to his music, public ignorance of works beyond those in the national-romantic style, and the label "national hero."

278. Lange, Ina. *Skilda tiders musikmästare: Händel, Beethoven, Chopin, Sibelius, Studier över deras liv och verk* [Music Masters of Different Periods: Händel, Beethoven, Chopin, Sibelius, Studies of Their Life and Work]. Stockholm: P. A. Norstedt & Söners, 1913. 207 p.

An enthusiastic essay addressed to Swedish-reading music lovers who wish to follow an interest in four of the "greats." The author was a Finnish concert pianist who was also known as a writer (Lange penned her Swedish-language novels such as *Luba* under the pseudonym "Daniel Sten"). In this book each man receives his own chapter, although, unlike the others, Sibelius's is called not by his name but by the title "Något om Finsk Musik" [Something about Finnish Music] (pp. 170–205). A brief review of Finnish music history, with portraits of important figures, serves as the background for the discussion of Sibelius, who is described as the composer of the most distinctive symphonies of our time.

279. Parmet, Simon. "Sibelius' ställning i samtiden" [Sibelius's Position in Our Time]. *Nya Argus* 48 (1955): 303–06.

Placing Sibelius against the background of an idyllic Finland unspoiled by civilization, conductor Parmet offers a birthday tribute that praises Sibelius for setting equally well both the Finnish and Swedish languages in his music, mentions the music's deep connections to the country's struggle against foreign tyranny, and stresses his position as the country's first composer to achieve international significance. Yet most of all, Parmet feels, the strong and individual personality evident in his music puts Sibelius among the great figures of musical composition.

280. Ringbom, Nils-Eric. "Är Jean Sibelius musik universell, och är den aktuell?" [Is Jean Sibelius's Music Universal and Is It Current?]. *Nya Argus* 53 (1950): 273–76.

In this essay, often reprinted in magazines for the general reader, Ringbom considers Sibelius's music in three periods of development, his influence, and his critical position, and concludes that his music belongs both to the present and to the future.

281. Ringbom, Nils-Eric. "Sibelius' ställning i tiden" [Sibelius's Position in Time]. *Nya Argus* 41 (1948): 133–34.

Considers the composer's position in the larger picture of music's history and concludes, as above, that by not consciously belonging to any school or style, Sibelius thereby belongs both to the present and to the future.

282. Setälä, E[mil] N[estor]. "Sävelten mahtaja" [The Mighty of Tones]. *Kalevalaseuran vuosikirja* 7 (1927): 226–30.

Transcription of a speech by Setälä (1864–1935), a member of Parliament, husband of Helmi Krohn (see no. 193), and Sibelius's neighbor at Järvenpää, given at Helsinki University on Kalevala Day (February 2) in 1926. In Sibelius's music, the author observes, Finland's nature, her unique culture, and her people are embodied for all the world to hear through means more powerful than could be effected by any politician or diplomat. Setälä's speech indicates how deeply Finns had come to identify Sibelius with the national consciousness in the twentieth century.

283. Tolonen, Jouko. "Sibelius: säveleepikko" [Sibelius: Tone Epic]. *Suomalainen Suomi*, 1957: 462–64.

Written immediately after Sibelius's death, the essay addresses the question of his importance. Sibelius, says the author, is great in Finland because he expressed in his music the power and serenity of Finnish nature and the noble spirit of his people. Yet Sibelius is great beyond the borders of Finland because of his symphonies, a genre which is the high point of epic music. As Sibelius himself said, "I love this life infinitely, and it must stamp everything I compose," so with their imprint of life the symphonies have transcended the purely national to speak to the whole world.

FRANCE AND BELGIUM

284. Fantapié, Anja, and Henri-Claude Fantapié. "Jean Sibelius." In *Boréales, revue du centre de recherches inter-nordiques*. Numéro special: La musique finlandaise, nos. 26, 27, 28, 29 (1983): 760–770.

This "article" is really a series of essays valuable for the fresh French perspective they offer on Sibelius. The authors begin with a biographical chronology and then discuss Sibelius's production in three periods. In the most interesting essays the authors place Sibelius within the larger history of Western music, discuss

Sibelius vis-à-vis romanticism, impressionism, and symbolism; examine Sibelius the melodist (with frequent references to artist Claude Monet), and discuss three aspects of the composer's legacy in Finland. Short discography and bibliography.

285. Fantapié, Henri-Claude. "Jean Sibelius et la France, au miroir des écrits musicographiques 1900–1965" [Jean Sibelius and France, Mirrored in Writings about Music, 1900–1965]. *Boréales, revue du centre de recherches inter-nordiques* 54/57 (1993): 59–82; 58/61 (1994): 215–19.

An evaluation of Sibelius's position in France through French writings about music. Enormously useful, both for the annotated bibliography of sources from 1898 to 1982 and for the author's thoughtful, interpretive essay.

286. Fragny, Robert de. "Jean Sibélius et Paul Dukas" [Jean Sibelius and Paul Dukas]. *Résonances, Le spectateur Lyonnais*, May 1965: 25–26.

Homage to two musicians having an anniversary year. Sibelius is called "the Bruckner of Finland." "Hats off to Sibelius," says the author, for contributing to the artistic revelation of his "little country" [Finland is in fact 25 percent larger than the United Kingdom]. Fragny also offers explanation for the French disdain of Sibelius.

287. Leibowitz, René. *Sibelius, le plus mauvais compositeur du monde* [Sibelius, the Worst Composer in the World]. Liège: Aux Editions Dynamo, 1955. 6 p.

Leibowitz's few pages of text have received far more attention, no doubt owing to his audacious title and contentious arguments, than the quality of his essay deserves. The author, a student and propagandist of the Second Viennese School, reveals more about himself than about Sibelius. His vindictive words are important chiefly for indicating those who did not support Sibelius and why.

For a response, see Alfhild Forslin, "En fransk-tysk dispyt om Sibelius" [A French-German Dispute over Sibelius]. *Minerva*,

November 17, 1965: 1–2. This response appeared in Finnish as "Ranskalais-saksalainen väittely Sibeliuksesta," *Pieni musiikkilehti*, 1966, no. 3: 8–9. See also no. 288.

288. Oramo, Ilkka. "Sibelius, le plus mauvais compositeur du monde" [Sibelius, the Worst Composer in the World]. *Boréales, revue du centre de recherches inter-nordiques* 54/57 (1993): 51–58.

A Finnish theorist examines Leibowitz's pamphlet (no. 287) vis-à-vis Adorno's earlier "Glosse über Sibelius" (no. 292) and shows that Leibowitz simply recycled Adorno's insults under a new title.

289. "Ravel, critique" [Ravel the Critic]. *Musical: Revue du théâtre musical de Paris-Chatelet, L'orchestre, France* 4 (June 1987): 62–69.

An assortment of Ravel's opinions about his contemporaries, who are shown in photographs and drawings. A brief comment about Sibelius, quoted from the *New York Times*, August 7, 1927, calls the Finn a magnificent talent, although not a supreme artist, and a composer inspired by the Nordic realm from which he came.

290. Tyrväinen, Helena. "Suomalaiset Pariisin maailmannäyttelyiden 1889 ja 1900 musiikkiohjelmissa" [The Finns in the Music Programs of the Paris World's Fairs of 1889 and 1900]. *Musiikkitiede* 6 (1994): 22–74.

An important article that examines afresh the circumstances of Finland's participation in the Paris World's Fairs, the activities of Finland's musicians and especially the Helsinki Philharmonic Orchestra in this connection, and French reactions to the music of Sibelius. Taking into account the political atmosphere, the author uses evidence from French newspaper reviews and Finnish archival documents to demonstrate that the concerts were not the failures for Sibelius they are generally believed to have been. An English-language version of Tyrväinen's research, with emphasis on Sibelius, was presented at the Second International Sibelius Conference in Helsinki (November 1995) and will appear among those Proceedings.

291. Vidal, Pierre. “Sibelius révélé par le disque” [Sibelius Revealed on Record]. *Boréales, revue du centre de recherches inter-nordiques* 54/57 (1993): 83–88.

Thoughtful discussion, going well beyond the confines of the title, of reasons for the infrequent appearance of Sibelius's music in the concert halls of France.

GERMANY

292. Adorno, Theodor W. “Glosse über Sibelius” [Comments About Sibelius]. In *Gesammelte Schriften*. Vol. 17, *Musikalische Schriften IV. Moments musicaux: Impromptus*, 247–52. Frankfurt-am-Main: Suhrkamp Verlag, 1982. ML60.A27 1978 v. 4 ISBN 3-518-57610-0

A blistering attack on Sibelius, in which his scores are described as “dürftig und böotisch [sic].” The article originated (without the title above) as a review of Bengt de Törne's *Sibelius: A Close-Up* (no. 176) in *Zeitschrift für Sozialforschung* 7 (1938): 460–63. Adorno's piece voices the extreme irritation of many adherents of the Second Viennese School with what they viewed as Sibelius's unwarranted and dangerous popularity.

293. [Batka, Richard]. “Richard Batka om Jean Sibelius” [Richard Batka on Jean Sibelius]. *Finsk musikrevy* 2 (1906): 416–20.

Translation into Swedish of a lecture given about Sibelius in the Deutsches Landestheater in Prague, November 21, 1906. Batka reveals a surprising early enthusiasm among German-speaking people for Sibelius. The lecturer evokes Wagner and emphasizes Sibelius's loyalty to his national roots, thereby suggesting the source of the appeal to Teutonic audiences.

294. Brüll, Erich. “Der Klassiker Sibelius: Einige Gesichtspunkte” [The Classic Sibelius: Some Viewpoints]. *Musik und Gesellschaft* 9 (1971): 582–88.

In this short but thoughtful article, Brüll situates prevailing German opinions and earlier German research on Sibelius in the context of Marxist-socialist thought and attempts to discard the notion of the composer as a hopelessly antiquated romantic. He sees instead a politically disinterested individualist whose artistic struggles and compositional skill enabled him to achieve a kind of classic balance, both in form and between "absolute" and "program" music. A photograph of a middle-aged Sibelius with a full head of hair writing at his desk in Ainola replaces the *Greis* image with which the composer is usually represented.

295. Göhler, Georg. "Orchesterkompositionen von Jean Sibelius" [Orchestral Compositions of Jean Sibelius]. *Kunstwart*, September 1, 1908: 261–69. A shortened version of this article appeared in *Mitteilungen der Musikalienhandlung Breitkopf & Härtel*, November 1908: 3826–33, and in *Deutsche Militär-Musiker-Zeitung* 31 (1909/26): 1–2; (1909/27): 1–2; (1909/28): 1–2. The article has been translated into Finnish as "Jean Sibeliuksen varhaisemmat orkesterisävellykset," *Kalevalaseuran vuosikirja* 6 (1926): 13–26.

The reasons for the many times this article was recycled are not hard to seek: Göhler's was a welcoming German voice that found Sibelius a refreshing antidote to "Strauss mania." He suggests that within Sibelius's "national" art lies the kind of authentic quality that appeals to all people, a belief he attempts to demonstrate by reviewing the orchestral works, beginning with the one he considers the most nationalistic (*Finlandia*) and proceeding to the abstract, Symphonies no. 1–3.

296. Krellmann, Hanspeter. "Plädoyer für Sibelius" [Pleading for Sibelius]. *Musica* 24 (1970): 442–44.

A defense of Sibelius against those who have charged the composer with being an anachronism. The author points out that in his geographical and spiritual isolation, Sibelius could have become another Max Bruch or Karl Goldmark but instead became much more. He says that, aside from the Concerto for Violin, Sibelius's music is hardly known in Germany, and he provides a short discography of symphonies and tone poems.

297. Tawaststjerna, Erik. "Über Adornos Sibelius-Kritik" [Concerning Adorno's Sibelius Criticism]. *Studien zur Wertungsforschung* 12 (1979): 112–24. Delivered as a lecture during the symposium "Th. W. Adorno und die Musik," October 14, 1977, Hochschule für Musik und darstellende Kunst, Institut der Wertungsforschung in Graz. Translated into Finnish as "Adornon Sibelius-kritiikistä," *Musiikki* 7 (1977): 1–14.

Tawaststjerna places Adorno's vitriolic remarks about Sibelius in context by examining the critic's background, his conception of music, and his cultural and political situation.

298. Thaer, Günther. "Sibelius ja nykypäivien Saksa" [Sibelius and Contemporary Germany]. *Valvoja-aika* 14 (1936): 121–23.

An explanation for the failure of Sibelius's compositions to captivate German listeners. Despite the fact that Germany, like Finland, belongs to the Northern world, the thoroughly "Finnish" character of the music together with what Germans perceive as the poverty of melodic invention and formal structure have contributed to the lack of appreciation of Sibelius. The author predicts a new direction for this music in Germany, although he surely would have been surprised to know that a half a century would lapse before the new direction got underway.

299. Trojahn, Manfred. "Ein verpasstes Jubilaeum" [A Missed Anniversary]. *Musica* 41 (1987): 424–46.

A consideration of Sibelius's fate, especially in Germany, on the occasion of the thirtieth anniversary of the composer's death. The view advanced here is that, far from being a late romantic, Sibelius is the radical father of modernism.

HUNGARY

300. Nyyssönen, Juho, and Iván Schiffer. *Jean Sibelius*. Budapest: Rózsavölgyi és Társa Bizománya, 1936. 53 p.

A seventieth birthday appreciation, this little book contains two essays in Hungarian about the composer interlarded with passages from the *Kalevala* translated into Hungarian and accompanied by a conventionally sombre photograph of Sibelius. Approximately one third of the book is devoted to a list of works by opus number.

SWEDEN

301. Alin, Sven. "'Tycker ni om Sibelius?' Synpunkter på Sibelius' internationella roll" ['Do You Like Sibelius?' The Idea of Sibelius's International Role]. *Tidsspegel*, 1984: 9–15. The article also appears as "Sibelius: ett svårt namn för europeiskt musikliv!" [Sibelius: A Difficult Name for European Music Life!], in *Svenskbygden* 64 (1985): 62–66.

Swedish pianist Sven Alin considers the extreme positions taken on Sibelius, from that of René Leibowitz to those of British and North American enthusiasts, and concludes that knowledge of Finnish nature, atmosphere, and culture are necessary for understanding the composer's music.

302. Hambraeus, Axel. "Jean Sibelius." In *Mästare i tonernas värld: en samling musikerporträtt*, 167–71. Uppsala: J. A. Lindblads Förlag, 1933. The volume went through numerous editions, the sixth appearing in 1963.

Son of the organist of the same name, the author originally intended his "collection of musical portraits" for children, and his text is thus quite general. Among composers from Bach to Strauss, Sibelius appears as a crowning finish. Hambraeus's observation, that Sibelius's name is perhaps the greatest among living composers, is an indication of his stature in Sweden in the 1930s.

303. Nyblom, C. G. *Jean Sibelius*. Kortfattade lefnadsteckningar om framstående tonsättare, III. Stockholm: Elkan & Schildknecht, Emil Carelius, 1916. 18 p. ML410.S54N9 1916

An appreciative essay about the life and works on the occasion of the composer's fiftieth birthday. Nyblom's piece presents Sibelius as the incarnation of the Finnish people's character, their struggles, their cares, and their hopes.

304. Ottelin, Odal. "Jean Sibelius." In *Tolv nordiska porträtt*, 55–72. Stockholm: Tidningen Studiekamraten, 1945.

In this laudatory Swedish-language essay, which appears within the framework of chapters on Hans Christian Andersen, Björnstjerne Björnson, and Edvard Grieg, the author emphasizes the importance to Sibelius of Swedish-language poets such as Runeberg and of Northern nature, a matter treated in a section of its own. No music examples or bibliography, but a photograph of Väinö Aaltonen's bust of Sibelius appears on page 24 in the context of the chapter that discusses the visual representations of Northern artists.

305. Pergament, Moses. *Vandring med Fru Musica* [Wanderings with Lady Music]. Stockholm: P. A. Norstedt, 1943. 259 p. Translated into Finnish by Eeva Kangasmaa as *Retkiä musiikin maailmassa* (Turku: Uuden Auran Osakeyhtiön Kirjapaino, 1945).

A biographical essay about Sibelius (pp. 214–24) by conductor and brother of Simon Parmet in which the author emphasizes the composer's progress from Finnish roots, especially the *Kalevala*, to being a composer for all mankind.

UNITED KINGDOM

306. Cardus, Neville. "Sibelius." In *Ten Composers*, 153–66. London: Jonathan Cape, 1944. 166 p. Revised and enlarged as *Composers Eleven*, 238–55 (New York: Braziller, 1959). Reprint. Freeport, N.Y.: Books for Libraries Press, 1970. ML390.C3 1970 ISBN 0-8369-1554-2. Translated into Swedish by Kajsa Rootzén as *Tio tondiktare* (Stockholm: Lujs, 1947).

A very personal interpretation of Sibelius who appears in the company of other nineteenth- and twentieth-century composers, from Schubert to Delius. The Finn is described as "the most masculine and fortifying composer of all our contemporaries" and "simple yet subtle." More enduring perhaps than the subjective comments is the interpretation of a solid yet troubled composer in the drawing by Milein Cosman that accompanies the essay.

307. Cardus, Neville. "Sibelius." In *The Concert-Goer's Annual*, no. 2: 24–27. Edited by Evan Senior. New York: Doubleday, 1958.

A discussion of Sibelius as a symphonist, with parallels drawn to Bruckner: the music of both is described as "non-erotic," unegotistical, and often made from the simplest raw material. Cardus suggests that only with time can Sibelius's place among the universal masters be assessed.

308. Colles, H[enry] C[ope]. "Jean Sibelius." In *Great Contemporaries: Essays by Various Hands*, 396–407. London: Cassell, 1935. An American edition appeared as *Men of Turmoil: Biographies by Leading Authorities of the Dominating Personalities of Our Day* (New York: Minton, Balch, 1935). D412.G7

Among essays on Adolf Hitler, Lawrence of Arabia, and George Bernard Shaw, the one on Sibelius is important as a period piece, depicting Sibelius's impact on the British in the mid-twentieth century. The author (1879–1943), a scholar and teacher, was also a music critic at *The Times* and edited both the third and fourth editions of *Grove*'s dictionary. A conspicuous conservatism and insularity are in evidence when Colles proclaims Britain to be the only country outside Finland likely to place Sibelius among the century's great composers.

309. Elliot, John Harold. "Jean Sibelius: A Modern Enigma." *Chesterian* 12 (1931): 93–100. Partially reprinted in *An Anthology of Musical Criticism*, edited by Norman Demuth (London: Eyre & Spottiswoode, 1947), 328–29.

Writing in the house journal for the firm of J. & W. Chester, which on occasion published Sibelius's music, Elliot compares Sibelius's originality of conception and design to Berlioz. He maintains that for the English, the "original character of his music as a whole—still presents an enigma yet to be solved."

310. Gray, Laura. "Sibelius and England." In *The Sibelius Companion*, 281–96. Edited by Glenda Dawn Goss. Westport, Conn.: Greenwood, 1996. ML410.S54S53 1996 ISBN 0-313-28393-1

An intelligent examination of the reasons for the so-called Sibelius cult in England and the subsequent decline of the composer's reputation there. The author (no relation to Cecil) supports her findings with British critical writings, some difficult to obtain today, ranging from the first responses to Sibelius at the beginning of the century to opinions in the 1990s. She also explores the critics' theories of Sibelius's symphonic methods, particularly the widely-discussed notion of "germ motives."

311. Layton, Robert. "Sibelius in England." *Music in Britain, A Quarterly Review* 70 (1965): 14–17.

Concise but useful assessment of the popularity of the Finnish composer in England, which the author attributes to supportive conductors, critics, and scholars, and to recordings.

312. Legge, Walter. "Sibelius's Position Today." *Monthly Musical Record* 65 (1935): 224–26.

An appreciative evaluation by the founder of the Sibelius Society in Great Britain. Legge considers Sibelius against the background of twentieth-century music, its audiences, and the technology that made gramophone recordings possible.

313. Lorenz, Robert. "Afterthoughts on the Sibelius Festival." *Musical Times*, January 1939: 13–14.

An attempt to provide a critical evaluation of Sibelius's achievement in the face of the enthusiastic biographies, studies, and analytical notes available in the 1930s. While the incidental music earns high marks, Lorenz objects to Sibelius's repeated use of basic formulas and to what he describes as "many irritating and depressing effects of frustration." Lorenz's piece is discussed in a larger context in the Introduction, p. xv.

314. McMullin, Michael. "Sibelius: An Essay on His Significance." *Music Review* 46 (1985): 199–211.

McMullin suggests that Sibelius's melodic inventiveness, his advancement of symbolism through integration of orchestration and form, and a philosophy of life "independent of time and place" are essential ingredients in defining his importance. He provides an analysis of the first movement of Symphony no. 5 in an appendix.

315. Mellers, Wilfrid. "Sibelius at Ninety: A Revaluation." *The Listener*, December 1955: 969.

Mellers considers Sibelius to have investigated the evolution of themes from their constituent parts and pared down symphonic structure to its bare bones, but wonders whether his "religious sensibility without a faith" and his music may be spiritually and technically dead ends.

316. Raynor, Henry. "Sibelius: An Attempted Postscript." *Chesterian* 34 (1959): 16–23.

An aptly titled essay in which the author, by his own admission prejudiced against the composer, attempts to explain Sibelius's position in musical history. The essay is an early example of the backlash against Sibelius that occurred in England after the composer's death.

317. Vaughan Williams, Ralph. "Sibelius." *R.C.M. Magazine* 51 (1955): 58–60.

Contributed at the request of *R.C.M. Magazine* to honor Sibelius's ninetieth birthday, Vaughan Williams's piece is a ringing endorsement of the music of Sibelius, who "has shown us that there is an inexhaustible store of juice in the old orange if we only know how to suck it." Defending Sibelius against those who complain about the quantity of mediocre works, he muses that it takes 1,000 routine compositions to make a single masterpiece—and from Sibelius have come no fewer than seven symphonies, *Tapiola*, *En saga*, and *Voces intimae*.

318. Westrup, J. A. "Jean Sibelius." *Musical Times*, November 1957: 601–03.

Written as an obituary, Westrup's article gives a British scholar's assessment of the composer's achievement ("compelling individuality which somehow fuses the most incongruous elements into a coherent whole . . . ") and a brief consideration of the propaganda and criticism to which Sibelius has been subjected.

UNITED STATES

319. Downes, Olin. "Jean Sibelius." *New Music Review and Church Music Review* 13 (July 1914): 358–61; (August 1914): 403–07; (September 1914): 442–46.

In an extensive article of great zeal ("Out of the North has come a new prophet: Jean Sibelius . . . "), Downes, at the time critic for the *Boston Post*, reviews Sibelius's background and orchestral works in the wake of the composer's June 1914 visit to the United States. Most of the critic's later turns of phrase ("with a seven-league stride, the hero theme appears"; the "skirling of winds"; Sibelius's "racial inheritance") and his judgments ("The music of Sibelius is even more important to men than to art") already are in place here as is the assertion that Sibelius told him the Fourth Symphony was composed in one week (a claim later proved false; see no. 175).

320. Price, Lucien. "Portrait of Sibelius at Järvenpää." In *We Northmen*, 354–66. Boston: Little, Brown, and Co., 1936. D965.P846. First published in *Yale Review* 24 (1934): 356–69.

Written by a Boston reporter, this article is less a portrait of Sibelius than an explanation of what many North Americans perceived in his music: "manliness, loyalty, courage, and a certain rough honesty, salted with humor." The title of the volume in which Price's article appears suggests the importance of the Nordic kinship that many Americans believed they shared with Finns.

321. Rosenfeld, Paul. "Sibelius." In *Musical Portraits: Interpretations of Twenty Modern Composers*, 245–55. New York: Harcourt, Brace and Howe, 1920; London: Kegan Paul, Trench, Trubner & Co., 1922.

Reprint. Freeport, N.Y.: Books for Libraries Press, 1968. ML390.R78 1968

Rosenfeld turns his full literary prowess upon Sibelius in this essay, providing some of the most vivid wind and nature images ever written about the composer. The critic especially approved of the Fourth Symphony ("More definitive, it cannot be"), which he describes with whiplash intensity. Later, Rosenfeld turned against the Finn and in a vilifying essay in *The New Republic* (April 21, 1941) called him "that overstuffed bard."

322. Saminsky, Lazare. "Sibelius, A Mind Two-Dimensional." In *Music of Our Day: Essentials and Prophecies*, 193–204. New enlarged edition, New York: Thomas Y. Cromwell Co., 1939. ML197.S18 1939

Saminsky's stated purpose is to counter the "strange hysteria of worship" surrounding Sibelius and demonstrate that his genius was merely regional. He criticizes the music's lack of harmonic movement, the motives "without a future," and the inability to inspire followers.

C. Influence

See also nos. 372, 394, 454

323. Anderberg, Thorild. "Et försvar for Stenhammar" [A Defense of Stenhammar]. *Dansk Musiktidsskrift* 21 (1946): 62–63.

A response to Niels Viggo Bentzon (no. 324), with whom the author disagrees on several points. Anderberg believes that the musical production of Swedish composers Lars-Erik Larsson and Dag Wirén both clearly show the influence of Sibelius and suggests that Bentzon has too readily dismissed the Finn's importance, especially to composers in eastern Sweden.

324. Bentzon, Niels Viggo. "Jean Sibelius og hans nordiske samtid" [Jean Sibelius and His Northern Contemporaries]. *Dansk Musiktidsskrift* 21 (1946): 37–39.

Composer Bentzon considers the influence of Sibelius vis-à-vis his northern contemporaries and successors and finds the music indebted to Tchaikovsky, more Finnish than Nielsen's is Danish, and less significant to contemporary composers than that of Brahms.

For a response, see no. 323.

325. Heiniö, Mikko. "Sibelius, Finland, and the Symphonic Idea." *Finnish Music Quarterly*, 1990, nos. 3–4: 10–13.

An insightful consideration of Sibelius's influence in Finland, the importance of symphonic music in that country, and an explanation of the crucial position the symphony as a genre has occupied there. Heiniö, himself a composer, observes that Sibelius's "organic quality," whereby an entire work developed "logically" from a concise musical idea, became a favorite notion among Finnish composers.

326. Kaipainen, Jouni. "À l'ombre de Sibelius" [In the Shadow of Sibelius]. *Finnish Music Quarterly*, Numéro special en français, 1990: 24–29.

A brief review of some of Finland's other important composers vis-à-vis Sibelius, from Erkki Melartin and Selim Palmgren to Aarre Merikanto and Uuno Klami, the latter two active until 1958 and 1961 respectively. Illustrated, including a full-page reproduction of one of Yousuf Karsh's photographs of Sibelius.

327. Klotins, Arnold. "La rencontre entre la musique de Jean Sibelius et celle de Claude Debussy en Lettonie, au début du XXe siècle et ses conséquences" [The Encounter with the Music of Jean Sibelius and Claude Debussy in Lettonie at the Beginning of the Twentieth Century and Its Consequences]. *Boréales, revue du centre de recherches inter-nordiques* 54/57 (1993): 19–24.

A look at how young composers of Lettonie absorbed features of impressionism in their music, which the author believes came through their contact with the music of Sibelius and Debussy. Music examples.

328. Lloyd, Stephen. "E. J. Moeran: Some Influences on His Music." *Musical Opinion*, February 1981: 174–77.

A consideration of the potent influences, Sibelius among them, on the English composer Moeran (d. 1950). The impact of Sibelius is said to be evident in aspects of orchestration, in the use of "germ themes," and in certain uses of ostinato and hammerstroke chords. No examples but passages from selected works are mentioned.

329. Mäckelmann, Michael. "Integration und offene Gestalt: Zu Jean Sibelius und Allan Pettersson" [Integration and Open Form: To Jean Sibelius and Allan Petterson]. In *Allan Pettersson Jahrbuch 1987*, 5–22. Edited by Michael Mäckelmann. Wuppertal, Germany: Internationale Allan Pettersson Gesellschaft, 1987. ML410.P425A45

Working from the premise that no composer creates in isolation, the authors represented in this yearbook have sought to explore the influences, from Jean Sibelius to Charles Ives, on Swedish composer Allan Pettersson (1911–1980). Mäckelmann's essay on Sibelius concludes that, while one cannot overtly claim Sibelius as a direct source of inspiration, Pettersson's music inclines toward certain traits also found in the music of the Finn, such as compression of musical material and ostinato accompaniment figures underlying long-spun melodic lines. The author also sees Sibelius's integration of thematic-motivic unity and formal development as a precursor to Pettersson's open formal conception, which he calls *freien Verlaufsformen*.

330. Matthews, David. "Living Traditions." *Musical Times* 134 (1993): 189–91.

An active British composer's view of Sibelius. Matthews cites Sibelius's "particular solution to the problem of romanticism" as especially important and talks of the specific ways in which he believes his own music to be indebted to the Finn.

331. Nørgård, Per. "Sibelius og Danmark" [Sibelius and Denmark]. In *Suomen musiikin vuosikirja 1964–65*, 67–70. Helsinki: Otava, 1965. With English summary.

A Danish composer's assessment of the importance of Sibelius to composition in Denmark. Although up until 1950 the Finn seems to have meant little to young Danish composers, owing to a widespread allegiance to the aesthetic principles of Carl Nielsen, the writer finds a positive attitude toward Sibelius since midcentury, facilitated by fresh analytical approaches to his music.

332. "Sibelius tänään" [Sibelius Today]. *Rondo*, 1965, no. 6: 4–5.

Five Finnish composers, Einar Englund, Osmo Lindeman, Tauno Marttinen, Aulis Sallinen, and Erkki Salmenhaara, discuss "What Sibelius means to me."

333. Wallner, Bo. "Sibelius och den svenska tonkonsten: en konturteckning" [Sibelius and Swedish Composition: An Outline]. In *Suomen musiikin vuosikirja 1964–65*, 91–113. Helsinki: Otava, 1965. With English summary.

A demonstration of Sibelius's profound impact upon Swedish musical composition by the biographer of Wilhelm Stenhammar. Although not admired by all (the Fourth Symphony, for instance, sparked heated debate about the nature of modernism), Sibelius nevertheless proved fundamentally important to such men as Stenhammar, Hilding Rosenberg, Moses Pergament, Dag Wirén, and others, particularly through his orchestral technique. The author supports his points with music examples and quotations from composers' letters and reviews.

* * *

D. Sibelius in Music Histories

334. Adler, Guido. *Handbuch der Musikgeschichte* [Compendium of Music History]. 2d edition. Berlin: Wilmersdorf, 1930. 2 vols. Vol. II: 1125–26. ML160.A3 1930

In Adler's famous history book Sibelius appears in the chapter on modern composers in a section about Finland contributed by Toivo Haapanen. The influence of earlier composers such as

Tchaikovsky is mentioned, but Sibelius, who is treated generously by his countryman, is recognized as individual in his musical expression and epoch-making in Finland.

335. Austin, William W. *Music in the 20th Century from Debussy through Stravinsky*. New York: Norton, 1966. 708 p. Pp. 96–103. ML197.A9

A readable synopsis of Sibelius's life that recognizes the evolution of his style beyond nationalism and illustrates musical characteristics with examples from *Pelléas et Mélisande*. The reproachful tone, however, emphasizes the conventional aspects of Sibelius whom Austin describes as naïve and "baffled by his own adventure."

336. Bauer, Marion. *Twentieth Century Music: How It Developed, How to Listen to It*. New York: G. P. Putnam's Sons, 1933. xii, 349 p. Pp. 187–91. Revised edition, 1947. Reprint. New York: Da Capo Press, 1978. ML197.B29 1978 ISBN 0-306-77503-5

In an explanatory volume intended to guide bewildered listeners through the labyrinth of modern music, Bauer's brief treatment of Sibelius is notable primarily for its inclusion in the portion entitled "Looking Forward." Bauer (1887–1955) was a composer herself; she had studied with Nadia Boulanger and others and had championed American music, being a co-founder of the American Music Guild and a board member of the League of Composers. Most of her sympathetic treatment of Sibelius is based on Cecil Gray's writings, and she mistakenly asserts that Sibelius composed eight symphonies.

337. Bauer, Rudolf. *Das Konzert: Lebendige Orchestermusik bis zur Gegenwart* [The Concert: Living Orchestral Music Up to the Present]. Berlin: Safari-Verlag, 1955. 802 p. Pp. 465–76. MT125.B28

Written for the non-specialist, this book is a general history of the orchestral music that is often heard on record and in the concert hall and is organized by composer, beginning with Handel and extending to Messiaen. A chapter is devoted to Sibelius (pp. 465–

76) in which brief mention is made of the tone poems, and each of the symphonies is discussed with reference to *echte* symphonic form. Music examples.

338. Berger, Melvin. *Masters of Modern Music*. New York: Lothrop, Lee & Shepard, 1971. 256 p. ML3930.A2B498

Of the four parts in which the author discusses fourteen twentieth-century composers, Sibelius appears in "Music in the Mainstream" along with Strauss, Hindemith, Prokofiev, Copland, and Britten. As with the other composers, Sibelius receives his own chapter in which biography and musical issues are summarized.

339. Copland, Aaron. *Our New Music*. New York: McGraw-Hill, 1941. xiv, 305 p. Revised as *The New Music 1900–1960*. New York and London: MacDonald, 1968. 194 p. ML197.C66 1968

American composer Aaron Copland (1900–1990) took a dim view of Sibelius in 1941 and had not revised his opinion by the second edition of his book. Peevishly calling the composer a "hangover from the 1890s" both times, in 1941 Copland said that Sibelius was a "folk composer"; by 1968 the real issue is acknowledged: resentment, fostered by the critics who insisted that no composer of the stature of a Sibelius or a Stravinsky could be found in America. Includes a short discography.

340. Davies, Laurence. "The Sibelius Conspiracy." In *Paths to Modern Music: Aspects of Music from Wagner to the Present Day*, 155–68. London: Barrie & Jenkins; New York: C. Scribner's Sons, 1971. ML196.D4 1971b ISBN 0-214-65249-1

A less than flattering summary of Sibelius's life and works in which the author views the last thirty-five years of the composer's life as a "gigantic conspiracy to preserve his fame." Davies suggests that although Sibelius was one of the greatest composers of the century, he ought to have had the sense and integrity to avoid the cul-de-sac of exploiting his position as the leader of a minority culture. Brief references to Sibelius also appear in the chapter on Mahler.

341. Demuth, Norman. *Musical Trends in the 20th Century*. London: Rockliff, 1952. Reprint. Westport, Conn.: Greenwood, 1975. xvii, 359 p. Pp. 253–64. ML197.D37 1974 ISBN 0-8371-6896-1

In a chapter devoted to Sibelius (one of five so-called "Composers in Isolation" who also include Bartók, Stravinsky [!], Eugene Goossens, and Willem Pijper), the author assesses Sibelius's position in England, discusses and illustrates the character of the Sibelian melody, and uses the notion of the "germ theme" to address matters of thematic expansion and symphonic development. Although somewhat dated in its style and information, the essay reveals how Sibelius was viewed and understood by the English around the middle of the twentieth century.

342. Ewen, David. *The Complete Book of 20th Century Music*. New York: Prentice-Hall, 1952; revised edition, 1959, 1961. S.v. "Sibelius." MT90.E9 1959

Intended for the layman, Ewen's book gives brief biographical information for contemporary composers together with descriptions of major works composed since 1900. The Sibelius entry, however, is badly out of date and contains unfortunate errors of dates and other facts.

343. Ewen, David, comp. and ed. *Composers of Today: A Comprehensive Biographical and Critical Guide to Modern Composers of All Nations*. New York: H. W. Wilson Co., 1934; 2d edition, 1936. xii, 332 p. S.v. "Sibelius." ML105.E94C6 1936

Ewen's *Guide* represents the first attempt in the United States to provide a comprehensive dictionary of composers active in the twentieth century. Each composer is portrayed with a photograph and an essay that incorporates the critical comments of distinguished authorities. Ewen gives the pronunciation of Sibelius's name for North Americans as "sī-bāl'yŭs," a pronunciation few Finns would recognize; in Finland, both "-i's-" are short as is the "-e-," and slightly more emphasis is put on the first syllable. As often happened during the 1930s, a work list mentions eight completed symphonies (perhaps the result of Sibelius's repeated promises to deliver the work).

344. Foulds, John. *Music To-day: Its Heritage from the Past, and Legacy to the Future*. London: Ivor Nicholson and Watson, 1934. 391 p. Pp. 316–24 especially. ML197.F79M8

Foulds, who recalls meeting the composer in 1903, waxes metaphysical about the music, which he describes as shot through with "deva vibrations." In prose that defies summation, he concludes, " . . . had but Sibelius the soul-force to shake off the lower devic vibrations and transcend those of even country, continent, hemisphere . . . what unimaginable splendours would have then been ours."

345. Gray, Cecil. *A Survey of Contemporary Music*. "Jean Sibelius," 184–93. London: Humphrey Milford for Oxford University Press, 1924; 2d edition, 1927. Reprint. Freeport, N.Y.: Books for Libraries Press, 1969. ML197.G7 1969 ISBN 0-8369-1294-2

Gray surveys contemporary music by discussing a dozen composers prominent in the 1920s and providing his idiosyncratic evaluations of each. Calling Stravinsky "little more than an artistic weathercock" and Schoenberg the last commanding figure in the history of romanticism, Gray characterizes Sibelius as primitive and finds among his works a curious amalgam in which the well-crafted and the vulgar jostle within a single masterpiece, the Fourth Symphony.

346. Grout, Donald Jay, and Claude V. Palisca. *A History of Western Music*. 4th edition. New York: Norton, 1988. xi, 910 p. Pp. 782–84. ML160.G87 1988 ISBN 0-393-95627-X

The most famous of American music history books affords Sibelius brisk but surprisingly sympathetic treatment. The composer's innovations are viewed as embodying the idea of "coalescing themes," Symphony no. 7 is considered the acme of formal unity, and Symphony no. 4 is thought to be the quintessence of Sibelius. A half page of musical examples demonstrates thematic transformations in this symphony.

347. Harman, Alec, with Anthony Milner and Wilfrid Mellers. *Man and His Music: The Story of Musical Experience in the West.* London: Barrie & Jenkins, 1988. 1,245 p. Pp. 928–34 et passim. ML160.H2840 1988 ISBN 0-7126-2001-X

In a discussion essentially unchanged from the original edition (issued in four parts, 1957–1959), the authors compare and contrast Sibelius with Delius, Nielsen, and Wagner in a benevolent view of the Finn as a symphonist whose silence after *Tapiola* expressed a spiritual impasse in European history. Music examples from Symphony no. 4.

348. Horton, John. *Scandinavian Music: A Short History.* London: Faber & Faber; New York: Norton, 1963. Reprint. Westport, Conn.: Greenwood, 1975. 184 p. ML310.H67 1975 ISBN 0-8371-6944-5

A survey of the music history of Scandinavia for the English-language reader. The chapter entitled "Jean Sibelius and Carl Nielsen" compares and contrasts the life and works of the two Northern composers born the same year, and another discusses "Finnish Music After Sibelius." Illustrated with photographs and music examples, although none from Sibelius's music. A short bibliography suggests further reading in English.

349. Lambert, Constant. *Music Ho! A Study of Music in Decline.* London: Faber & Faber; New York: Scribner, 1934. Reprint. 1936. Revised edition, 1937, 1941, 1943, 1947, 1948; 3d edition, 1966, with an introduction by Arthur Hutchings. Reprint. London: Hogarth Press, 1985. 342 p. ML197.L22 ISBN 0-7012-0603-9 (pbk)

First published just three years after Cecil Gray's *Sibelius*, Lambert's *Music Ho!*, its title borrowed from Shakespeare's *Antony and Cleopatra*, crested a wave of Sibelius popularity among Anglo-Saxons. The remarkable number of times the book was reissued and revised indicates something of its significance. While Lambert considered many twentieth-century musical issues from French composers to jazz, he crowned his volume with three chapters devoted to Sibelius whom he judged, along with Schoenberg, to be the most important composer of the twentieth century and the most important symphonist since Beethoven. For many intellectuals, Lambert together with Gray seriously overstated Sibelius's importance at the expense of other significant composers. To their enthusiasm together with Olin Downes's in America is often attributed the severe negative reaction against Sibelius that began in the early 1940s.

350. Leichtentritt, Hugo. *Music, History and Ideas.* Cambridge, Mass.: Harvard University Press, 1950. xxv, 296 p. Pp. 215, 264–65. ML160.L53 1950

Although mention of Sibelius is brief, it is significant for the deeply favorable opinion proffered. A German musicologist who taught at Harvard University from 1933–1940, Leichtentritt developed the book from his Harvard lectures. His position on Sibelius places him in the minority among intellectuals in North America in the 1940s and 1950s.

351. Leichtentritt, Hugo. *Music of the Western Nations.* Edited and amplified by Nicolas Slonimsky. Cambridge, Mass.: Harvard University Press, 1956. 324 p. Pp. 218–20. ML160.L54

Sibelius receives sympathetic if somewhat romanticized treatment in Leichtentritt's history, which was completed after his death by Slonimsky and organized along national lines. Finns will surely be interested to read that "they feel an animal joy of living . . . [and] are capable of transports of ecstasy," traits reflected in Sibelius's music. The music is considered in two general categories, the intensely national and the "European in essence," which, according to the authors' view, nevertheless strongly suggests Northern nature.

352. Maasalo, Kai. *Suomalaisia sävellyksiä* [Finnish Compositions]. 2 vols. Helsinki: Werner Söderström Osakeyhtiö, 1964–1969. Vol. I, 226 p. Pp. 129–224.

The last chapter in the first of a two-volume history of Finnish composition that explores composers from Erik Tulindberg (1761–1814) to Yrjö Kilpinen (1892–1959), the Sibelius essay, written by the man who directed the Finnish Broadcasting Company from 1956 and introduced many unfamiliar Sibelius works through his broadcasts, provides an extended consideration of Sibelius's music in Finnish. The author proceeds by genre, beginning with the symphonies, symphonic poems, and other orchestral works and continuing through the Violin Concerto, the theater music, the chamber compositions, the piano, violin, and cello music, and the songs and choral pieces. Maasalo's keen insight, the historical perspective of his history overall, and the short, apt music examples make this a very useful discussion.

353. Maasalo, Kai. *Suuri sinfoniamusiikki Haydnista Sibeliukseen* [Great Symphonic Music from Haydn to Sibelius]. Helsinki: Werner Söderström Osakeyhtiö, 1956. 310 p. Pp. 242–87.

In this survey of the symphony, which has been characterized as the Finnish counterpart to Tovey's essays, the last chapter is devoted to Sibelius. *Kullervo* and all seven symphonies are discussed and illustrated by their principal themes. The composer is depicted as evolving from romantic beginnings and is viewed along with Mahler as the leader of symphonic music in our time. The author draws certain parallels with Beethoven, finding themes to be the point of departure in the symphonies of both composers. He observes, however, that Sibelius's themes are distinguished by their "organic" growth into a series of musical events.

354. Morgan, Robert P. *Twentieth-Century Music: A History of Musical Style in Modern Europe and America.* New York: Norton, 1991. xvii, 554 p. Pp. 120–23 et passim. ML197.M675 1990 ISBN 0-393-95272-X

In a scant three pages (half of one occupied by a portrait of the composer, half of another by a discussion of Carl Nielsen), Sibelius's symphonies are characterized as "essentially conservative—even antimodernist . . . ", an assessment that illustrates how time reshapes perceptions: it was written by a professor at Yale University, the institution whose faculty members had regarded Sibelius so highly among the modernists in 1914 that they awarded the composer an honorary doctorate. A bibliography but the sources for Sibelius are not current.

355. Niemann, Walter. *Die Musik Skandinaviens* [The Music of Scandinavia]. Leipzig: Breitkopf & Härtel, 1906. xi, 155 p. Pp. 136–42. ML310.N66

With a dedication to Edvard Grieg, this volume examines the leading role played by composers from Denmark, Norway, Sweden, and Finland in folk and art music. As Niemann said repeatedly, both here and elsewhere, Sibelius's music is a pure example of regional art. Illustrations and music examples.

356. Ranta, Sulho. *Musiikin historia* [History of Music]. 2 vols. Jyväskylä: Gummerus, 1956. Vol. II, pp. 653–56 et passim.

Sibelius appears briefly in the chapter on Finland, thereby affording a picture of the composer vis-à-vis his contemporaries Robert Kajanus, Erkki Melartin, and Armas Järnefelt. There is a photo of a scowling, old Sibelius.

357. Schonberg, Harold C. *The Lives of the Great Composers*. London: Davis-Poynter Ltd., 1971. 599 p. Pp. 385–87 et passim; revised edition, New York: Norton, 1981. Pp. 409–11. ML390.S393 1981 ISBN 0-393-01302-2. Translation of 1971 edition by Gerhard Aschenbrenner as *Die grossen Komponisten: Ihr Leben und Werk* (Königstein: Athenäum, 1983).

In his few, disparaging pages on Sibelius, Schonberg, former music critic for the *New York Times*, belittles the Finn while commending his contemporary Carl Nielsen ("more universal," "not as determinedly nationalistic"). Schonberg says virtually nothing about Sibelius's life or his music, but interprets instead the attitude toward Sibelius among intellectuals after World War II, of which his own piece is symptomatic. His withering concluding comment in 1981 was that Sibelius "deserves to occupy an honorable place among the minor composers." A portrait of the old Sibelius accompanies the text.

358. Searle, Humphrey, and Robert Layton. *Britain, Scandinavia, and The Netherlands*. Twentieth Century Composers, vol. III. Edited by Nicolas Nabokov and Anna Kallin. London: Weidenfeld & Nicolson; New York: Holt, Rinehart, and Winston, 1972. xvi, 200 p. Pp. 138–52. ML390.S445 B7 1973 ISBN 0-03-003381-0

Chapter 9, entitled "The Great Scandinavian Symphonists: Sibelius and Nielsen," offers a summary of events in Sibelius's life and a review of his musical accomplishments. No music examples or notes.

Rev.: *American Reference Books Annual* 5 (1974): 389.

359. Slonimsky, Nicolas. *Music Since 1900*. 5th edition. New York: Schirmer, 1994. S.v. "Sibelius." ML197.S634 1994 ISBN 0-02-872418-6

In this deliciously overstuffed volume, which consists of a Descriptive Chronology (a catalogue of selected events relating to music from January 1, 1900 through December 1991) and a group of Letters and Documents, a number of entries concern Sibelius and his music. These can be located through the well-crafted index. Items range from a transcription of the Yale University commemorative words about Sibelius in 1914 to the startling news that in 1938 a copy of *Finlandia* was buried in a time capsule beneath the fairground of the New York World's Fair together with, of all things, John Philip Sousa's *Stars and Stripes Forever* and the swing piece, *Flat Foot Floogie*. Accompanying instructions direct the capsule to be opened in 500 years. Although most of the Sibelius entries belong to the Descriptive Chronology, the composer also appears, rather pejoratively described, under "Neo-Romantics" in the "Dictionary of Terms."

360. Viney, Basil. *From Monteverdi to Sibelius: A Short History of Music for All Lovers of the Art*. London: Allenson & Co., 1936. 160 p. Pp. 133–34. ML160.V6F93

The subtitle indicates the general nature of this history, which deals with Sibelius in two short pages in the chapter on the twentieth century. Described as "a much greater master" than Debussy, Stravinsky, or Schoenberg, Sibelius is ranked as one of the three greatest symphonists since Schumann, with Franck and Dvořák completing the triumvirate.

361. Whittall, Arnold. *Music Since the First World War*. London: J. M. Dent; New York: St. Martin's Press, 1977. vii, 277 p. Pp. 18–24 et passim. ML197.W55 ISBN 0-312-55492-3. The most recent edition, published by Oxford University Press in 1995, appeared too late for examination here.

In the first of two chapters on symphonic music, Whittall gives Sibelius brief but sympathetic treatment along with such contemporaries as Carl Nielsen, Ralph Vaughan Williams, Gustav Holst, Albert Roussel, and Maurice Ravel. Directing his attention to the last three symphonies and *Tapiola*, Whittall draws his analytical points from the work of Robert Simpson and emphasizes the composer's radical treatment of form and motion. Music examples.

362. Whittall, Arnold. *Romantic Music: A Concise History from Schubert to Sibelius*. London, New York: Thames & Hudson, 1987. 192 p. Pp. 182–83. ML196.W55 1987 ISBN 0-500-01401-9

Sibelius makes only the briefest of appearances here, but the choice of his music to delineate the time frame and the understanding with which he is placed vis-à-vis Romanticism are notable exceptions in the writing of English-language music histories.

Rev.: *Music & Letters* 69 (1988): 270–72; *Music Review* 47 (1986–87): 298–300; *Music Review* 51 (1990): 236–37 (of paperback edition); *Musical Times*, September 1987: 495; *Times Literary Supplement*, 1987: 845.

363. Wörner, Karl H. *Musik der Gegenwart: Geschichte der neuen Musik* [Music of the Present: History of New Music]. Mainz: B. Schott's Söhne, 1949. 264 p. Pp. 44–48. ML197.W7

Of interest primarily for including a chapter on Sibelius in a "history of new music." Wörner, like Walter Niemann, emphasizes Sibelius's national and conservative traits. He says that the composer formed no school and believes that he hardly advanced orchestration beyond *Lohengrin*, yet he observes with some surprise that the music has endured in the concert hall.

V
Special Categories

There are several categories of bibliographical literature about Sibelius that do not neatly dovetail into one of the major classifications. Grouped together here, these begin with symposia and conference proceedings and move to the increasingly literary: periodical issues featuring Sibelius; catalogues and studies of the library at Ainola; and finally, books, short stories, and poems in which the composer has appeared over the last century.

Until recently, collected volumes with scholarly studies devoted to Jean Sibelius were rare and conferences dedicated to the composer unheard of. Indeed, the single find was Gerald Abraham's *Sibelius: A Symposium*, first published in 1947 and re-issued in numerous editions for some thirty years. It was only in 1990, with the First International Sibelius Conference, held in conjunction with Helsinki University's 350th anniversary, that conditions began to change. Suddenly, in the last decade of the twentieth century a flurry of scholarly activity has swirled around Sibelius; thus far, there have been four international conferences on the composer, two in Finland, and one each in France and Germany, and reports of these meetings have either been published or are projected. Several smaller seminars have taken place in countries as far apart as Sweden and Canada. There has also been the publication of a new symposium (see no. 366).

The first conference on Sibelius to be held in France is also the first to issue an account in published form (see no. 365). The Proceedings of the First International Sibelius Conference, held in Helsinki in August 1990, were brought out too late for inclusion here, but they are available through the Sibelius Academy in Helsinki as will be those of a second Sibelius conference held in the same city in November 1995. Meiningen, Germany, was host to a meeting devoted to reception history (February 24–27, 1994), and this report is also promised. There have been presentations about Sibelius within larger conferences as well, the proceedings of which have not been published. Two of the more interesting, both by Robert Layton, are "Sibelius and England," presented before the International Music Congress at the University of Jyväskylä in Finland, June 30, 1965, and "Some Reflections on Bartók and Sibelius," presented before the Bartók-Kodály Symposium, Indiana University, Bloomington, April 5–7, 1982. International activity of this kind spells a new era for Sibelius studies. One hopes that what Finland must necessarily lose by the invasion of foreign elements will be richly repaid by the greater understanding of a composer whose music the world has embraced as its own.

Although collected volumes devoted to Sibelius have been rare abroad, in Finland the picture has been quite different. As early as 1915 entire periodical issues were given over to the composer, a practice that continued as Sibelius's importance to Finland was reinforced by the century's political events. In these journals and magazines, one finds a wide variety of materials, not all of which can be considered "scholarly" or even "studies." They range from poetry and open letters of congratulation to Sibelius to honeyed reminiscences and ingratiating eulogies, but there are also considered analyses and valuable illustrations. Aside from the information they provide, such issues stand as documents of their time. They offer an opportunity for sounding out Finland's cultural climate at a given historical moment and a means of measuring perceptions of Sibelius in the homeland.

Below, the few symposia and published conference proceedings are followed by annotations of periodicals devoted wholly or in substantial part to Sibelius. When significant articles in these periodicals have been annotated separately, cross-references indicate the entries. Analyses of contents of many publications before 1965 may be found under the periodical's title in Blum, no. 1.

A. Symposia and Conference Proceedings

364. Abraham, Gerald, ed. *Sibelius: A Symposium*. London: Lindsay Drummond, 1947. 188 p. text; 28 p. music examples; reissued 1948, 1952, London: Oxford University Press, 1952. Published in the U.S. as *The Music of Sibelius*. New York: Norton, 1947. Reprint. New York: Da Capo Press, 1975. ML410.S54A5 ISBN 0-306-70716-0

Although most of the information has been updated by more recent research, Abraham's *Sibelius* is important as the first attempt to undertake comprehensive study of the composer's works. That this symposium should have taken place in England indicates the great stature Sibelius enjoyed there and the interest he generated among England's leading musical figures. There is a Chronology, a Bibliography, and a work list. Chapters, annotated separately, include Gerald Abraham, "The Symphonies" (no. 557), Eric Blom, "The Piano Music" (no. 513), David Cherniavsky, "Special Characteristics of Sibelius's Style" (no. 435), Astra Desmond, "The Songs" (no. 684), Scott Goddard, "The Chamber Music" (no. 500) and "The Choral Music" (no. 717), Ralph Hill, "Sibelius the Man" (no. 182), and Ralph W. Wood, "The Miscellaneous Orchestral and Theatre Music" (no. 534).

Rev.: In addition to the reviews cited in Blum (no. 1), p. 1, see *The Music Journal* 34 (1976): 14.

365. *Boréales, revue du centre de recherches inter-nordiques: Colloque international Jean Sibelius* [Review of the Center of Inter-Nordic Research: Jean Sibelius International Colloquium]. 54/57 (1993). 192 p.

Presentations delivered at the Third International Conference on Sibelius (March 31–April 1, 1993) and the first to be given in France, with special emphasis on the composer's relationship to that country. Individual contributions, annotated separately, include Henri-Claude Fantapié, "Jean Sibelius et la France, au miroir des écrits musicographiques 1900-1965" (no. 285), Arnold Flotins, "La rencontre entre la musique de Jean Sibelius et celle de Claude Debussy en Lettonie, au début du XXe siècle et ses conséquences" (no. 327), Veijo Murtomäki, "L'ultime trilogie orchestrale de

Sibelius: 'Fantaisie symphonique' et la recréation de la symphonie classique au XXème siècle" (no. 446), Leo Normet, "Sibelius, en avance ou en retard sur son epoque" (no. 448), Ilkka Oramo, "Sibelius, le plus mauvais compositeur du monde" (no. 288), Eero Tarasti, "Sibelius et Wagner" (no. 466), Pierre Vidal, "Sibelius révélé par le disque" (no. 291).

366. Goss, Glenda Dawn, ed. *The Sibelius Companion.* Westport, Conn.: Greenwood, 1996. 449 p. ML410.S54S53 1996 ISBN 0-313-28393-1

Perspectives on Sibelius ranging from special studies of individual works to issues of research and reception. The volume includes new biographical finds, discussion of Sibelius and the theater, a chronological work list, a lengthy register identifying poets, performers, and other personalities associated with the composer, a collection of Sibelius's sayings (the chapter entitled "Observations on Music and Musicians") with the source for each identified, and a bibliography. Individual chapters, annotated separately, include Fabian Dahlström, "Sibelius Research" (no. 2), Goss, "Chronology of the Works of Jean Sibelius" (no. 18), Laura Gray, "Sibelius and England" (no. 310), David Haas, "Sibelius's Second Symphony and the Legacy of Symphonic Lyricism" (no. 603), James Hepokoski, "The Essence of Sibelius: Creation Myths and Rotational Cycles in *Luonnotar*" (no. 545), Kari Kilpeläinen, "Sibelius's Seventh Symphony: An Introduction to the Manuscript and Printed Sources" (no. 639), Veijo Murtomäki, "'Symphonic Fantasy': A Synthesis of Symphonic Thinking in Sibelius's Seventh Symphony and *Tapiola*" (no. 445), Daniel Politoske, "The Choral Music" (no. 727), Peter Revers, "Jean Sibelius and Vienna" (no. 215), Erkki Salmenhaara, "The Violin Concerto" (no. 666), Valerie Sirén, "The Songs" (no. 702), Eero Tarasti, "Sibelius and Wagner" (no. 467), William A. Wilson, "Sibelius, the *Kalevala*, and Karelianism" (no. 491).

367. *Sibelius-Mitteilungen.* Edited by the Deutschen Sibelius-Gesellschaft (1958–1967). 12 vols.

A publication of the second of the Sibelius societies that have been formed in Germany, this one founded by Sibelius scholar Ernest Tanzberger in association with the composer's publisher, Breitkopf & Härtel. The Society's journal, usually issued once a year, contains lists of Sibelius recordings, information, and reports on Sibelius festivals, book reviews, brief scholarly articles, and even short musical compositions. Most of the contents through 1964 are listed on p. 66 in Blum (no. 1). A 100th anniversary issue, published in February 1966, included press notices on the Fifth German Sibelius Festival in Essen, Karttunen's article "Sibelius als Liederkomponist" (no. 688), a photograph of the Sibelius plaque in Rapallo, and Gerd Sievers' review of Blum's bibliography.

B. Periodicals Devoted Wholly or in Part to Sibelius

368. *Aulos,* 1925. 59 p. + unnumbered pages.

A Christmas publication of *Suomen musiikkilehti*, dedicated to Sibelius on the occasion of his sixtieth birthday. Together with portraits, drawings, a facsimile of *Souda, souda, sinisorsa*, and Eeli Granit-Ilmoniemi's genealogical chart of the composer's ancestors (see no. 188), the issue includes such recollections of Sibelius as Karl Flodin's famous description "First Meeting," here translated into Finnish (annotated as no. 116), and tributes in prose and poetry from Robert Kajanus, Leo Funtek, Ture Rangström, Ida Ekman, and many others. Often humorous drawings of composers, critics, and other well-known contemporary figures are found among the unnumbered pages of advertisements.

369. *Euterpe*. 1901–1905.

Finland-Swedish cultural publication founded and edited throughout its short life by Karl Flodin. Although it began as a music journal, *Euterpe* soon became an organ for music, theater, and literature and even played a certain role in the struggle against Russian influence. From the first issue, which appeared January 4, 1901, until the last, the pages of *Euterpe* are filled with information about Helsinki's cultural life and the matters that claimed the attention of its artists. Where Sibelius specifically is concerned, the first work list ever published appeared in *Euterpe* on September 13, 1902 (see no. 16). There are also articles about his symphonies by Flodin and reviews of performances of his works.

370. *Finnish Music Quarterly*, 1990, nos. 3–4.

One-hundred-twenty-fifth anniversary issue with many illustrations including the cover portrait, facsimiles of music and letters, an editorial on Sibelius's significance, and a chart illustrating a chronology of the works. Articles annotated individually include Kim Borg, "How to Sing Them: Some Thoughts on the Interpretation of Sibelius' Songs" (no. 681), Fabian Dahlström, "The Early Chamber Music of Jean Sibelius" (no. 498), Martti Haapakoski, "The Concerto That Holds a Record" (no. 48), Mikko Heiniö, "Sibelius, Finland, and the Symphonic Idea" (no. 325), Antero Karttunen, "Roots: Sibelius, Finland, and the Town of Hämeenlinna" (no. 189), Robert Keane, "'Höstkväll': Two Versions?" (no. 691), Joonas Kokkonen, "The National and International Sibelius" (no. 277), Friedhelm Krummacher, "Voces intimae: Das Streichquartett op. 56 und die Gattungstradition" (no. 505), Minna Lindgren, "I've Got Some Lovely Themes for a Violin Concert" (no. 665), Veijo Murtomäki, "On the Nature of Sibelius's Late Style" (no. 443), Ainomaija Pennanen, "The Fourth Symphony: A State of Mind" (no. 620), Maija Suhonen, "Catalogue of Sibelius Monographs 1906–1989" (no. 6), Erik T. Tawaststjerna, "The Piano Music of Sibelius" (no. 522).

371. *Kalevalaseuran vuosikirja* 6 (1926). Helsinki: Werner Söderström Osakeyhtiö, 1926. 228 p.

In honor of the composer's sixtieth birthday, the Kalevala Society Yearbook printed a portrait of the composer, a dedication, open letters of congratulations from Nordic composers and conductors, including Carl Nielsen, Christian Sinding, and Hugo Alfvén, a translation into Finnish of Georg Göhler's "Orchesterkompositionen von Jean Sibelius" (no. 295), and excerpts from laudatory newspaper articles from around the world published the previous December (1925) and also translated into Finnish.

372. *Kirkko ja musiikki,* 1965, no. 5.

Anniversary issue with cover portrait by Karsh of Ottawa and short articles on Sibelius's musical origins; Sibelius and nature; Sibelius as symphonist; works for men's choir (including a wonderful drawing of the composer in Robert Westerlund's guestbook); Sibelius and Vienna; Sibelius as song composer; *Musique religieuse*; problems of interpreting the piano sonatas; Sibelius and chamber music; *The Maid in the Tower*; and a consideration of the composer's influence.

373. *Musiikki*, 1950, no. 9.

Honoring the composer's ninetieth birthday, the journal depicted Sibelius in a cover photograph and published a eulogy by Eino Roiha entitled "Jean Sibeliuksen maailmanmaine" [Jean Sibelius's World Reputation].

374. *Musiikkitieto,* 1935, nos. 9–10.

Devoted entirely to Sibelius, the issue features a cover photograph, memoirs by colleagues and students, a review of Karl Ekman, Jr.'s newly published Sibelius biography, and numerous illustrations.

375. *Musiikkitieto*, 1940, nos. 5–6.

Most of the issue, which reproduces Eero Järnefelt's 1892 portrait of Sibelius on the cover, is devoted to the composer. Among the memoirs and congratulatory letters, a special feature is Aune Lindström's contribution (pp. 93–96), where various paintings and sculptures of Sibelius are shown and their artists and owners identified.

376. *Musiikkitieto*, 1945, nos. 9–10.

Eightieth anniversary issue featuring Kalervo Kallio's sculpture of Sibelius on the cover and many tributes, from Robert Kajanus (whose piece is reprinted from *Aulos* [1925]) to Olin Downes, some of whose reviews are here translated into Finnish.

377. *Musiikkiviesti*, 1955, no. 11b.

Partially devoted to Sibelius. A picture of Matti Haupt's marble relief of the composer is displayed on the cover. There are brief reports on Fazer as Sibelius's publisher and the state of recordings of the music.

378. *Musiikkiviesti*, 1957, no. 11.

An issue dedicated to Sibelius. Among the illustrations is a facsimile of the composer's choral arrangement of *Finlandia* in manuscript. Articles include reflections on how Sibelius's music speaks to the Finnish nation and on the wider critical reception of his works. There is also a one-page compilation of the composer's sayings, translated into Finnish.

379. *Musikern: Sibelius-nummer*, December 1, 1925.

A birthday issue abundantly illustrated with photographs, tributes from contemporaries, and articles, a number of which also appeared in *Musiikkitieto*, 1925.

380. *Musikrevy* 5 (1950).

Features a cover photograph, a memoir of Sibelius by Lili Foldes, Nils-Eric Ringbom's oft-reprinted essay on the phases in Sibelius's development (annotated as no. 432), and an essay on Sibelius and the United States.

381. *Musikrevy: Jean Sibelius 90 år* 10 (1955).

Cover photograph together with an essay on the "unbohemian" Sibelius by Lennart Reimers, articles about Sibelius's contemporary Wilhelm Stenhammar and the Göteborg Orchestra, and articles by Bengt Essén and Bo Wallner, "Tuonelas svan" (no. 541), and Bengt Pleijel, "Sibelius på skiva" (no. 57).

382. *Musikrevy: Specialnummer om Finland* 21 (1966).

A photograph by Fred Runeberg serves as cover portrait. Other Sibelius-related illustrations include facsimiles of a letter and a telegram to Tor Mann. There are appreciations from the Ambassadors of Finland and Sweden and articles by Joonas Kokkonen; Erik Tawaststjerna on Sibelius's Wagner crisis (no. 204); Nils-Eric Ringbom's familiar article on the composer's phases of development (no. 432); Tor Mann's reminiscence of meeting Sibelius; Antero Karttunen on the songs (no. 688); Einari Marvia on Finland's music before Sibelius; and Bengt Pleijel's consideration of Sibelius from abroad.

383. *Musikrevy* 47 (1992).

Cover portrait and the first four articles devoted to Sibelius, one of which is annotated as no. 216, Fabian Dahlström's "Tystnaden i Järvenpää: Några randanmärkningar." A second article discusses Sibelius biographer Erik Tawaststjerna, with the remaining two being short personal recollections.

384. *Musikvärlden* 1 (December 1945).

An illustrated issue largely devoted to Sibelius, including cover photo. Articles are in the nature of reminiscences by those who knew the composer, including Tor Mann, Antti Favén, Ture Rangström, and Nils-Eric Ringbom.

385. *Nordic Sounds: Nomus*, 1990, no. 4.

Jean Sibelius 125th anniversary issue including cover sketch, editorial, reprint of Finnish President Urho Kekkonen's Sibelius obituary, and an article by Robert Keane entitled "Sibelius' Orchestral Songs" (no. 692).

386. *Nya Argus* 28 (1935).

This Swedish-language periodical for culture and politics began in 1908 in Helsinki, initiated by Sibelius's contemporary and friend Werner Söderjhelm and Guss Mattson. Until 1911 its title was simply *Argus*. Founded as an organ for Finland-Swedish cultural life, *Argus* became an outlet for ideas of the Euterpist circle, publishing the writings of Emil Zilliacus, Gunnar Castrén, Elmer Diktonius, and others. Sibelius's name appears frequently in its pages, sometimes in reviews of books and music, sometimes in dedicated articles (see, for example, the annotations given as nos. 274, 280, 494, and 613). In this, the year of his seventieth birthday, Sibelius was eulogized by Sigurd Frosterus whose article "Gallen-Kallela, Sibelius: randanteckningar kring Kalevalajubileet" (annotated as no. 475) was also published in the issue together with Elmer Diktonius's poem *Symfoni i ord* dedicated to the composer (see no. 404). Blum (no. 1) lists other Sibelius-related contents through different issues.

387. *Nya Argus* 48 (1955).

Cover reproduces Eero Järnefelt's 1908 lithograph of Sibelius with the lead article (pp. 303–306) being Simon Parmet's "Sibelius ställning i samtiden" (no. 279), an admiring assessment of Sibelius's genius.

388. *Österreichische Musikzeitschrift* 20 (1965).

A 100th-anniversary illustrated issue devoted to Sibelius and featuring a cover portrait by Akseli Gallen-Kallela, articles by performers and composers, lists of planned Sibelius concerts, brief bibliography of literature on Sibelius, a short compilation of the composer's sayings, and a list of significant events in music that took place in the year of Sibelius's birth. These events included the premiere of Wagner's *Tristan und Isolde* ("the most notable and far-reaching music historical event of the 19th century") and the births of Paul Dukas, Carl Nielsen, and Alexander Glazunov.

389. *Pieni musiikkilehti*, 1965, no. 6.

100th-anniversary volume devoted entirely to Sibelius. Along with the usual complement of fond and flattering recollections, there are articles on Sibelius as a youth, on op. 113, on the violin compositions, on music critic Evert Katila and Sibelius, on Sibelius as a dance composer, and the German text of *Kullervo*. Photographs and music examples.

390. *Rondo*, 1965.

Centennial publication, almost all of which is devoted to Sibelius. There is a schedule of Sibelius "occasions" planned for December 1965 both in Finland and around the world and information on the Sibelius Violin Competition. Some articles are annotated separately; see "Sibelius tänään" (no. 332); "Jean Sibeliuksen sinfonialevytykset" (no. 50); Antero Karttunen, "Sibeliuksen yksinlauluista" (no. 687); Taneli Kuusisto, "Ydinmotiivin asema Sibeliuksen V sinfoniassa" (no. 631).

391. *Suomen musiikkilehti*, December 1925.

An issue in honor of the composer's sixtieth birthday, which includes a cover portrait, translations of articles from Swedish and English (including Donald Francis Tovey's program notes on the Violin Concerto), birthday wishes in prose and poetry, and the complete music of *Romanssi* for violin and piano, identified as "a youthful composition." Annotated separately is Väinö Joensuu's article, "Mestari oppipoikana" (no. 200), a remembrance of Sibelius's student years.

392. *Suomen musiikkilehti*, December 1935.

An illustrated anniversary issue at a time when the journal was edited by Heikki Klemetti (1876–1953), composer, choral director, and fierce champion of the Finnish language. It is thus not surprising to find that one of the contributions is a group of seven Sibelius songs translated from Swedish and English into Finnish. Klemetti himself contributed other articles, most of which are in the nature of birthday notes and reminiscences. Together with eulogies and congratulatory letters from around the world, the issue contains articles on the piano works, the songs, the compositions for violin, and various special topics including "Sibelius and Wagner," the *March of the Finnish Jaeger Battalion* (*Jääkärimarssi*), and a recollection of the birth of the three-voice *Nostalgia* (*Kotikaipaus*), annotated as no. 723. Illustrated with numerous photographs and several music facsimiles.

393. *Suomen musiikkilehti*, December 1940.

In this 75th-anniversary issue, again edited by Heikki Klemetti, there is a somewhat tongue-in-cheek treatment of the composer, who is depicted in a number of humorous illustrations. The issue contains short biographies of some of the artists in Sibelius's circle, a memoir of the first performance of the *Song of the Athenians* (*Athenarnes sång*), and facsimiles of portions of *The Lover* (*Rakastava*) in the version for chorus and orchestra, and the *March of the Finnish Jaeger Battalion (Jääkärimarssi*).

394. *Suomen musiikkilehti*, 1945, nos. 8–9.

Eightieth birthday issue featuring a cover photograph, a eulogy by Yrjö Suomalainen, Eino Roiha's thoughts on the Fourth Symphony, Selim Palmgren's recollections of Sibelius's influence on him as a young composer, a few paragraphs on Sibelius and Finland's amateur musicians, and a poem.

395. *Suomen musiikin vuosikirja 1964–65*. Helsinki: Otava, 1965. 200 p.

A 100th anniversary volume. There are many special articles; annotated separately, these include Olavi Ingman, "Sonaattimuoto Sibeliuksen sinfonioissa" (no. 570), Tauno Karila, "Uusi näkökulma Sibeliuksen Sadun esteettiseen tulkintaan" (no. 537), Robert Layton, "Sibelius and the Gramophone" (no. 54), Per Nørgård, "Sibelius og Danmark" (no. 331), Leo Normet, "Uusi ja vanha Sibeliuksen ensimmäisessä ja toisessa sinfoniassa" (no. 601), John Rosas, "Bidrag till kännedomen om tre Sibelius-verk" (no.

532), Dag Schjelderup-Ebbe, "Sibelius og Norge" (no. 99), and Bo Wallner, "Sibelius och den svenska tonkonsten: en konturteckning" (no. 333). In addition, the issue provides a report on the Sibelius Museum in Turku, mentions concerts planned for the Sibelius Week (May 15—June 4, 1965), and lists presentations to be read at the International Music Congress in Jyväskylä, Finland, among which several concern Sibelius.

396. *Tidning för musik* 5 (1915).

The first periodical to devote an entire issue to Sibelius on the occasion of his birthday. The volume includes a poetic hommage from Ernst V. Knape whose text *People from Land and Sea* (*Män från slätten och havet*) had earlier been given a choral setting by Sibelius; articles reflecting Otto Andersson's biographical research on Sibelius, including a chronology and one of the earliest work lists (annotated as no. 11); a memoir of rehearsals of *Snöfrid* (no. 729); and reports on Sibelius festivals at home and abroad together with many photographs.

397. *Uusi musiikkilehti*, 1955, no. 9.

Photographs include those by Tuovi Nousiainen (cover portrait), Fred Runeberg, and others; a poetic eulogy entitled "Laulu titaaneista" [A Song of Titans] by Toivo Lyy; homages by Martti Similä and Jussi Jalas; and some dozen articles; annotated separately, these include Jussi Jalas, "Sibeliuksen sinfoniat ja 'Kultainen leikkaus'" (no. 572), Joonas Kokkonen, "Piirteitä Sibeliuksen pianomusiikista" (no. 515), Ilmari Krohn, "Jean Sibeliuksen 'Timantti hangella'" (no. 694), Taneli Kuusisto, "Kirkkomusiikillisia kosketuskohtia Jean Sibeliuksen sävellystuotannossa" (no. 525), Armas Maasalo, "Miten Sibeliuksen Oma maa syntyi" (no. 724), Einari Marvia, "Jean Sibeliuksen musikaalinen sukuperintö" (no. 192), "Olin Downesin kirjeitä Sibeliukselle" (no. 224), Martti Pajanne, "Muusikkojen muistelmia mestarista orkesterinjohtajana" (no. 196), Simon Parmet, "Siirtymien ja temponvaihteluiden muotoilu Sibeliuksen musiikissa" (no. 495), Väinö Pesola, "Jean Sibelius kuorosävellystensä kuvastimessa" (no. 726), Tauno Pylkkänen, "Sibeliuksen sinfonioitten soitinnuksesta" (no. 450), Sulho Ranta, "Jean Sibelius ja näyttämön musiikki" (no. 656).

* * *

It has yet to be widely appreciated how profoundly Sibelius was affected by literature, perhaps because many of the works he knew were originally written in languages so difficult for non-Finns to follow. The impressive scope of his reading is suggested by the splendid array of volumes in his home library as even a short browse through the catalogues listed here will confirm. Meanwhile, for more than a century Sibelius's own life has enlivened novels, poems, and short stories. The earliest appeared in 1891. As recently as 1993, the mystery of the Eighth Symphony spawned a new novel. There are also the many passing references to Sibelius by writers as diverse as Noel Coward and Jack London, not to mention various poems dedicated to him and short stories named after titles of his compositions. None of these would be considered scholarly sources, yet they are of interest, for they show how profoundly Sibelius's life and music have captured the imagination of twentieth-century men and women. Although it has not been possible to compile a list of every reference to Sibelius in literature, included here are some significant examples of writings that owe their origins or aspects of their plots to the composer's life and work.

* * *

C. Sibelius's Library and Related Studies

398. Ellilä, E. J. "Säveltäjän kirjasto" [A Composer's Library]. *Kirjastolehti* 47 (1954): 150–55.

A report on the library at Sibelius's home of Ainola, giving a general account of the kinds of books, a physical description of their care and surroundings, and a narrative summary of specific works about Sibelius. Photographs depict the composer in his library and in various publications. For a catalogue of the library, see no. 400.

399. *Jean Sibeliuksen kirjaston luettelo 2* [Catalogue 2 of the Library of Jean Sibelius]. Helsingin Yliopiston Kirjaston Monistesarja 13. Helsinki: Helsinki University Library, 1985. 25 p.

A companion catalogue to no. 400, this inventory lists the 457 volumes that had mainly been the property of Aino Sibelius and her daughters. Most of the volumes are in Finnish and Swedish, although there are occasional English-language volumes, fewer still in French and German, together with translations of such authors as Mark Twain, George Eliot, Charles Dickens, and Jonathan Swift. There is no music here, only literature. The compiler has provided a useful index to authors who wrote dedications to one or another family member.

400. *Jean Sibeliuksen kirjaston luettelo/Förteckning över Jean Sibelius' Bibliotek/Catalogue of the Library of Jean Sibelius.* Helsingin Yliopiston Kirjaston Monistesarja 7. Helsinki: Helsinki University Library, 1973. 186 p.

An alphabetical catalogue of the 2,928 literary publications found in Sibelius's library at Ainola together with transcriptions of all personal dedications. There is a separate index to authors of dedications. For publications found in the library of Aino Sibelius and the daughters, see no. 399.

401. Mäkelä-Henriksson, Eeva. "Die Bibliothek von Jean Sibelius in seinem Haus Ainola" [The Library of Jean Sibelius in his House at Ainola]. *Bibliophilie und Buchgeschichte in Finnland: aus Anlass des 500. Jubilaums des Missale Aboense*, 96–101. Edited by Esko Häkli and Friedhilde Krause. Berlin: Deutsche Staatsbibliothek Berlin and Helsinki University Library, 1988. Z167.B5 1988 ISBN 3-7361-0035-3

An essay on the materials found in Jean and Aino Sibelius's home library and catalogued in nos. 399 and 400.

* * *

D. Sibelius in Literature

402. Aho, Juhani. *Yksin* [Alone]. Helsinki: Werner Söderström Osakeyhtiö, 1890. 159 p. PH355.A427Y38. Translated into Danish by Åge Meyer as *Alene* (Copenhagen: P.G. Philipsen, 1892).

Novel in which the first-person narrator is left alone when the woman he loves becomes engaged to another, one "Toivo Rautio." Set in familiar corners of Helsinki and Paris, the thinly disguised fiction is based on the author's real-life love for Aino Järnefelt, whom he lost to Sibelius.

403. Carpelan, Bo. *Axel: roman.* Helsingfors: Holger Schildt Förlag; Stockholm: Bonniers, 1986. Translated into English by David McDuff as *Axel: A Novel* (Manchester: Carcanet, 1989). 374 p. PT9875.C35 A913 1989. ISBN 0-85635-808-8; translated into Finnish by Kyllikki Villa as *Axel: romaani* (Helsinki: Otava, 1987); translated into French by C.G. Bjurström and Lucie Albertini ([Paris?]: Gallimard, 1990).

Historical novel in which the narrative alternates with fictional diary entries by the author's uncle, the curious Baron Axel Carpelan. Axel Carpelan's devotion to Sibelius and his uncannily apt musical advice to the composer are well known, and the novelist gives both his uncle and Sibelius human dimensions against a background of Finland's fin-de-siècle culture and politics. The English translator has added commentary in the form of notes. These together with the translation, however, must be used with care. The reader is cautioned to proceed with the *Swedish Book Review*'s critique in hand; it provides a wealth of corrective detail that will certainly interest the Sibelius scholar.

Rev. of English-language translation: *Music & Letters* 71 (1990): 123; *Musical Times* 130 (1989): 413–14; *Swedish Book Review*, 1991, no. 1: 55–58.

404. Diktonius, Elmer. "Symfoni i ord" [Symphony in Word]. *Nya Argus* 28 (1935): 266–67.

A poem dedicated to Sibelius. Stanzas are organized like the movements of a symphony (*Introduction*, *Andante*, *Scherzo*, and *Finale*).

405. Järnefelt, Arvid. *Vanhempieni romaani* [My Parents' Story], 3 vols. Helsinki: Werner Söderström Osakeyhtiö, 1928–30. Reprint. 3 volumes in 1, Helsinki: Werner Söderström Osakeyhtiö, 1976. 606 p. PH355.J27Z475 1976. ISBN 951-0-007868-9

A Swedish translation of vol. 1 by Sibelius's friend Bertel Gripenberg appeared as *Mina föräldrars roman* (Helsingfors: Holger Schildt Förlag, 1929); revised translation by Thomas Warburton (Helsingfors: Holger Schildt Förlag, 1988). ISBN 951-50-0443-8. Vols. 2–3 translated by Thomas Warburton (Helsingfors: Holger Schildt Förlag, 1989). ISBN 951-50-0450-0

An historical fiction about the large family into which Sibelius married. The parents of the title, Elisabeth and Alexander Järnefelt, begot nine children in the course of their busy lives. One became a Tolstoyan and is the author here. His story is rich with particulars about Finland's political and cultural life and about Sibelius's contemporaries, such as Juhani Aho, the young writer who fell in love with the much older Elisabeth and later became Sibelius's rival for Aino's hand.

406. Lundberg-Nyblom, Ellen. "Valse triste." *Ord och bild* 19 (1910): 99–107.

A short story inspired by Sibelius's famous composition.

407. Paul, Adolf. *En bok om människa* [A Book About a Human Being]. Stockholm: Albert Bonniers Förlag, 1891. 287 p. PT2631.A74

Dedicated to Jean Sibelius, Paul's book depicts the artist Sillén, of delicate sensibility and bohemian habits, who has sometimes been regarded as modelled upon Sibelius. The portrait is not always flattering. Selected passages from the novel have been translated into English in Harold E. Johnson's *Jean Sibelius* (no. 159).

408. Saroyan, William. "Finlandia." In *Love*, 100–07. New York: Lion Library Editions, 1955. PZ3.S246

The irreverent William Saroyan (1908–1981), prolific American author and playwright who first came to widespread attention during the 1930s, recalls visiting Helsinki, the impact of hearing *Finlandia* there, and his brash decision to call on Sibelius. If the naïve observations and profane language make one reluctant to call this "literature," the piece does manage to suggest the power of *Finlandia*, here exerted upon a writer known for his mastery of the vernacular.

409. Sillanpää, Frans Emil. "Jean Sibeliukselle 8.XII.1945" [To Jean Sibelius, 8.XII.1945]. [N.p., n.p.]. 5 p.

In a birthday tribute, Sillanpää (1888–1964), the only Finnish author to win the Nobel Prize for Literature, recalls the first time he met Sibelius.

410. Suomalainen, [Karl Gustaf] Samuli. *Andante, akkordeja iltahämyssä* [Andante, Chords in Twilight]. Helsinki: Otava, 1903.

A book of essays and short stories dedicated to Sibelius in which three of the pieces, *Aleksis Kiven satu* (Aleksis Kivi's Tale), *Impromptu*, and *Sydämeni laulu* (Song of My Heart) have connections with the composer, the first two most directly. A Sibelius-like young composer, "Johannes Seppälä," discusses with his friend, conductor "Robert Kajava," the revision of *En saga*, which, in the story, has been based upon Aleksis Kivi's *Seven Brothers*. For a discussion of this book vis-à-vis Sibelius's music, see no. 537.

411. Trotter, William R. *Winter Fire*. New York: Dutton, 1993. 485 p. PS3570.R596W56 1993 ISBN 0-525-93581-9. Translated into Finnish by Eva Siikarla as *Talven tuli* (Helsinki: Werner Söderström Osakeyhtiö, 1994). 466 p. ISBN 951-0-19832-3

A novel in which a German officer, Erich Ziegler, a conductor in civilian life, is assigned to Finland during World War II and meets Sibelius. Ziegler becomes obsessed with obtaining the score of the Eighth Symphony. The story unfolds against graphically narrated battle scenes, delicately portrayed Finnish nature, and Ziegler's love affair with the Sibelius family's mystical and beautiful servant Kyllikki.

Rev.: *New York Times Book Review*, May 16, 1993.

412. Wachler, Dietrich. *Väinämöinens Wiederkehr: Ein phantastischer Sibelius-Roman* [Väinämöinen's Return: A Fantastical Sibelius Novel]. Altenberge: Horizonte, 1986. 313 p. PT2685.A33V35 1986

Described by its author as the first German novel about Sibelius and the *Kalevala*, Sibelius's music is cited as the work's source of inspiration. The story is based upon the composer's life and includes such well-known events as his meeting with Mahler, his trip to North America, and the premiere of *Tapiola* by Walter Damrosch. There are also fictitious characters, who are based upon real-life personalities, and a great deal of fictional dialogue.

VI
The Music

Men, and indeed some women, have been writing about and analyzing the music of Sibelius since his works began to be heard in the late nineteenth century. Not surprisingly, the instrumental works, primarily the symphonies and tone poems, have received the lion's share of attention. It is only in the past decade that the great quantity of vocal music, some of it of surpassing beauty, has begun to be seriously addressed by scholars. Consequently, some important studies that go beyond the numerous "I was there when they sang . . . " accounts are at last being made available for the songs and the choral music.

The writings about Sibelius's music reveal in microcosm some of the general trends and issues in musical discussion that have engaged critics, scholars, and theorists over the past century. These issues range from nationalistic interpretations to germ motive theories to the more recent application of Schenkerian analysis. The reader must take note of the time and country of the writer in order to assess where a particular study belongs in this history. One must also be prepared to encounter everything from the merely descriptive, and sometimes quite fanciful, to the extremely technical investigation addressed to the specialist only.

This portion of the *Guide* begins with manuscript studies and sources for finding the music in facsimile followed by research dealing with aspects of style and performance practice. Thereafter, the sections are organized by genre, with general investigations coming first, followed by those devoted to individual works. Owing to various circumstances, including revisions that transformed incidental music into tone poem (as with *Finlandia*) and inconsistencies in the ways

Sibelius himself referred to his works (*Kullervo*, for instance, which is variously called both symphony and tone poem), some compositions may reasonably be placed in several categories. Since a research guide is not the place to debate such matters, the decisions made here have been taken for the sake of bibliographic clarity and should not be construed to reflect a definitive analytical classification. Titles of all works mentioned will be found through the index. It should be remembered that most biographies, and many biographical articles, also discuss the music, since it is the music that made the life worthy of so much investigation. Thus, in an important sense, this part of the *Guide* simply amplifies what has already been begun.

A. Manuscripts: Studies and Facsimiles

Studies of Sibelius's music manuscripts, and what the primary sources can reveal about the compositional process, have only recently become part of the literature. Although the list of these studies is small, the gains have been great. The research by Kari Kilpeläinen, for example, has provided the means for dating works with greater accuracy and for identifying previously unsuspected connections between compositions.

The great majority of Sibelius's surviving music manuscripts are preserved today in Finland. However, it is possible to study selected pages of manuscripts and first prints in facsimile. Although facsimile editions of the music are outside the present scope, the manuscript studies given in this section are followed by references to published books and articles that include facsimiles of the composer's music. Many of these sources are readily available in American university libraries. It should also be emphasized that nearly every biography and analytical article ever written about Sibelius contains a page or two of music in facsimile. Many Finnish periodicals, such as those listed in the section "Special Categories," offer facsimile material in abundance. Even newspapers have, on occasion, published the composer's music: pages from three different manuscripts, *The Ferryman's Brides* (*Koskenlaskijan morsiamet*), Symphony no. 4, and *Mazurka* for violin, op. 81, were published on December 8, 1955, in their original size in Helsinki's now-defunct *Uusi Suomi*. Since a complete inventory of every page in facsimile would form a catalogue of its own, no attempt has been made to establish a comprehensive list or to cross reference all sources. The selections given here, however, should make it possible for anyone, with a minimum of effort, to be able to examine some manuscript leaves in Sibelius's hand.

1. MANUSCRIPT STUDIES AND RELATED READING

See also no. 21

413. Josephson, Nors S. "Die Skizzen zu Sibelius' 4. Symphonie (1909–1911)" [The Sketches of Sibelius's 4th Symphony]. *Die Musikforschung* 40 (1987): 38–49.

A detailed study based on manuscript material in the Helsinki University Library. The author shows that work on Symphony no. 4 took place in three stages, during which the symphony became increasingly modern. Initial sketches were followed by keyboard or short scores, after which the composer made drafts of the full score. The early stages were characterized by late romantic traits, thick doublings, and numerous repetitions. Music examples from the sketch material are included and an outline of the second version of the Symphony's last movement.

414. *Katalog des Archivs von Breitkopf & Härtel, Leipzig* [Catalogue of the Archives of Breitkopf & Härtel, Leipzig]. Edited by Wilhelm Hitzig. I. Musik-Autographe (mit einem Noten-Faksimile). Leipzig: Breitkopf & Härtel, 1925. II. Brief-Autographe. Leipzig: Breitkopf & Härtel, 1926. 50 p. ML97.B727

Bibliographic description of selected autograph letters and manuscripts in the archives of Breitkopf & Härtel, arranged chronologically. Although Sibelius is not mentioned among the letters, five of his musical autographs (*Impromptu*, *Tulen synty*, *Teodora*, *Valse triste*, and *In memoriam*) are listed on pp. 41–45. The manuscripts' size and format are given together with the number of pages and the publisher's engraving number.

415. Kilpeläinen, Kari. "Jean Sibeliuksen käsikirjoituksista" [About the Manuscripts of Jean Sibelius]. *Musiikkitiede* 4 (1992): 128–33.

An evaluation of the work to be done in the field of Sibelius studies made at the outset of the author's inventory of Sibelius's music manuscripts. For his completed catalogue, see no. 21.

416. Kilpeläinen, Kari. "Sibeliuksen sävellysten luettelointi ja teoksen ongelma" [Cataloguing Sibelius's Compositions and the Problem of the Work]. *Musiikkitiede* 3 (1991): 75–92.

Sibelius's frequent revisions and his ambivalence about the worth of certain compositions inevitably create problems for scholars today, not the least of which concern which version should be considered final. Kilpeläinen gives an insightful discussion of these problems, drawing on his extensive work with the sources and explaining the surprising and little-known history of a great many compositions. An article to be used alongside the author's invaluable catalogue, no. 21.

417. Kilpeläinen, Kari. "The Helsinki University Library Collection of Sibelius Manuscripts." *Finnish Music Quarterly*, 1990, nos. 3–4: 72–75.

A report devoted largely to the sources donated to the Helsinki University Library by the Sibelius family in 1982. The findings are more fully discussed in the introduction to the author's catalogue, no. 21.

418. Kilpeläinen, Kari. *Tutkielmia Jean Sibeliuksen käsikirjoituksista* [Research on Jean Sibelius's Music Manuscripts]. Studia Musicologica Universitatis Helsingiensis 3. Helsinki: Helsinki University, 1991. 303 p. ML410.S54K55 1991 ISBN 951-45-6138-4

A dissertation devoted to three main issues: the correct dating of Sibelius's compositions; the changes and eliminations Sibelius made in his opus numbers; and the manuscript sources of Symphony no. 7. Discussion in the first two sections suggests that the older Sibelius revised the dates of certain works in order to appear to posterity in a better light. The third section traces the genesis of Symphony no. 7 from the first sketches to the revised printed score. There is an abstract in English and bibliographies of music sources and secondary literature. The material on Symphony no. 7 has been revised and appears in English; see no. 639.

Rev.: *Rondo*, 1992, no. 6: 41.

419. Sipilä, Pekka. "Fazerin käsikirjoitukset yliopiston kirjastolle" [Fazer's Manuscripts to the University Library]. *Pieni musiikkilehti*, 1988, no. 1: 4–5.

An announcement on the occasion when Finland's venerable music house of Fazer deposited some 4,000 composer manuscripts in the Helsinki University Library. Among the treasures were such materials as Sibelius's *Surusoitto*, the funeral music composed for Akseli Gallen-Kallela. A facsimile of a page of this work.

2. MUSIC IN FACSIMILE

420. *Catalogue of Valuable Printed Books, Music, Autograph Letters and Historical Documents . . . Which Will Be Sold by Auction by Sotheby & Co. May 11–12, 1970*, 159–63. London: Sotheby & Co., 1970. 168 p.

Catalogue descriptions of a collection of Sibelius autograph manuscripts sold along with nine letters from Sibelius to Bertel Gripenberg. A facsimile of the first page of *Oma maa* is included.

421. *Jean Sibelius: Käsikirjoituksia* [Jean Sibelius: Manuscripts]. Edited by Lauri Solanterä. Text by Eino Roiha. Translated into Swedish by Erik Bergman; translated into English by Paul Sjöblom. Helsinki: R. E. Westerlund, 1945. ML96.4.S5

Excerpts from twelve manuscripts belonging to the Helsinki publisher R. E. Westerlund and representing music from 1895 to 1925. The works include *Oma maa*; *Julvisa*, op. 1, no. 4; *Arioso*; *Humoresque*, op. 40; *Harpspelaren*, op. 34, no. 8; *Reconnaissance*, op. 34, no. 9; *Danse caractéristique*, op. 79, no. 3; *Aubade*, op. 81, no. 4; *Humoresque*, op. 87, no. 1; *Blåsippan*, op. 88, no. 1; *Fågelfängaren*, op. 90, no. 4; and *Intrada*, op. 111a. With each is a short commentary in three languages (Finnish, Swedish, and English) giving facts of publication and remarks about the music. A frontispiece reproduces a portrait of Sibelius by Akseli Gallen-Kallela.

422. *Musical Autographs from Monteverdi to Hindemith*. Vol. II. Edited by Emanuel Winternitz. Princeton, N.J.: Princeton University Press, 1955. 196 plates [pages unnumbered]. ML96.4.W5

Plate 178 reproduces page 23 from *Swanwhite*, "Prinsen ensam" [The Prince Alone].

423. *Musiker Handschriften von Schubert bis Strawinsky* [Music Manuscripts from Schubert to Stravinsky]. Edited by Martin Hürlimann. Zürich: Atlantis, 1961, p. 87. 184 p. A translation, by Ernst Roth, appeared as *Composers' Autographs*. Vol. 2: *From Schubert to Stravinsky*. 181 p. + index. London: Cassell, 1968, p. 87. ML96.4.C64 v. 2

Page 23 from the autograph of Symphony no. 4, showing the hymn theme from the slow movement.

424. Patten, Nathan van. *Catalogue of the Memorial Library of Music, Stanford University*. Stanford, California: Stanford University, 1950, p. 245. ML136.S8S8.

Shows a facsimile of the first two pages of *Teodora*.

425. *Små flickorna* [Young Girls], in *Lucifer*, 1920: on unnumbered pages.

Sibelius's four-and-a-half page manuscript of the song to words of Hjalmar Procopé preceded by Antti Favén's drawing of the composer.

426. *Till trånaden* [To Longing], in *Lucifer*, 1913: 2.

Facsimile of the one-page manuscript.

427. *Valsette*, in *Lucifer*, 1912: 8.

Facsimile of the one-page manuscript of op. 40, no. 1.

B. Stylistic Studies

1. GENERAL

428. Andersson, Otto. "Jean Sibelius: Några konturer" [Jean Sibelius: Some Outlines]. *Tidning för musik* 2 (1912): 239–41.

A perceptive early discussion of Sibelius's music vis-à-vis Finland's two language groups with particular attention given to vocal compositions. Andersson observes that ultimately it was Finnish nature that played the greatest role in Sibelius's artistic creation.

429. Furuhjelm, Erik. "Sibelius säveltaiteilijana" [Sibelius as a Composer]. *Valvoja* 35 (1915): 600–24.

An assessment of Sibelius's compositional skills in a broad consideration that encompasses songs and incidental music as well as orchestral works. Furuhjelm's evaluation is particularly interesting as an appraisal by a musically knowledgeable contemporary who saw Sibelius's competition in 1915 as Richard Strauss.

430. Jyrhämä, Outi. "Sibeliuksen sinfonioiden sarja ja uudet tuulet" [Sibelius's Symphonic Series and New Currents]. *Rondo*, 1982, nos. 5–6: 12–18.

The author's subtitle "Sibelius: From Romantic to Classic, From National to Universal" summarizes the theme of this sweeping review of the composer's stylistic development, which also takes into consideration the more general question of composition in Finland after 1913.

431. Niemann, Walter. "Jean Sibelius und die Finnische Musik" [Jean Sibelius and Finnish Music]. *Die Musik* 13 (November 2, 1913): 195–206. Appeared in Swedish as "Sibelius och den finska musiken." *Tidning för musik* 4 (1914): 2–7, with commentary by Erik Furuhjelm, pp. 8–9. A different article from the essay of the same title in *Signale für die musikalische Welt* (see no. 606).

A short survey of the composer's music with repeated emphasis on his Finnishness, whether in works directly based on the *Kalevala* or in the symphonies which, while lacking "organic, logical development" and other acceptable German traits, are redeemed by their fundamental Nordic qualities. It was articles such as these that caused biographer Erik Tawaststjerna to suggest that Sibelius must have begged to be delivered from his friends.

432. Ringbom, Nils-Eric. "Sibelius' utvecklingsskeden" [Sibelius's Stages of Development]. *Musikrevy* 5 (1950): 265–70; reprinted in *Musikrevy* 21 (1966): 192–96; appeared in Finnish as "Sibeliuksen kehityskaudet" in *Uusi musiikkilehti*, 1955, no. 9: 4–8.

Sibelius's overall production is considered in three phases: a *Sturm und Drang* period infused with Finland's awakening national consciousness, a time when Sibelius's music was overwhelmingly programmatic; a more personal phase that coincides with the beginning of the new century and evident as early as Symphony no. 2; and synthesis, beginning with Symphony no. 5. Music examples.

433. Salmenhaara, Erkki. "Nuori Sibelius ja 1890-luku: Suomalaisen sävelkielen synty" [Young Sibelius and the 1890s: The Birth of Finland's Musical Language]. *Rondo*, 1982, no. 4: 11–17.

A thoughtful consideration of the forces that shaped Sibelius's mature style. For full annotation, see no. 202.

434. Touchard, Maurice. "Un musicien finlandais: Sibelius" [A Finnish Musician: Sibelius]. *La nouvelle revue* 35 (1914): 55–65.

Touchard's survey of Sibelius and his work emphasizes the symphonic poems, the songs, the theater music, and the piano music. The author views Sibelius as having profound roots in his native soil, and he draws parallels with Verdi. In a strangely prescient observation for 1914, Touchard, while describing the composer as having participated in the emancipation of tonality, wonders whether, based on the evidence of his recent compositions, Sibelius's muse may have deserted him.

2. ASSORTED COMPOSITIONAL ISSUES

435. Cherniavsky, David. "Special Characteristics of Sibelius's Style." In *The Music of Sibelius*, 141–76. Edited by Gerald Abraham. New York: Norton, 1947. ML410.S54A5

A study of the music's "general characteristics and gradual development" with adroit comparisons to Beethoven and emphasis in the analytical portions on what the author considers most important about Sibelius: his tendency to evolve themes from one or two "thematic germs," a tendency explained as "a natural culmination of all progress up to this time."

436. Cherniavsky, David. "The Use of Germ Motives by Sibelius." *Music & Letters* 23 (1942): 1–9.

A now-famous article in which the notion of Sibelius and the "germ motive" was first developed: in the author's words, a "really organic manner of imparting unity originated by Beethoven." Cherniavsky believed that Sibelius first used germ motives in Symphony no. 2 in the form of the falling fifth accented on the higher note. He demonstrates other germ motives with music examples from *Voces intimae* and Symphony no. 6. By achieving unity with the germ motive, he concludes, Sibelius made his greatest contribution to form.

437. Collins, M. Stuart. "Germ Motives and Guff." *Music Review* 23 (1962): 238–43.

Collins's title aptly describes his opinion of the analytical ideas of the most influential English writers on Sibelius, Cecil Gray, Gerald Abraham, and David Cherniavsky, whom he finds unconvincing and who, he implies, are at least partially responsible for the poor opinion Sibelius suffers among critics. Collins takes particular issue with Cherniavsky's "germ-motive theory" for failing to illuminate the works' larger purpose and suggests a re-evaluation of the seven symphonies on the composer's own terms. Music examples.

438. Harris, Simon. "Chord-forms Based on the Whole-tone Scale in Early Twentieth-century Music." *Music Review* 41 (1980): 36–51.

A revealing examination of selected passages from the music of Debussy, Sibelius (*Tapiola*), Stravinsky, Bartók, and members of the Second Viennese school. The comparison suggests that around 1900 new chord forms were evolving in the musical language at the very time that the chord's traditional role began to disintegrate. Harris's evidence, especially valuable for the "whole view" he has undertaken, indicates that the stylistic changes of the early twentieth century cut across generations and backgrounds and were implicit in the harmonic language of romanticism. Music examples.

439. Hollander, Hans. "Stilprobleme in den Symphonien von Sibelius" [Style Problems in the Symphonies of Sibelius]. *Musica*, 1965, no. 1: 1–4.

The author maintains that the reasons for the decline in popularity of Sibelius, whom he considers one of the most vital creative personalities of new music, are ill defined and suggests that Sibelius's romanticism forms part of the problem. The seven symphonies, he observes, are not stylistically all that different from one another, with the masterful summation of Symphony no. 7 clearly foreshadowed as early as Symphony no. 2. He then discusses how the seeds of Sibelius's mature style may be found in his earlier work.

440. Howell, Timothy B. "Jean Sibelius and the Fourth Dimension." *Sibelius-Akatemian Aikakauskirja SIC 1993*, 97–113. Edited by Veijo Murtomäki. Helsinki: Sibelius Academy, 1993. ISBN 952-9658-16-8

An examination of how Sibelius controls musical time, which the author emphasizes is still a relevant issue in composition, with reference especially to Symphonies no. 4, 5, and 7 and to *En saga* and *Tapiola*. Music examples and diagrams.

441. Lyle, Watson. "The 'Nationalism' of Sibelius." *Musical Quarterly* 13 (1927): 617–29.

Observations such as Sibelius "discards Teutonized harmony of the blocky type," incorrect spellings, and faulty translations of titles indicate how difficult it has been to obtain accurate information about Sibelius in English, even from respected scholarly journals. Sibelius's nationalism is dealt with only in an imaginary way. Illustrated with a pen-and-ink sketch of the composer.

442. Matter, Jean. "Quelques aspects de l'être symphonique de Sibelius" [Some Aspects of the Symphonic Being of Sibelius]. *Schweizerische Musikzeitung/Revue musicale suisse* 106 (1966): 31–36.

Among the aspects of the composer's "symphonic being" discussed and illustrated with music examples are a) similarities between symphony and symphonic poem; b) dance elements (and the author reminds us of the parallel in Mahler's music); c) string backgrounds against which woodwind plaints may be heard; d) the atmosphere of Finland's nature, so strong that the author proposes the term *symphonie paysage* for this music (as opposed to the term *symphonie destinée* applied to Mahler's symphonies); e) the *Kalevala* and features of the Finnish language, manifest in themes that prolong the first note; and f) elements of classicism, evident in the composer's admirable economy of means and adherence to certain traditional values.

443. Murtomäki, Veijo. "On the Nature of Sibelius's Late Style." *Finnish Music Quarterly*, 1990, nos. 3–4: 50–57. Appeared in Swedish as "Om stilkaraktären under Sibelius sista skaparperiod." *Finnish Music Quarterly, Specialnummer på svenska*, 1992: 12–18.

An argument for viewing Sibelius's mature orchestral style as a synthesis, in which differences between symphony and symphonic poem are minimized with both genres illustrating the same compositional vision. Facsimile of a page from *Tapiola*.

444. Murtomäki, Veijo. "Sibelius-analyysin nykytila: ongelmia, haasteita, mahdollisuuksia" [The Present State of Sibelius Analysis:

Problems, Challenges, Possibilities]. *Sävellys ja musiikinteoria 1/92*, 1–9. Helsinki: Sibelius Academy Composition and Music Theory Division, 1992.

A valuable review of the types of analytical approaches that have been applied to Sibelius's music heretofore, from the notorious methods of Ilmari Krohn and Ernst Tanzberger through recent work (1991) of such writers as Timothy B. Howell and Eero Tarasti. The author provides some evaluation of the strengths of the different analyses and identifies areas of Sibelius study particularly in need of investigation.

445. Murtomäki, Veijo. "'Symphonic Fantasy': A Synthesis of Symphonic Thinking in Sibelius's Seventh Symphony and *Tapiola*." In *The Sibelius Companion*, 147–166. Edited by Glenda Dawn Goss. Westport, Conn.: Greenwood, 1996. ML410.S54S53 1996 ISBN 0-313-28393-1

An important, well-documented discussion of the interconnections among Sibelius's late symphonic trilogy: Symphonies no. 6 and 7 and *Tapiola*. Consideration is given to the meaning of "fantasy" in the composer's works and to the musical sources for the idea of fantasy. The nature of program music is discussed in this context, and there are detailed structural analyses, especially of *Tapiola*. Music examples.

446. Murtomäki, Veijo. "L'ultime trilogie orchestrale de Sibelius: 'Fantaisie symphonique' et la recréation de la symphonie classique au XXème siècle" [The Final Orchestral Trilogy of Sibelius: 'Symphonic Fantasy' and the Recreation of the Classic Symphony in the Twentieth Century]. *Boréales, revue de centre de recherches inter-nordiques* 54/57 (1993): 103–08.

A conference presentation which appears revised and expanded in *The Sibelius Companion*; see no. 445.

447. Nilova, Vera. "Sibeliuksen aika Suomen musiikissa" [Sibelius's Time in the Music of Finland]. *Carelia*, 1992, no. 11: 116–25.

Setting out to discuss traits of Sibelius's music that are also found in the cultures of other countries, the author embraces an amazing number of issues within the scope of this short article: landscape, magic, "*Kalevala*, Sibelius and Joyce," history, myth, and metaphor. Originally written in Russian and translated here by Kerttu Kyhälä-Juntunen, with a bibliography of Russian-language sources.

448. Normet, Leo. "Sibelius, en avance ou en retard sur son époque" [Sibelius, Ahead of or Behind His Time]. *Boréales, revue de centre de recherches inter-nordiques* 54/57 (1993): 25–29.

The author selects progressive passages from the symphonic works to challenge the frequently advanced image of Sibelius as a composer behind the times.

449. Pike, Lionel. "The Tritone in Sibelius's Symphonic Music." *Soundings* 5 (1975): 82–96.

A discussion of the role played by music's most notorious interval in Symphonies no. 3 and 4. The author views the tritone as a constructive force in Symphony no. 3, a destructive force in Symphony no. 4. Music examples from the former. The identical discussion is reproduced as part of Chapter V in the same author's *Beethoven, Sibelius and the 'Profound Logic'* (no. 583).

450. Pylkkänen, Tauno. "Sibeliuksen sinfonioitten soitinnuksesta" [On the Instrumentation of Sibelius's Symphonies]. *Musiikkitieto*, February 1942: 20–22; March 1942: 36–37. Reprinted in *Uusi musiikkilehti*, 1955, no. 9: 27–32.

Short, personal consideration of Sibelius's orchestration, proceeding by choirs, strings, woodwinds, brass, and percussion, with a brief separate section devoted to the harp used in Symphonies no. 1 and 6. The one music example (not reproduced in the later version of the article) is a facsimile of the opening measures of the Fourth Symphony's *Scherzo*.

451. Reid, Sarah Johnston. "Tonality's Changing Role: A Survey of Non-Concentric Instrumental Works of the Nineteenth Century." Ph.D. diss., University of Texas at Austin, 1990. vii, 316 p.

The author explains that her major objective has been to identify "non-concentric" works, that is, compositions which close in a key other than the one in which they began. This process is seen as an important step toward the destruction of tonality, and thus a useful review of theoretical definitions, with emphasis on the ideas of Heinrich Schenker, Paul Hindemith, and Arnold Schoenberg, precedes the musical discussion. Among the twenty-two composers of non-concentric works written before 1900, Sibelius is represented by his *King Christian* and *Karelia Suites*, *Finlandia*, *En saga*, and *Lemminkäinen's Return* (here called *Lemminkäinen's Homefaring*). Reid establishes a new and interesting context for Sibelius's music and presents her ideas in a clear writing style. Music examples and a bibliography rich in sources on tonality.

452. Ringbom, Nils-Eric. "Sibelius och Impressionismen" [Sibelius and Impressionism]. *Finsk tidskrift* 143 (1948): 104–12.

The author defines impressionism, of which he believes there is only one representative, Debussy, and then considers in what measure the term may be applied to Sibelius's music. The article is extracted from the author's *Jean Sibelius, A Master and His Work* (no. 169) and may be read there in English in the chapter entitled "Impressionistic Harmonies."

453. Ryynänen, Teuvo. "Beethoven, Sibelius ja synkoopin ulottuvuudet" [Beethoven, Sibelius, and Aspects of Syncopation]. In *Sibelius-Akatemian Aikakauskirja SIC 1993*, 135–60. Edited by Veijo Murtomäki. Helsinki: Sibelius Academy, 1993. ISBN 952-9658-16-8

An investigation into the little-explored field of syncopation in Sibelius's symphonic works preceded by a clarifying discussion of syncopation as used by Mozart, Beethoven (especially in the *Eroica* Symphony), Brahms, Schubert, and Berlioz. Various types of syncopation are distinguished, including "structural syncopation" and "rhythmic dissonance," the latter term borrowed from Lionel Pike (no. 583). Particular emphasis is given to connections between Sibelius and Beethoven, justified by the analytical diagram of the *Eroica*'s first movement found in one of Sibelius's sketchbooks and reproduced here.

454. Ryynänen, Teuvo. "The 'Domino-Principle' in the Symphonies of Sibelius." *Proceedings from the Nordic Musicological Congress, Turku/Åbo 15.–20.8.1988*, special issue of *Musiikki*, 1989: 208–13.

The author discusses one aspect of "germ motives" in Sibelius's symphonies, here referred to as the "domino principle." Ryynänen makes the provocative suggestion that Sibelius was influenced in this manner of composition through Brahms's example and that Sibelius's method in turn is the model for the later Finnish composer, Paavo Heininen.

455. Tammaro, Ferruccio. "L'imperativo' nella musica di Sibelius" [The Imperative in the Music of Sibelius]. *Nuova rivista musicale italiani* 8 (1974): 14–35.

Tammaro, who has written a biography of the composer (no. 173) as well as a book about his symphonies (no. 589), here argues that for Sibelius, the obligation to create—to think, to work, to order his ideas—constituted the "imperative" in his music. This imperative is discernable in the concentration and the intuition the composer brought to his task, things that constitute the Sibelian passion. According to Tammaro, the composer's view of life, which he loved so dearly, was tempered with the knowledge that living involves sadness and suffering as much as joy and passion. This idea is especially evident in *Luonnotar*, where the gift of life is accompanied by pain and anguish.

456. Tawaststjerna, Erik. "Sibeliuksen innoituksen lähteistä" [Starting Points for Sibelius's Inspiration]. *Valvoja* 81 (1961): 23–27.

A demonstration of programmatic associations or inspiration for certain "absolute" works of Sibelius by way of three examples: the composer's jottings mentioning "Don Juan" on the manuscript of Symphony no. 2; diary entries that link the finale of Symphony no. 5 with the flight of swans and nature mysticism; and Sibelius's dream, while composing the Sonatina in E major for violin, of once again being twelve years old and an aspiring virtuoso. The author sees a paradox in Sibelius's ostensibly romantic and programmatic sources of inspiration and his creation of symphonic monuments of absolute music.

457. Truscott, Harold. "A Sibelian Fallacy." *Chesterian* 32 (1957): 34–43.

The first essay to challenge Cecil Gray's "discovery" that Sibelius composed by introducing thematic fragments, building them into a whole, and dispersing them again (see no. 567). Truscott questions both this interpretation and its subsequent reincarnations at the hands of Wilfred Mellers (in his article "Sibelius and the Modern Mind," *Music Survey* 1 [1949]) and Donald Tovey, pointing out that these writers fail to mention the fundamental component of symphonic form, namely tonality.

458. Wood, Ralph. "Sibelius's Use of Percussion." *Music & Letters* 23 (1942): 10–23.

A survey of the way Sibelius handled percussion instruments. Wood shows that while Sibelius was a moderate in his use of percussive "extras," he was a pioneer in his writing for timpani, which he used as much for color as for rhythm. Numerous instances in the orchestral scores that demonstrate the variety and originality of this aspect of Sibelius's orchestration are listed.

3. COMPARATIVE STUDIES: SIBELIUS VIS-À-VIS OTHER COMPOSERS

See also nos. 194, 392

459. Dahlström, Fabian. "Grieg und Finnland" [Grieg and Finland]. *Studia musicologica Norvegica* 19 (1993): 77-85.

In a volume containing the papers presented at the International Edvard Grieg Symposium in 1993, Dahlström examines the connections between the famed Norwegian composer and Sibelius. He mentions their personal contacts and uses music examples to demonstrate Grieg-like passages in Sibelius's early chamber works.

460. Garden, Edward. "Sibelius and Balakirev." *Slavonic and Western Music: Essays for Gerald Abraham*, 215–18. Edited by Malcolm Hamrick Brown and Roland John Wiley. Russian Music Series 12. Ann Arbor, Mich.: UMI Research Press; Oxford: Oxford University Press, 1985. ML55.A18 1985 ISBN 0-8357-1594-9

Garden refutes the oft-mentioned influence of Balakirev's First Symphony on Sibelius's *Lemminkäinen and the Maidens of the Island,* but he makes a case for the work's influence on Sibelius's Symphony no. 3. The argument rests on stylistic rather than thematic similarities.

461. Hintze, Dmitry. "Sibelius ja venäläiset klassikot" [Sibelius and the Russian Classics]. *Kirkko ja musiikki* 14 (1966): 9–11.

Partly written in response to the Sibelius biography by Alexandr Stupel (in Russian and therefore, excluded here), Hintze considers and rejects most of that writer's evidence for the alleged influence on Sibelius of such composers as Rimsky-Korsakov, Glazunov, Borodin, Mussorgsky, and Tchaikovsky.

462. Jeanson, Gunnar. "Carl Nielsen och Jean Sibelius: en jämförande studie" [Carl Nielsen and Jean Sibelius: A Comparative Study]. *Nordens kalender 1934*: 44–54.

Jeanson's comparison is presented from the point of view of a musically intelligent observer in the 1930s for whom an important question concerned which composer was more significant to music in Sweden. For Jeanson, Sibelius's subjectivism and use of primitive musical elements are partly explained by his culture and romantic orientation, including contact with the music of Tchaikovsky, whereas Nielsen's unsentimental approach looked toward the future. The full-page photograph of Sibelius, clearly contemporary with the article, is of particular interest for showing that the composer, although going bald, still had at least some of his hair.

463. Matter, Jean. "Sibelius et Debussy" [Sibelius and Debussy]. *Schweizerische Musikzeitung/Revue musicale suisse* 105 (1965): 82–87.

A provocative essay in which the author compares the two composers biographically, mentioning their similarities in age, their 1909 meeting in London, and the position each occupies as representative of his people. More fascinating, however, are the musical comparisons, illustrated with examples showing that Sibelius seems to echo Debussy. For a response to Matter's viewpoint, see no. 468.

464. Mellers, Wilfrid. "Delius, Sibelius, and Nature." *Romanticism and the 20th Century (from 1800)*, 123–34. London: Rockliff, 1957; Fair Lawn, New Jersey: Essential Books, 1957. Revised edition, 1988. ML196.H3 1988 ISBN 0-712-62050-8

A comparative essay, into which Nielsen is also introduced, beginning from the premise that because "Finland had never had a musical tradition," Sibelius, like Delius, began composing in the accepted European idiom. The author finds another parallel in that both men were well over thirty before either produced "any music we could recognize as theirs." Better understanding of Finland's musical history and the now widely available recordings of *Kullervo* (1892) disprove Mellers' assessments. However, he shows clear insight into Sibelius's Wagnerian debt, widely denied at the time he was writing. His observations about the composer's symphonic procedures reflect the "coalescing fragment" theory widely in vogue in the 1950s. Two short music examples from Symphony no. 4.

465. Seebohm, Reinhard. "Pfitzner und sein Zeitgenosse Sibelius" [Pfitzner and his Contemporary Sibelius]. *Mitteilungen der Hans Pfitzner-Gesellschaft* 25 (1969): 1–10.

An examination of musical parallels between Hans Pfitzner and Jean Sibelius, who, though unacquainted and outwardly dissimilar, are viewed as representing the same stage in the history of music. The author considers such similarities as motivic unification, fusion of movements, and use of modal polyphony in Palestrina-like music, the latter illustrated by the single music example taken from Sibelius's Symphony no. 6 (in the last movement of which it is stated that the motive B-A-C-H is interwoven). The author finds important affinities between these composers in the deep artistic comprehension and the near-religious fervor which both men brought to the act of musical creation.

466. Tarasti, Eero. "Sibelius et Wagner" [Sibelius and Wagner]. *Boréales, revue du centre de recherches inter-nordiques* 54/57 (1993): 89–102.

A conference presentation revised and expanded in *The Sibelius Companion*; see no. 467 for annotation.

467. Tarasti, Eero. "Sibelius and Wagner." *The Sibelius Companion*, 61–76. Edited by Glenda Dawn Goss. Westport, Conn.: Greenwood, 1996. ML410.S54S53 1996 ISBN 0-313-28393-1

A consideration of biographical and especially musical connections between Sibelius and Wagner with particular reference to Symphony no. 4. Despite Sibelius's vehement denials, the composer revealed his Wagnerian debt in certain aspects of orchestration, in his harmonic language, and in a temporal sense.

468. Tawaststjerna, Erik. "Sibelius möte med Debussy i London 1909" [Sibelius's Meeting with Debussy in London, 1909]. *Suomen musiikin vuosikirja 1967–1968.* Helsinki: Otava, 1968, 31–39. With English summary. Appeared in German as "Jean Sibelius und Claude Debussy: Eine Begegnung in London 1909," translated by F. Nikolowski. In *Colloquium Leoš Janáček et musica europaea*, 307–19. Brno: 1968.

The meeting described by the title is related in the same author's biography (no. 175), where a fuller account may be read in

English (vol. II: 105–09). The Swedish version, however, preserves Sibelius's original language in the letters to Carpelan and in the diary excerpts quoted. The article also serves as a response to Jean Matter (see no. 463), who had argued that Sibelius copied Debussy. While affirming the composers' musical similarities, Tawaststjerna points out that impressionistic qualities may be found in Sibelius's music in the 1890s, well before he heard works by Debussy.

469. Tawaststjerna, Erik. "Sibelius und Bartók: Einige Parallelen" [Sibelius and Bartók: Some Parallels]. In *International Musicological Conference in Commemoration of Béla Bartók 1971*, 121–35. Edited by Jószef Ujfalussy and János Breuer. Melville, N.Y.: Belwin Mills, joint edition with Editio Musica Budapest, 1972. ML410.B26I61. Appeared in Finnish as "Sibelius ja Bartók: eräitä yhtymäkohtia," *Musiikki* 1 (1971): 5–15.

A comparison whose point of departure is Bartók's essay about folk music's influence on art music. The author applies Bartók's three categories of influence to Sibelius's works and finds that 1) Sibelius seldom used direct quotations from folk melody, although his few arrangements of Finnish folk songs for piano bear certain resemblances to Bartók's arrangements of Hungarian folk music; 2) in *Kullervo* and in *Kalevala*-inspired tone poems Sibelius created original melodies that sometimes emulate Finnish folk song; and 3) the symphonies have moments that seem to breathe a Finnish atmosphere, revealing Sibelius's musical mother-tongue to have been unmistakably Finnish. The comparisons are made particularly tantalizing by the connections believed to exist between Finnish and Hungarian folk music as well as by the affinities between the languages.

C. Sibelius and Folk Music

As every Sibelius music lover and scholar knows, the titles, background, and sometimes texts of a significant number of the composer's works are taken from the great Finnish epic, the *Kalevala*. Still other texts come from the collection of Finnish lyric poetry known as the *Kanteletar*. Today these titles are usually taken to mean the editions of the poems collected and forged into a whole by Elias Lönnrot and published in 1835 and 1849 (the *Kalevala*) and 1840–1841 (the *Kanteletar*). The poems, however, (sometimes called runes, from the Finnish word *runo* meaning poem) have been recited and sung for centuries. Ideally, one should read the *Kalevala* in its original Finnish, for the power of its alliterative style and trochaic tetrameter are not readily translated. Whenever translations are made, feelings run high as to their relative merits. Today there are translations into forty-five different languages; most can be located through the valuable reference volume compiled by Rauni Puranen entitled *The Kalevala Abroad: Translations and Foreign Language Adaptations of the Kalevala* (Helsinki: Suomalaisen Kirjallisuuden Seura, 1985). In the present section some important English translations of the *Kalevala* and *Kanteletar* poetry are given, followed by literature on the fascinating subject of Sibelius and folk music.

1. ENGLISH-LANGUAGE EDITIONS OF FINNISH FOLK POETRY

470. *Finnish Folk Poetry, Epic: An Anthology in Finnish and English.* Edited and translated by Matti Kuusi, Keith Bosley, and Michael Branch. Helsinki: Suomalaisen Kirjallisuuden Seura, 1977. 607 p. PH401.E3F5 ISBN 951-717-087-4

A free translation (one that ignores the original meter and rhyme) of poems from *Suomen kansan vanhat runot* (The Ancient Poems of the Finnish People), authentic folk materials collected in Finland, Karelia, and Ingria, and originally published in 33 volumes. English translations are given parallel to original texts. Singers of the poems are identified together with the location and date each poem was heard and the folklorist who recorded it. Introductory material includes an extensive essay on the poetry, including its history, the role played by Elias Lönnrot in its collection, the types of poetry and their structure, and matters of performance. Commentaries provide detailed information about each poem or group of related poems, and a Name Index identifies people and places with cross-references to their locations in the texts.

471. *Kalevala: The Land of Heroes*. Translated by W. F. Kirby. London: 1907. Reprint. With an introduction by M. A. Branch. London and Dover, New Hampshire: Athlone Press, 1985. xxxiv, 667 p. PH324.E5K5 1985. ISBN 0-485-11258-2. An edition of Kirby's translations with illuminations and paintings by Akseli Gallen-Kallela appeared in 1986, Helsinki: Werner Söderström Osakeyhtiö.

Branch's introduction (pp. xi–xxxiv) is highly recommended. For some readers, this translation by the eminent entomologist William Forsell Kirby (1844–1913) follows the *Kalevala*'s metrical pattern too slavishly. See, however, the list of merits of Kirby's translation in Ernest J. Moyne, *Hiawatha and Kalevala: A Study of the Relationship Between Longfellow's "Indian Edda" and the Finnish Epic* (Helsinki: Suomalainen Tiedeakatemia, 1963), p. 113.

472. *The Kalevala: Epic of the Finnish People*. Translated by Eino Friberg. Editing and Introduction by George C. Schoolfield. Illustrated by Björn Landström. Helsinki: Otava, 1988. 408 p. PH324.E5F7 1988 ISBN 951-1-10137-4

A translation that largely preserves the alliterative style and trochaic tetrameter of Lönnrot's verses and illustrated with Landström's color pictures and black-and-white designs. The front matter includes the translator's essays on the significance of the *Kalevala* to the Finnish people and the structure of the epic. There is also an extremely informative essay by the editor on American translators of the *Kalevala* and comparisons of the nature of Friberg's translation with Kirby's (no. 471), in which the general problem of translating the musical qualities of the original verses is addressed. A useful bibliography and glossary of important names.

2. STUDIES OF SIBELIUS AND FOLK MUSIC

See also nos. 138, 469, 520, 551, 564, 582, 647

473. Aho, Kalevi. *Suomalainen musiikki ja Kalevala* [Finnish Music and the *Kalevala*]. Suomalaisen Kirjallisuuden Seura, vol. 426. Helsinki: Suomalaisen Kirjallisuuden Seura, 1985. 140 p. ML3619.A46 1985 ISBN 951-717-414-4

Along with addressing directly Sibelius's *Kalevala*-inspired works from *Kullervo* to *Tapiola* (pp. 12–18, et passim), the author, a leading composer in Finland today, traces the epic's importance to Finnish musical composition from Filip von Schantz's *Kullervo* Overture (1860) to the avant-garde of the late twentieth century. Sibelius is viewed as standing near the beginning of a long and rich tradition that continues right down to the present. Plentifully illustrated with music examples as well as photographs of composers.

474. Fellerer, Karl Gustav. "Nordische Volks- und Kunstmusik im 19. Jahrhundert" [Nordic Folk- and Art Music in the 19th Century]. In *Beiträge zur Musikgeschichte Nordeuropas: Kurt Gudewill zum 65. Geburtstag*, 212–20. Edited by Uwe Haensel. Wolfenbüttel and Zurich: Möseler, 1978. ML55.G88 1978

An examination of how the romantic nationalistic movement in central Europe affected composers in Scandinavia, from Gade and Grieg to Svendsen and Sibelius. Fellerer places Sibelius in a much larger folk music context than has generally been done. He observes that many Scandinavians pursued musical studies in Germany, and many of their compositions, like Sibelius's *Kullervo*, bear the stamp of Nordic folksong. No music examples but copious notes.

475. Frosterus, Sigurd. "Gallen-Kallela, Sibelius: randandteckningar kring Kalevalajubileet" [Gallen-Kallela, Sibelius: Random Remarks About the Kalevala Jubilee]. *Nya Argus* 28 (1935): 93–96; 107–10. Revised and reprinted as "Kalevalas reinkarnationer" [The *Kalevala*'s Reincarnations] in *Stålålderns Janusansikte och andra essäer*, 229–59. Helsingfors: Söderström & Co., 1935.

An essay on the occasion of the *Kalevala*'s 100th anniversary by a sympathetic and artistically prominent contemporary. The first part is devoted to Gallen-Kallela's *Kalevala* paintings and the second, to Sibelius's *Kalevala* compositions. While the author finds that Gallen-Kallela's paintings give the *Kalevala* a kind of second flowering, he says that Sibelius, in striving for the pure tone world in his symphonies, has grown wings and strength from his experiences with the *Kalevala*; like the phoenix, he observes, Sibelius's music rises from the *Kalevala*'s fertile ashes.

476. Gorog, Lisa de, with the collaboration of Ralph de Gorog. *From Sibelius to Sallinen: Finnish Nationalism and the Music of Finland.* Contributions to the Study of Music and Dance, no. 16. Westport, Conn.: Greenwood, 1989. 252 p. ML269.5.D4 1989 0-313-26740-5

The authors explore the importance of folk poetry and folksong to Sibelius's music from the perspectives of a cultural historian and linguist. Using examples from music and poetry, they establish a valuable context: Finland's pre-Sibelian, oral music tradition on the one hand, and the numerous later Finnish composers heir to the Sibelian legacy, on the other. The interesting thesis, that Sibelius demonstrated the value of the national folk heritage to Finnish art music just as the Mighty Five had done for Russian music, is unfortunately not borne out by the rather naïve discussion of the music. For annotation of the concluding discography, see no. 46.

Rev.: *Ethnomusicology* 35 (1991): 119–21; *Fontes artis musicae* 37 (1990): 282–83; *Scandinavian Studies* 63 (1991): 500–02.

477. Gregory, Robin. "Sibelius and the Kalevala." *Monthly Musical Record*, March/April 1951: 59–62.

The performance in England of two unpublished movements of the *Lemminkäinen Suite* prompted this cursory review of major Sibelius works that draw their texts or programmatic inspiration from the *Kalevala*. Although superseded today by more detailed studies, Gregory's essay suggests how few such works were known in England at midcentury.

478. Kurkela, Vesa. "Sibelius, Klemetti, Kangas ja Andersson: suomalaisten säveltäjien käsityksiä kansanmusiikin sovittamisesta" [Sibelius, Klemetti, Kangas and Andersson: Ideas of Finnish

Composers About Arrangements of Folk Music]. *Synteesi* 7 (1988): 52–70.

Sibelius's university lecture of 1896 and his arrangements of six Finnish folksongs published in 1903 provide concrete evidence of his attitude to folk material, discussed here vis-à-vis the ideas of the fervently nationalist composer and conductor Heikki Klemetti and folk enthusiasts and researchers Knut Kangas and Otto Andersson. A useful bibliography provides sources for further reading.

479. Laitinen, Heikki. "Kalevalan kommentaarin runosävelmäliite vuodelta 1895" [The Folk Melody Supplement to the Kalevala Commentary from the Year 1895]. *Paimensoittimista kisällilauluun: Tutkielmia kansanmusiikista 1*, 157–92. Kaustinen: Kansanmusiikki-Instituutti, 1976. ISBN 951-95410-0-4

The fullest investigation available of Sibelius's activities collecting and editing folk melodies during the 1890s. This important study is filled with enormously interesting detail, carefully documented with reference to sources preserved in the archives of the Finnish Literary Society (Suomalaisen Kirjallisuuden Seura), the organization that sponsored Sibelius's research. The author provides valuable background to the research project, explores Sibelius's treatment of the material and his changing attitude toward his involvement with it, and gives music examples.

480. Oramo, Ilkka. "Vom Einfluss der Volksmusik auf die Kunstmusik: Ein unbekannter Aufsatz von Sibelius aus dem Jahre 1896" [Concerning the Influence of Folk Music on Art Music: An Unknown Essay by Sibelius from the Year 1896]. In *Bericht über den Internationalen Musikwissenschaftlichen Kongress Bayreuth 1981*, 440–44. Edited by Christoph-Hellmut Mahling and Sigrid Wiesmann. Kassel: Bärenreiter, 1984. ML36.I629 1981 ISBN 3-7618-0750-3

A Finnish version of the article appears as "Kansanmusiikin vaikutuksesta taidemusiikkiin: Sibeliuksen akateeminen koeluento vuodelta 1896," *Musiikki* 10 (1980): 106–22.

The author interprets Sibelius's view of the importance of folk music to art music in the context of prevailing European views of the 1890s. Sibelius's lecture delivered at Helsinki University (then Kaiser Alexander University) as part of his application for a position in 1896 serves as the basis for the discussion and provides Oramo the opportunity to compare Sibelius's views with Bartók's later writings on the same subject. For the complete text of Sibelius's lecture, see no. 482.

481. Salmenhaara, Erkki. "Kalevala, Sibelius ja Suomen säveltaide" [Kalevala, Sibelius and Finland's Musical Art]. *Musiikki* 15 (1985): 75–92. The article also appears in the Kalevala Society Yearbook celebrating the 150th anniversary of the *Kalevala*; see "Kirjokannesta kipinä: Kalevalan juhlavuoden satoa." *Kalevalaseuran vuosikirja* 66 (1985): 186–200.

Useful discussion of the *Kalevala*'s importance to art in Finland as a background to Sibelius's works inspired by the epic. A welcome bibliography provides many sources about the *Kalevala* and music.

482. Sibelius, Jean. "Några synpunkter beträffande folkmusiken och dess inflytande på tonkonsten/Joitakin näkökohtia kansanmusiikista ja sen vaikutuksesta säveltaiteeseen" [Some Observations About Folk Music and Its Influence on Art Music]. *Musiikki* 10 (1980): 86–105.

Sibelius's lecture, delivered at Helsinki University in 1896, in its original Swedish together with a Finnish translation provided by Ilkka Oramo. Here one can verify the oft-described "improvisatory" nature of the text. More importantly, the text represents the only formal expression Sibelius ever gave of his aesthetic position.

483. Tarasti, Eero. "The *Kalevala* in Finnish Music." *Finnish Music Quarterly*, 1985, nos. 1–2: 12–18.

Brief consideration of the importance of Elias Lönnrot's great epic for composers in Finland, from Fredrik Pacius through modern Finns like Aulis Sallinen. Sibelius's *Kalevala*-inspired compositions such as the *Kullervo* Symphony are thereby placed in the broader context of Finland's musical and cultural history. Illustrated with pictures from operatic and theatrical performances of *Kalevala*-based works.

484. Tolonen, Jouko. "Jean Sibeliuksen koeluento ja molli-pentakordin soinnutus" [Jean Sibelius's Trial Lecture and the Minor-Pentachord Sound]. In *Juhlakirja Erik Tawaststjernalle 10.X.1976./Festskrift till Erik Tawaststjerna.* Edited by Erkki Salmenhaara, 79–92. Acta musicologica Fennica 9. Keuruu: Otava, 1976. ML55.T39 1976 ISBN 951-1-04106-1

A discussion of modal and pentatonic elements in Sibelius's scores set against the background of the composer's lecture on Finnish folk music given in 1896. Music examples, many from works of the 1890s, illustrate the essay.

485. Väisänen, A. O. "Eräistä säveltäjäin kansansävelmäaiheista" [About the Folk Music Motives of Certain Composers]. *Kalevalaseuran vuosikirja* 15 (1935): 270–79.

A discussion by the eminent ethnomusicologist A. O. Väisänen (1890–1969) of the similarities between *En saga* and certain Finnish folk melodies. Mention is also made of Finnish folk influence on *Kullervo*, illustrated, among other ways, by the third movement's 5/4 meter. Music examples.

486. Väisänen, A. O. "Jean Sibelius 8.12.1865-20.9.1957." *Kalevalaseuran vuosikirja* 38 (1958): 5–8.

A eulogy stressing the composer's relationship to the *Kalevala* and the Kalevala Society. The author believes his own research has demonstrated the influence of folk music on Sibelius's melodies, which seem to show family resemblances to folk song, yet he recognizes Sibelius's distinctive individuality.

487. Väisänen, A. O. "Kalevala ja säveltaide" [The *Kalevala* and Musical Composition]. *Kalevalaseuran vuosikirja* 27–28 (1947–48): 303–22.

A review of compositions inspired by the *Kalevala* with emphasis on Sibelius. Bibliography.

488. Väisänen, A. O. "Kanteletarta sävellettynä" [The *Kanteletar* in Music]. *Kalevalaseuran vuosikirja* 31 (1951): 87–96.

Short historical review of musical settings of texts from the *Kanteletar* with references to Sibelius.

489. Väisänen, A. O. "Poimintoja Sibeliuksen tematiikasta kansanmusiikkia silmällä pitäen" [Excerpts from Sibelius's Themes with Reference to Folk Music]. *Kalevalaseuran vuosikirja* 36 (1956): 286–98.

Using thematic examples from Sibelius's symphonies and symphonic poems to illustrate his points, the author emphasizes how such features of Finnish folk music as minor mode, thematic tetrachords and pentachords, characteristic rhythms, and changeable structures were all used by Sibelius.

490. Väisänen, A. O. "Sibelius ja kansanmusiikki" [Sibelius and Folk Music]. *Kalevalaseuran vuosikirja* 16 (1936): 276–88.

Despite the claim published the previous year in Ekman's biography (no. 154) that Sibelius encountered genuine Finnish folk melodies only after he completed *Kullervo*, Väisänen asserts that Sibelius in fact heard Larin Paraske sing Finnish folk poems as early as the fall of 1891 and jotted down his ideas. The author discusses rhythmic and melodic characteristics of folk music found in Sibelius's works, illustrated with examples from the music and from Karelian melodies.

491. Wilson, William A. "Sibelius, the *Kalevala*, and Karelianism." In *The Sibelius Companion*, 43–60. Edited by Glenda Dawn Goss. Westport, Conn.: Greenwood, 1996. ML410.S54S53 1996 ISBN 0-313-28393-1

Essential reading for anyone who wishes to understand the term "Karelianism," its complex historical background, and the role of both Sibelius and the *Kalevala* in the country's burgeoning national consciousness. The article, the only source in English to deal with this important topic, is expertly written and refreshingly well documented, based as it is on valuable Finnish sources.

D. Studies in Performance Practice

See also nos. 52, 56, 143, 372, 519, 549, 577, 582, 608, 620, 637, 681, 696, 697

492. Cherniavsky, David. "Sibelius's Tempo Corrections." *Music & Letters* 31 (1950): 53–55.

Annotated as no. 493.

493. "Metronomimerkinnät Sibeliuksen sinfonioihin" [Metronome Markings for Sibelius's Symphonies]. *Musiikkitieto*, 1943: 12. An English-language version is David Cherniavsky's "Sibelius's Tempo Corrections." *Music & Letters* 31 (1950): 53–55.

A table of approximate tempo markings for the seven symphonies supplied by Breitkopf & Härtel and based on Sibelius materials in their possession. In the *Music & Letters* article, Cherniavsky adds his own views, including the suggestion that the gradual acceleration of tempo in the last three symphonies is rooted in the way Sibelius's symphonies "grow organically like natural organisms."

494. Parmet, Simon. "Ur en essä om interpretationen av Sibelius' musik" [From an Essay on the Interpretation of Sibelius's Music]. *Nya Argus* 42 (1949): 133–37.

A conductor's remarks on tempo, dynamics, and phrasing with particular reference to *En saga* and *Swan of Tuonela*.

495. Parmet, Simon. "Siirtymien ja temponvaihteluiden muotoilu Sibeliuksen musiikissa" [Movement and Design of Tempo Changes in Sibelius's Music]. *Uusi musiikkilehti*, 1955, no. 9: 24–26.

The conductor-author discusses problems of interpretation with reference to passages from Symphony no. 1. Some of the same ideas may be found in his book on the symphonies of Sibelius (no. 582).

496. Sibelius, Jean. "Tempo Markings in Sibelius' Tapiola." *Finnish Music Quarterly*, 1991, no. 3: 20–21.

Facsimile of a letter from Sibelius to Artur Rodzinski, written in German and dated August 20, 1934, in which the composer gives metronome markings for different sections of *Tapiola*.

497. Väisänen, Risto. "Sibeliuksen tempot: *Tapiola* ja kuudes sinfonia" [Sibelius's Tempos: *Tapiola* and the Sixth Symphony]. In *Sibelius-Akatemian Aikakauskirja SIC 1993*, 161–75. Edited by Veijo Murtomäki. Helsinki: Sibelius Academy, 1993. ISBN 952-9658-16-8

Noting that recent recordings of *Tapiola* by Finnish conductors differ dramatically in their durations (14'48 vs. 21'03), Väisänen sets out to examine the evidence for Sibelius's tempos. Although his particular focus is *Tapiola* and Symphony no. 6, he provides the most complete study of the topic of Sibelius's tempos to date based on the composer's letters, Sibelius's own tempo and metronome markings (he typically spoke of "duration" rather than metronome numbers), and testimony of those to whom Sibelius spoke about such matters, including Jussi Jalas and Santeri Levas. He deals with the issue of how and why certain interpretations arose and persist (a matter in which Kajanus's recordings played an important part) and the vexed problem of the tempos in Symphony no. 6, which Sibelius himself changed.

E. Genre Studies

1. CHAMBER MUSIC

See also nos. 372, 635

General Studies

498. Dahlström, Fabian. "The Early Chamber Music of Jean Sibelius: Some Remarks On Its Reception History." *Finnish Music Quarterly*, 1990, nos. 3–4: 18–23.

A useful, up-to-date review of the chamber works, a survey of the periods in which they were composed, and observations on their performances in Finland.

499. Dahlström, Fabian. "Sibelius' Early Chamber Music." *Fazer Music News*, Spring 1991: 6–7.

A valuable look at the chamber works composed between 1885 and 1888, which the author divides into two categories: those written under the supervision of Martin Wegelius and those written independently of this teacher. Also considered are such matters as the works' premieres and subsequent performance history and their opus numbers, which varied with the composer's whim. Illustrations show the trio of the Sibelius siblings and an infrequently reproduced portrait of the composer by Sigurd Wettenhovi-Aspa from 1892.

500. Goddard, Scott. "The Chamber Music." In *The Music of Sibelius*, 91–96. Edited by Gerald Abraham. New York: Norton, 1947. ML410.S54A5

Survey, a substantial portion of which is devoted to *Voces intimae*. More recent events, including the gift of many of Sibelius's youthful chamber works to the Helsinki University Library, invalidate much of the essay.

501. Rosas, John. *Otryckta kammarmusikverk av Jean Sibelius* [Unpublished Chamber Music by Jean Sibelius]. Acta Academiae Aboensis. Humaniora XXIII.4. Åbo: Åbo Akademi, 1961. 89 p. AS262.A3 vol. 23, no. 4

A study of Sibelius's unpublished chamber works is by definition a study of his early style. Rosas' essay is based on materials in the Sibelius Museum, some made available only after the composer's death. The author provides descriptive analyses of fourteen chamber works, most of which are believed to come from the years 1885–1891, and draws various conclusions regarding the influence of earlier masters of chamber music on Sibelius. Although subsequent research has since altered the chronological picture, Rosas was the first to examine this material in a scholarly fashion. Appendices list these unpublished works, their locations, and references made to them by previous authors. Along with music examples there is a still useful index of personal names and a short but important bibliography directing attention to related materials in newspapers and periodicals around the turn of the century.

Rev.: *Suomen musiikin vuosikirja* (1960–61): 65–68.

Studies of Individual Works

502. Kilpeläinen, Kari. "Onko 'Fuuga Martin Wegeliukselle' Fuuga Martin Wegeliukselle?" [Is the 'Fugue for Martin Wegelius' the Fugue for Martin Wegelius?]. *Musiikkitiede* 3 (1991): 128–34.

An important study based on close examination of the composer's manuscripts in which the author demonstrates that the fugue named for the composer's early teacher in fact originated as the last movement of the Quartet in A minor.

Voces intimae

503. Blom, Eric. "Sibelius." In *Cobbett's Cyclopedic Survey of Chamber Music*, compiled and edited by Walter Wilson Cobbett. With supplementary material edited by Colin Mason, 2d edition. Vol. 2: 416–19. London: Oxford University Press, 1963. ML1100.C7

Limited to a discussion of *Voces intimae*, with themes from each of the movements illustrated in music examples.

504. Fredriksson, Risto. "Voces intimae." *Kollega*, 1966: 26–30.

Cursory description of Sibelius's mature quartet with music examples showing principal themes. In Finnish.

505. Krummacher, Friedhelm. "Voces intimae: Das Streichquartett op. 56 und die Gattungstradition" [Voces intimae: The String Quartet op. 56 and the Genre's Tradition]. *Finnish Music Quarterly*, 1990, nos. 3–4: 36–43. Another version of the article appeared in *Musica* 45 (1991): 360–67.

An examination of Sibelius's best-known quartet with emphasis on the first movement set against the background of the genre's history. The author suggests that such things as the homophonic style and the programmatically suggestive title, both of which go against traditional conventions of quartet writing, contributed to the misunderstanding of Sibelius by such critics as Theodor Adorno. Music examples.

506. Ringbom, Nils-Eric. "Vår tids musik: V. Voces intimae" [Music of Our Time: V. Voces intimae]. *Musikvärlden*, 1948, no. 7: 210–11. Reprinted, without the music examples, in the same author's *Sibelius: Symphonies, Symphonic Poems, Violin Concerto, Voces intimae. Analytical Notes* (Helsinki: Fazer, 1955), 30–31.

Brief analysis of *Voces intimae* emphasizing Sibelius's introspective disposition at the time of its composition. Music examples.

2. MARCHES AND MUSIC FOR BRASS

See also nos. 392, 393

507. Heikinheimo, Veikko. "Kun Jääkärimarssin sanat syntyivät" [When the Words to the March of the Jaeger Battalion Were Born]. *Vapaussodan invaliidi*, 1958, nos. 2–3: 17–20. Reprinted with additional illustrations in *Uusi Aura*, October 28, 1962.

The story behind the birth of Heikki Nurmio's three stanzas, which won his battalion's competition for a marching song (described as the "most powerful marching song ever written by a Finnish man") and then sent to Sibelius who set the words to music. Illustrated with the complete poem, Lieutenant Nurmio's picture, and a facsimile of a page from the notebook in which the poem was drafted.

508. Helasvuo, Veikko. "Jean Sibelius ja Porilaisten marssi" [Jean Sibelius and the March of the Men of Pori]. *Uusi musiikkilehti*, 1957, nos. 7–8: 20–21.

A report on the discovery of one of Sibelius's autographed arrangements of this traditional march tune, which came to light when the library of the Helsinki Philharmonic Orchestra moved to new headquarters in 1952. There are facsimiles of the first and last pages. The author also mentions other arrangements of the march, including one by Robert Kajanus which may predate that of Sibelius.

509. Karjalainen, Kauko. "Sibeliuksen Allegro torviseptetille" [Sibelius's *Allegro* for Brass Septet]. *Sulasol*, 1987, no. 1: 8–9.

A discussion of a newly found work for Eb cornetto, Bb cornetto I and II, Eb alto horn, Bb tenor horn, Bb euphonium, and Eb Basso. The work is thought to be Sibelius's, although only the letters *-n -l -s* of the composer's name can be seen. The *Allegro* seems to have been composed for the Society for Culture and Education (*Kansanvalistusseura*), for a festival competition in the 1880s.

For a follow-up article, see no. 512.

510. Lagus, Ernst. "Björneborgarnes Marsch: en musik- och kulturhistorisk essay" [March of the Björneborgers: A Musical and Cultural-Historical Essay]. *Johan Ludvig Runebergs hundraårsminne: Festskrift den 5 Februari 1904*, 305–44. Svenska Litteratursällskapet i Finland, no. 62. Helsinki: SLS, 1904.

The rather extraordinary history behind the march, once called *Bonaparte's March* and known in Finnish as *Porilaisten marssi*, that inspired words by poets Johan Ludvig Runeberg and Zacharias Topelius, a painting by Albert Edelfelt, and musical arrangements by composers from Fredrik Pacius to Sibelius. Sibelius in fact created two versions, but the first has been lost. Ernest Lagus (1859–1923), who wrote the essay, was an educator and noted cultural historian in Helsinki. Music examples.

511. Pekanheimo, Väinö. "Jääkärimarssin kopiot: 65 vuotta Jääkärimarssin kantaesityksistä Suomessa" [Copies of the March of the Jaeger Battalion: 65 Years After the Premiere of the March of the Jaeger Battalion in Finland]. *Sulasol*, 1983, no. 2: 24–26.

Short history of Sibelius's March of the Finnish Jaeger Battalion, its early performances, and how and by whom copies were made, some of which include changes from the original. Illustrated with facsimiles of selected measures of the music, photographs of the poet and copyists, and a program of January 19, 1918, with the composer's name prudently omitted.

512. Saari, Raimo. "Sibeliuksen Allegron jäljet johtavat Mäntyharjulle" [The Tracks of Sibelius's *Allegro* Lead to Mäntyharju]. *Sulasol*, 1987, no. 2: 16–17.

A postscript to no. 509.

3. WORKS FOR PIANO

See also nos. 372, 392

513. Blom, Eric. "The Piano Music." In *The Music of Sibelius*, 97–107. Edited by Gerald Abraham. New York: Norton, 1947. ML410.S54A5

A survey with emphasis on the author's choice of Sibelius's three most important piano works: the Sonata in F major, op. 12; *Kyllikki*; and the three Sonatinas, op. 67. Together with enthusiasm for these and selected other compositions are some familiar criticisms: filling in with tremolos instead of vital figuration, abrupt introduction of technical difficulties, "over-steep climaxes," and lapses into triviality.

514. Gould, Glenn. "Sibelius and the Post-Romantic Piano Style." *The Essential Piano Quarterly*, 1992/summer: 20–21. Originally appeared in *Piano Quarterly* 25 (1977/Fall): 22–27.

Sibelius was a special favorite of the famous Canadian pianist, who, in this short essay, maintains that the composer "never wrote against the grain of the keyboard" and far surpassed his Austro-German contemporaries Mahler, Webern, and Strauss in the ease and spontaneity with which he composed for the instrument. The most detailed musical remarks are reserved for *Kyllikki* and the three sonatinas of op. 67.

515. Kokkonen, Joonas. "Piirteitä Sibeliuksen pianomusiikista" [Features of Sibelius's Piano Music]. *Uusi musiikkilehti*, 1955, no. 9: 40–42.

Insights from a leading Finnish composer into the much-disparaged piano music. Kokkonen points out that hardly any other contemporary wrote in such a terse and linear style for the keyboard. Pictures of Sibelius at home, no music examples.

516. Niemann, Walter. *Die nordische Klaviermusik* [Nordic Piano Music]. Leipzig: Breitkopf & Härtel, 1918. 71 p.

In the chapter entitled "Finland" Sibelius occupies pride of place (pp. 64–68). Not surprisingly, Niemann emphasizes in the piano music the folk-like characteristics and nature impressions he found in Sibelius's orchestral works.

517. Shumway, Jeffrey. "A Comparative Study of Representative Bagatelles for the Piano since Beethoven." D.Mus. diss., Indiana University, 1981. iv, 98 p. text; 28 p. music.

The characteristics of Beethoven's bagatelles serve as the point of departure for examining the bagatelles of subsequent composers, including Sibelius's opp. 34 and 97 (see especially pp. 57–60 where Alexander Tcherepnin and Sibelius are discussed). The latter's music receives only cursory treatment, however, the works being characterized as of "rather mediocre artistic quality." The author finds that Beethoven was the single most influential factor on the bagatelles of his successors.

518. Tawaststjerna, Erik. *The Pianoforte Compositions of Jean Sibelius*. Helsinki: Otava, 1957. 104 p.

Equivalent to the first portion of the same author's *Ton och tolkning*, this English-language translation has the benefit of added illustrations and facsimiles of pages from the manuscripts of *Granen* and *Kyllikki*. For a fuller annotation, see no. 519.

519. Tawaststjerna, Erik. *Sibeliuksen pianosävellykset ja muita esseitä* [Sibelius's Piano Compositions and Other Essays]. Helsinki: Otava, 1955. 186 p. ML410.S56T23S

An edition appeared in Swedish as *Ton och tolkning: Sibelius-studier* [Music and Interpretation: Sibelius Studies]. Helsingfors: Holger Schildt Förlag; Stockholm: Wahlström & Widstrand, 1957. 132, [3] p. ML410.S54T2727 1957

A two-part study, the first dealing with style in the keyboard works, the second devoted to the interpretive idiosyncrasies of six Sibelius conductors and three performers of the Violin Concerto, namely, Isaac Stern, David Oistrakh, and Yehudi Menuhin. The piano music is classified into three main stylistic periods, the Kalevala-Romantic, the European-Classic, and the Universal, and the author indicates that the same periods hold equally true for the works in general. He demonstrates these and other parallels with such great composers for the piano as Chopin, Ravel, and Debussy. Illustrated with music examples.

520. Tawaststjerna, Erik. *Sibeliuksen pianoteokset säveltäjän kehityslinjan kuvastajana* [Sibelius's Piano Works as Reflection of His Compositional Development]. Helsinki: Otava, 1960. 154 p. ML410.S56T19

The author of Sibelius's most detailed biography began his Sibelius research by way of the piano compositions. In this book, his dissertation, the keyboard music is subjected to more stringent analytical treatment than in his other studies, each movement being given formal analysis based on the methods of Ilmari Krohn. The themes that would be espoused in the author's other books on the piano music, that the works divide into three periods which also correspond to those of the larger, symphonic works, are in place here, only the periods are called "romantic-realistic," "middle," and "late." There is also some discussion of the influence of folk music and, together with music examples and bibliography, a catalogue of piano compositions by opus number.

521. Tawaststjerna, Erik. "Sibelius pianokompositioner" [Sibelius Piano Compositions]. *Ord och bild* 65 (1956): 235–45.

Based on the author's larger study, a Swedish-language discussion of Sibelius's piano works grouped in three periods (now called the Kalevala-Romantic, the European-Classical, and the Universal) and a consideration of the "pianistic" quality of the composer's keyboard writing. No music examples for this Nordic cultural journal, but there is a facsimile of the first page from the manuscript of *Kyllikki*.

522. Tawaststjerna, Erik T. "The Piano Music of Sibelius." *Finnish Music Quarterly*, 1990, nos. 3–4: 66–71.

Lucid survey by the son of the biographer Erik Tawaststjerna, a pianist who has recorded the complete keyboard works of Sibelius. Acknowledging the piano works' three style periods, the author also considers arrangements and with keen insight discusses Sibelius's relationship to the instrument. Music examples.

4. RELIGIOUS MUSIC

See also nos. 372, 389

523. Ahtokari, Reijo, Eero Ekman, and Einari Marvia. *Näkymättömän temppelin rakentajat: Suomalaisen vapaamuurariuden historia* [Builders of the Invisible Temple: The History of Finnish Freemasons]. Helsinki: Otava, 1994. 319 p. ISBN 951-1-13459-0

Opening a previously secret record, the authors trace the history of Freemasonry in Finland from the middle of the eighteenth century. They furnish various details about Sibelius's Masonic connections throughout, and on pp. 227–44, Marvia deals specifically with Sibelius's *Masonic Ritual Music*, op. 113, whose history, settings, and arrangements are among the most complicated in the composer's oeuvre. He explains the work's origins, discusses the problem of dating, identifies the different poetic sources and translations, and follows the work's subsequent history, both in Finland and in America, where, in conjunction with the Masonic Lodge in New York, the history, performance, and publication of the composition took a new turn. Includes a facsimile of the work's opening hymn.

524. Kilpeläinen, Kari. "Detalji Sibelius-tutkimuksesta: mikä teos on Op. 107?" [A Detail in Sibelius Research: What Work Is Op. 107?]. *Musiikkitiede* 1 (1989): 88–93.

A review of the confusion in scholarly references to Sibelius's opus number 107, from Cecil Gray's *Sibelius* in 1931 through Fabian Dahlström's catalogue *The Works of Jean Sibelius* in 1987. On the basis of a work list written in Sibelius's own hand, Kilpeläinen shows that the composer variously used this opus number to refer to *God's Blessing* (*Herran siunaus*), to *Introductory Antiphons* (*Johdantovuorolaulut*), and to four other religious "ritual" works as well. The jumble surrounding the use of this number is, however, not yet resolved, and scholars are still seeking agreement on explanations.

525. Kuusisto, Taneli. "Kirkkomusiikillisia kosketuskohtia Jean Sibeliuksen sävellystuotannossa" [Points of Contact with Church Music in the Compositional Output of Jean Sibelius]. *Uusi musiikkilehti*, 1955, no. 9: 33–34.

A brief review of Sibelius's works that show either a stylistic orientation toward or a direct connection to church music. Included in the first group are the *Finlandia* hymn and the hymn in the finale of Symphony no. 3. To the second group belongs the *Masonic Ritual Music*. No music examples.

526. Sola, Wäinö. "Jean Sibelius as a Composer of Freemason Music." *Koilliskulma*, 1957, nos. 5–6: 7–9. A similar article appeared earlier in Finnish as "Jean Sibelius vapaamuurarimusiikin säveltäjänä," *Koilliskulma*, 1955: 4–6.

A personal memoir by singer and Sibelius's fellow Freemason, Finnish operatic tenor Wäinö Sola (1883–1961). Recalling Sibelius's improvisations, the singer claims a great deal of credit in the matter of Sibelius's Masonic music, saying that he, Sola, requested Sibelius to compose the work that came to be called

Musique religieuse, or *Masonic Ritual Music*. He also gives details about the American translation and publication of *Masonic Ritual Music*. The Finnish version discusses difficulties with royalty payments to the composer, owing to the different copyright laws in the United States. Of those royalties received, Sibelius donated half for the purpose of building an orphanage. In both versions the author relates an anecdote showing that the eighty-year-old composer was still composing, and with speed.

5. SYMPHONIC POEMS

General Studies

See also no. 569

527. Altenburg, Detlef. "La notion lisztienne de poème symphonique dans son interpénétration avec la conscience nationale à la fin du XIXe siècle et au début du XXe" [The Lisztian Idea of the Symphonic Poem in its Interpenetration with the National Conscience at the End of the XIXth Century and the Beginning of the XXth]. Translated from German by Michelle Biget and Serge Gut. In *Actes du Colloque International Franz Liszt (1811–1886)*, 287–95. Edited by Serge Gut. Published as *La revue musicale* 405/407 (1987).

A consideration of how certain aspects of Liszt's symphonic poems, such as *visée esthétique* and cyclicism, helped to shape national schools. A paragraph compares Sibelius's *Lemminkäinen Legends* with Smetana's *Má vlast* and *Finlandia* with Liszt's *Hungaria*.

528. Eeckhout, Antoon. *Muzikale exploraties, Tweede reeks: ouverturen en symfonische gedichtey* [Musical Studies, Second Series: Overtures and Symphonic Poems]. Mechelen, Leuven: De Monte, 1970. 106 p. MT90.E3

The second in a multivolume introduction to orchestral music directed to a general audience in which Sibelius is represented by *Finlandia*. The author gives a short descriptive outline of each work, using some thematic examples. Discography and definitions of musical terms.

529. Kloiber, Rudolf. *Handbuch der symphonischen Dichtung* [Handbook of the Symphonic Poem], 194–215. Wiesbaden: Breitkopf & Härtel, 1980.

A guide to symphonic poems from Berlioz and Liszt through Strauss and Respighi, including a discussion of thirteen Sibelius symphonic poems, among which are *Kullervo* and *Finlandia*. Although the musical observations are more descriptive than profound, the inclusion of more Sibelius works than any composer except Liszt forcibly conveys Sibelius's importance to the genre. The format is consistent throughout: some historical background is given for each symphonic poem followed by a brief description (labelled "Form and Content"), often showing principal themes.

530. Mäckelmann, Michael. "Sibelius und die Programmusik: Eine Studie zu seinen Tondichtungen und Symphonien" [Sibelius and Program Music: A Study of His Tone Poems and Symphonies]. In *Programmusik: Studien zu Begriff und Geschichte einer umstrittenen Gattung. Hamburger Jahrbuch für Musikwissenschaft*, vol. 6, 121–68. Edited by Constantin Floros, Hans Joachim Marx, and Peter Petersen. Hamburg: Laaber-Verlag, 1983. ISBN 3-921518-99-7

The author mentions Sibelius's uncomfortable position in the German world by contrast with his success in Anglo-Saxon countries and reviews the composer's relationship to the symphony and symphonic poem together with ideas about music and "programs" based on findings of other scholars and Sibelius's own statements. He then provides "semantic analyses" of two works: Symphony no. 4, in which the author explores musical and programmatic connections to the abandoned orchestral song *The Raven*; and *Tapiola*, analyzed as a set of variations, which both as a structural idea and in its four sections can be seen to reflect musically the four-line poem that accompanies it.

531. Murtomäki, Veijo. "On the Symphonic Poems by Sibelius." *Finnish Music Quarterly*, 1990, nos. 3–4: 48–49.

The author argues that Sibelius approached symphonic poems as if they were symphonies and that, rather than illustrating specific events, the composer took up instead where words leave off. There is a facsimile of a sketch of *En saga*.

532. Rosas, John. "Bidrag till kännedomen om tre Sibelius-verk" [Report on Receiving Information about Three Sibelius Works]. *Suomen musiikkin vuosikirja 1964–65*. Helsinki: Otava, 1965, 71–79. With English summary.

Based on manuscript material in the Sibelius Museum where Rosas was Director, a discussion of the *Karelia Suite*, *Spring Song* (*Vårsång*) and *Lemminkäinen and the Maidens of the Island* (*Lemminkäinen ja saaren neidot*). Rosas was among the first to shed light on the history of each work based on manuscript revisions and information found in reviews by Karl Flodin. He observes that the published *Karelia Suite* (here called *Carelia Music*) is shorter and somewhat different from the manuscript version, that *Spring Song* underwent at least two revisions, and that, of versions of the so-called *Lemminkäinen Suite*, the Sibelius Museum, in his opinion, owned the first.

533. Tanzberger, Ernst. *Die symphonischen Dichtungen von Jean Sibelius* [The Symphonic Poems of Jean Sibelius]. Würzburg: Konrad Triltsch Verlag, 1943. Musik und Nation IV. viii, 71 p. MT130.S5T3 1943

Tanzberger's systematic consideration of ten symphonic poems demonstrates a Lorenz-inspired concern for divining arch and bar forms. Rondo and strophic forms are also identified in two of the works. Liberally illustrated with music examples and formal outlines, the monograph contains a bibliography that is especially useful for its list of articles appearing in German newspapers and periodicals between 1935 and 1941.

534. Wood, Ralph W. "The Miscellaneous Orchestral and Theatre Music." In *The Music of Sibelius*, 38–90. Edited by Gerald Abraham. New York: Norton, 1947. ML410.S54A5

General observations in a survey of the tone poems and incidental music.

Studies of Individual Works

The Bard

See also no. 678

535. Oramo, Ilkka. "Jean Sibeliuksen sävelruno Bardi" [Jean Sibelius's Symphonic Poem *The Bard*]. *Musiikki* 12 (1982): 171–93.

To force *The Bard* into a conventional musical form such as Tanzberger's bar form analysis, the author argues, is to ignore the motivic structure of the work. Despite the generic name Sibelius gave it, *The Bard* is more "logical" than "plastic" and has symphonic characteristics. There is also a consideration of the ambiguity of the programmatic meaning of this "tone poem without a program" in light of its apparent source of inspiration, Runeberg's poem *Barden*.

En saga

See also nos. 215, 606

536. Furuhjelm, Erik. "Sibelius' tondikt 'En saga': musikalisk analys" [Sibelius's Tone Poem 'En saga': Musical Analysis]. *Finsk musikrevy* 4 (1905): 13–17.

Sibelius's first biographer and a composer himself, Furuhjelm was already writing about Sibelius's music before he began his biography. His "analysis" of the early tone poem *En saga* is interesting today primarily for its whimsical programmatic interpretation.

537. Karila, Tauno. "Uusi näkökulma Sibeliuksen Sadun esteettiseen tulkintaan" [New Perspective on the Aesthetic Interpretation of Sibelius's Saga]. *Suomen musiikin vuosikirja 1964–65*. Helsinki: Otava, 1965, 35–45. With English summary.

A discussion of *En saga* in light of a collection of essays and short stories entitled *Andante, Chords in Twilight* (see no. 410) by Samuli Suomalainen (1903), which fancifully portrays the tone poem as based on an episode in Aleksis Kivi's *Seven Brothers*. Karila discusses other essays in Suomalainen's book relating to Sibelius, introducing into his deliberation Gallen-Kallela's painting *Saga (Satu*, 1894), in which Sibelius and a fantastic landscape are depicted. Three music examples and the painting are shown, although the reproduction reverses the original orientation.

538. Murtomäki, Veijo. "Sibeliuksen *En saga*: Muodon ja ohjelmallisuuden ongelma" [Sibelius's *En saga*: The Problem of Form and Program]. *Näkökulmia musiikkii SIC 3*, 157–87. Edited by Kari Kurkela. Helsinki: Sibelius Academy, 1990. ML160.N22 1990 ISBN 951-370040-2

An examination of the structure of *En saga* in light of the Lisztian symphonic poem, with examples of transformed thematic material and Schenkerian graphs for both the 1892 and 1902 versions of the work. The author also discusses the programmatic meaning of *En saga*, remarking among other things on the difficulty of translating its title into Finnish: *satu*, which means "fairy tale" in Finnish, does not convey the same epic quality as the word *saga* in Swedish or English. Despite the suggestive title, the author believes that Sibelius's tone poem approaches the "absolute" symphony in structural ways.

539. Ringbom, Nils-Eric. *De två versionerna av Sibelius' tondikt "En saga"* [The Two Versions of Sibelius' Tone Poem "En saga"]. Acta Academiae Aboensis Humaniora XXII/2. Åbo: Åbo Akademi, 1956. 53 p. With English summary. AS262.A3 vol. 22, no. 2. A summary of the findings appears under the English title in *Finnish Music Quarterly*, 1987, no. 1: 2–10.

Ringbom was the first scholar to address the complicated question of Sibelius's revisions. He shows that between the first *En saga*, composed in 1892, and the version published by Breitkopf & Härtel in 1903, Sibelius significantly reduced the size of the work as well as the number of tempo changes and modulations while increasing the length of unbroken pedal points. Ringbom graphically demonstrates these differences in music examples, charts, and a lengthy diagram and provides a bibliography, particularly useful for its Scandinavian sources.

The Lemminkäinen Legends

540. Cherniavsky, David. "Two Unpublished Tone-Poems by Sibelius." *Musical Times*, August 1949: 272–75.

A report on *Lemminkäinen and the Maidens of the Island* and *Lemminkäinen in Tuonela*, whose scores had remained unavailable despite their premieres over fifty years before, in 1896. Cherniavsky examined the manuscripts while visiting Sibelius in the summer of 1948: he traces the "germ motives" within the main themes and offers an interpretation that attempts to capture the *Kalevala* background of the works. Music examples.

541. Essén, Bengt, and Bo Wallner. "Tuonelas svan" [*Swan of Tuonela*]. *Musikrevy* 10 (1955): 295–99.

A two-part discussion, in which first Essén deals with the *Swan*'s literary background in the *Kalevala*, drawing analogies between the myths of Lemminkäinen in the realm of the dead and Orpheus in the Underworld, after which Wallner takes up the nature of Sibelius's musical material and considers the ways in which it has been developed into his own distinctive language. Music examples.

542. Jacobs, Robert L. "Sibelius' *Lemminkäinen and the Maidens of Saari*." *Music Review* 24 (1963): 147–57.

Taking issue with Collins's dismissal of the germ motive as an analytical tool (no. 437), Jacobs offers his own programmatic interpretation of the *Lemminkäinen* tone poem, which he believes demonstrates the composer's use of "evolutionary thematicism." He uses numerous music examples to trace the thematic affinities of this work, which he finds imbued with the world of the *Kalevala*, with Symphonies no. 1, 2, and 4. The correct title of the work, it should be noted, is *Lemminkäinen and the Maidens of the Island*; for a discussion of the title confusion, see no. 159, pp. 71–72.

543. Raabe, Peter. "Zwei Legenden für Orchester von Jean Sibelius" [Two Legends for Orchestra by Jean Sibelius]. *Allgemeine Musik-Zeitung*, May 31/June 7, 1901: 379–84.

An analysis of *Swan of Tuonela* and *Lemminkäinen's Return* that includes music examples and a cameo portrait of Sibelius in Napoleonic pose (right hand inside his coat and over his heart). The essay was prompted by the Helsinki Philharmonic Orchestra's European tour the previous year during which these two works were played. The author was responsible for the Liszt Archive and later became widely known for his scholarship on Liszt (who appears on the cover of this issue).

544. Stockmeier, Wolfgang. *Die Programmusik*. Das Musikwerk 36. Cologne: Arno Volk, 1970. 124 p. M2.M945 Heft 36. Translated into English by A. C. Howie as *Program Music*. Anthology of Music 36 (Cologne: A. Volk Verlag; New York: MCA Music, 1970). 124 p. M2.M94512 no. 36

Eleven programmatic works, including Sibelius's *Lemminkäinen and the Maidens of the Island* (pp. 84–103), presented in a volume designed to define "program music" and trace its history from the fourteenth century to the twentieth. Although the musical discussion about Sibelius (pp. 26–28) is dated, Stockmeier's keyboard arrangement of the tone poem is a welcome study tool.

Rev.: *Musica* 25 (1971): 405.

Luonnotar

545. Hepokoski, James. "The Essence of Sibelius: Creation Myths and Rotational Cycles in *Luonnotar*." In *The Sibelius Companion*, 121–46. Edited by Glenda Dawn Goss. Westport, Conn.: Greenwood, 1996. ML410.S54S53 1996 ISBN 0-313-28393-1

A lively and fascinating look at *Luonnotar*, beginning with its text and continuing with a detailed analysis of its musical structure. The author offers a "gendered" interpretation of the work's meaning and demonstrates how this applies on various levels, using as supporting evidence the *Kalevala* text, the music's structure, and Sibelius's letters and diary entries.

546. Jyrhämä, Outi. "Kaksi myyttistä neitoa" [Two Mythical Maidens]. *Musiikki* 22 (1992): 67–86. The article appeared in Estonian as "Kaks müütilist neidu," in *Teater, muusika, kino*, 1991, no. 7: 14–25.

A comparison of Estonian composer Rudolf Tobias's ballade *Sest ilmaneitsist ilusast* with *Luonnotar*. Although both the composers and the works share certain similarities (Tobias had interested himself in his country's folk epic, the *Kalevapoig*, just as Sibelius was intrigued by the *Kalevala*), the author concludes that close inspection actually reveals the distinctive individuality of each man.

Nightride and Sunrise

547. A. C. [Axel Carpelan]. "Jean Sibelius: Nattlig Ritt och Soluppgång" [Jean Sibelius: Nightride and Sunrise]. *Tidning för musik* 1 (1911): 187–91.

A highly complimentary discussion of the tone poem written in 1908 and premiered in 1909 in St. Petersburg, by one of Sibelius's most loyal friends. Carpelan situates the work in the context of other Sibelius compositions whose titles, texts, or atmospheres suggest the magical world of myth and saga.

Oceanides (*Aallottaret*)

548. Dibelius, Ulrich. "Form und Impression: 'Die Okeaniden' von Jean Sibelius" [Form and Impression: 'The Oceanides' of Jean Sibelius]. *Neue Zeitschrift für Musik* 117 (1956): 689–92.

Observing that the change of name from *Rondo der Wellen* to *Oceanides* reflects the literary conception of the work, the author discusses the structure of *Oceanides*. He gives the main themes in examples and outlines a formal plan in which he finds a rondo element in the alternation of material in the two main (A and B) sections. He briefly compares the work with Debussy's *La mer*; whereas, according to Dibelius, Debussy worked from memory of the sea, Sibelius, never having taken a sea voyage, created out of his intuition. Sibelius's experiences of the sea, however, began in childhood, when he spent summers in the coastal town of Lovisa and extended through his own trans-Atlantic voyage to America, during which he made revisions to the score of *Oceanides*.

549. Fantapié, Henri-Claude. "*Aallottaret* de Jean Sibelius: une question de rhythmé" [The *Oceanides* of Jean Sibelius: A Question of Tempo]. *2e Trimestre* 27 (1992): 87–101. An English version of the article appears in the *Proceedings from the First International Jean Sibelius Conference, Helsinki, August 1990*, 41–64. Edited by Eero Tarasti. Helsinki: Sibelius Academy, 1995. ISBN 952-9658-38-9

> A consideration of various musical aspects of the tone poem from an interpreter's point of view, one that also takes into account some of the differences found in the manuscript in the Helsinki University Library. The heart of the essay is a "symbolic characterization" in which musical "objects" rather than "subjects" are described. The author concludes with a review of ways to determine tempo, with references made to Debussy.

550. Rosas, John. "Tondikten Aallottaret (Okeaniderna) Opus 73 av Jean Sibelius" [The Tone Poem *Aallottaret* (*Oceanides*) Opus 73 by Jean Sibelius]. In *Juhlakirja Erik Tawaststjernalle 10.X.1976./Festskrift till Erik Tawaststjerna*, 37–78. Edited by Erkki Salmenhaara. Acta musicologica Fennica 9. Keuruu: Otava, 1976. ML55.T39 1976 ISBN 951-1-04106-1

> This study of the first tone poem Sibelius composed for the United States reviews the circumstances of its commission together with Sibelius's experiences in the New World and then presents a comparative study of *Oceanides*' three versions. Plentifully illustrated with music examples and copies of programs from the first performance, in Norfolk, Connecticut, the article also contains a useful bibliography that includes numerous newspaper reviews.

Pohjola's Daughter

551. Fanselau, Rainer. "Jean Sibelius: Pohjolas Tochter op. 49" [Jean Sibelius: *Pohjola's Daughter*, op. 49]. In *Programmusik: Analytische Untersuchungen und didaktische Empfehlungen für den*

Musikunterricht in der Sekundarstufe, 217–35. Edited by Albrecht Goebel. Mainz: B. Schott's Söhne, 1992. ISBN 3-7957-0237-2

An expansive and important discussion of *Pohjola's Daughter* that explores the work's program, its relationship to the *Kalevala*'s text and melodies, and its style and structure. The author has examined Sibelius's letters to publisher Robert Lienau for the light they shed on the work and uses this evidence together with the composer's lecture on folk music and his music manuscripts to amplify his points. Two influences are traced in the tone poem's musical structure: the "Beethoven principle," namely, the development of motivic-thematic material from a fundamental cell, and the principle of variation derived from Finnish folk music, the latter demonstrated by comparisons of the opening cello theme to Finnish folk melodies. An outline, with the verses of the published program running parallel, shows a sonata form for the composition.

Tapiola

See also nos. 443, 445, 446, 496, 497

552. Mäckelmann, Michael. "Jean Sibelius: 'Tapiola,' Tondichtung op. 112" [Jean Sibelius: 'Tapiola,' Tone Poem, op. 112]. *Neue Zeitschrift für Musik* 147 (1986): 32–36.

A consideration of the structure of *Tapiola*. Outlines show a variation principle and a cyclic structure, while analogies are drawn to Sibelius's Symphonies no. 4 and 7. There is also a discussion of the program, with explanations of how Sibelius's four poetic lines generated certain aspects of the music.

553. Murtomäki, Veijo. "*Tapiola*: Sibeliuksen sinfonisen ajattelun päätepiste" [*Tapiola*: The End Point of Sibelius's Symphonic Thought]. In *Sibelius-Akatemian aikakauskirja SIC 1993*, 114–34. Edited by Veijo Murtomäki. Helsinki: Sibelius Academy, 1993. ISBN 952-9658-16-8

An investigation into Sibelius's last tone poem which the author believes synthesizes traits of its genre with that of the symphony. In exploring this relationship, he takes issue with an earlier analysis by Erkki Salmenhaara (no. 554). A revised version of the study, expanded to encompass Symphonies no. 6 and 7 and without the Salmenhaara criticisms, may be read in English; see no. 445.

554. Salmenhaara, Erkki. *Tapiola: Sinfoninen runo Tapiola Sibeliuksen myöhäistyylin edustajana* [*Tapiola*: The Tone Poem *Tapiola* as a Representative of Sibelius' Late Style]. Acta musicologica Fennica 4. Helsinki: Suomen Musiikkitieteellinen Seura, 1970. With English summary. 138 p. + chart on unnumbered foldout. MT130.S5S24

Against the background of three main trends of twentieth-century music—atonality, impressionism, and neoclassicism—the author finds Sibelius an unclassifiable original who created a new technique for composing symphonic music. Salmenhaara views the form of *Tapiola* as "organic process," a way of constructing music through the ongoing transformation of a basic germ motive. This process provides both the composition's working principle and its essence, giving rise to a monothematic work whose basic impulses are musical rather than programmatic. The author also demonstrates similarities between this method and Schoenberg's serial technique, both being musical projections of a fundamental series. Music examples include a chart to show the different transformations of the basic motive. Bibliography.

555. Tammaro, Ferruccio. "Sibelius e il silenzio di *Tàpiola*" [Sibelius and the Silence of *Tapiola*]. *Rivista italiana di musicologia* 12 (1977): 100–29.

An insightful examination of Sibelius's last tone poem for clues into the "silence of Järvenpää," the long, mostly fallow period at the end of Sibelius's life. Tammaro finds *Tapiola* to be the "music of silence," its opening motive (the single music example) the embodiment of stasis. He argues that with this great work the composer created a way of contemplating nature that transcends the nationalistic and romantic, immersing himself in an inner sound world that symbolized his real withdrawal.

556. Whittall, Arnold. "Sibelius' Eighth Symphony." *Music Review* 25 (1964): 239–40.

Viewing *Tapiola* as Sibelius's true Eighth Symphony, Whittall believes the tone poem portrays the inability to find alternatives, either musical or psychological. He chillingly describes this, Sibelius's last word on symphonic form, as "a musical death wish of formidable effectiveness."

6. SYMPHONIES

General Studies

See also no. 372

557. Abraham, Gerald. "The Symphonies." In *The Music of Sibelius*, 14–37. Edited by Gerald Abraham. New York: Norton, 1947. ML410.S54A5

A movement-by-movement consideration of each of the seven symphonies, using analytical concepts of such British writers as Cecil Gray and Donald Francis Tovey. Abraham emphasizes the importance of Alexander Borodin, whom he believed to have been of signal influence on Sibelius's early works, and stressed the simplicity of Symphony no. 5. The numerous music examples illustrating the discussion were unfortunately placed at the back of the volume, undoubtedly owing to cost-cutting measures caused by the war.

For a response to the assessment of Symphony no. 5, see no. 629.

558. Andersson, Otto. "Jean Sibelius och hans symfonier" [Jean Sibelius and His Symphonies]. *Tidning för musik* 1 (1910–1911): 155–60.

A brief, somewhat romanticized, biographical background followed by a review of the four symphonies Sibelius had composed at the time of writing. A number of Andersson's analytical points are taken from other writers, including Georg Göhler (no. 295) and Karl Flodin. Andersson endorses the view that Sibelius's music is neither German, French, nor Nordic but distinctly his own and thus fully representative of Finland.

559. Ballantine, Christopher. "A Revaluation of Sibelius' Symphonies." In *Music and Its Social Meanings*, 134–96. New York: Gordon and Breach Science Publishers, 1984. ML3795.B28 1984 ISBN 0-677-06050-5

Hegelian dialectic, imperialism, and Finland's political crises form the background for an evaluation of Sibelius's symphonic achievement and for explaining the mystery of Symphony no. 8. Music examples and a select bibliography.

Rev.: *Music Review* 46 (1985): 212–14 (mentioning Sibelius); *British Journal of Music Education* 4 (1987): 94–95.

560. Ballantine, Christopher John. "Tradition and Innovation in the Twentieth Century Symphony." Ph.D. diss., Cambridge University, 1971. vi, 350 p.

A study of trends in the genre using a phenomenological, or subjective, approach. Beginning with the rise of the symphony in the eighteenth century, the author frames his study with Mahler at the outset and serialists at the end, including selected British, Russian, and American symphonists along the way. Most of his third chapter, entitled "From Expansion to Integration: The Subjective Drama, I," is devoted to Sibelius (see pp. 95–118). After commenting on Symphony no. 7, which is characterized as giving "rise to a continually evolving monism" and viewed as Sibelius's endpoint, Ballantine turns to each of the remaining six symphonies and analyzes how the composer resolved the question of "dualism or conflict." The arguments are refined in the author's book on the symphony (no. 561). Bibliography but no music examples.

561. Ballantine, Christopher. *Twentieth Century Symphony*. London: Dennis Dobson, 1983. 223 p. ML1255.B27 1983 ISBN 0-234-72042-5

A theoretical examination of the twentieth-century symphony based on the genre's relationship to its past and influenced by the decision to include only those works actually called symphony and those that exhibit a large-scale exploration of dualism. Ballantine discusses all the Sibelius symphonies except the first (the only one composed before the twentieth century), demonstrating in the process the various ways in which Sibelius redefined traditional symphonic conflict.

Rev.: *Tempo* 148 (1984): 51.

562. Coad, Philip. "Bruckner and Sibelius." Ph.D. diss., Queens' College, Cambridge, England, 1985. 315, [2] p. ML410.S54C62 1985a

An expansive study of the musical relationship between two great symphonists that illustrates how Sibelius gradually transformed and assimilated ideas he learned from Bruckner's music into his own highly personal style. A range of works is examined, from *En saga* to the last orchestral compositions.

563. Coad, Philip. "Sibelius." In *A Companion to the Symphony*, 335–50. Edited by Robert Layton. London: Simon & Schuster, 1993. ML1255.C66 1993 ISBN 0-671-71014-1

A survey of the seven symphonies that emphasizes Sibelius's individuality. There is comparison and contrast with Tchaikovsky and speculation on reasons for the failure of the Eighth Symphony to appear. Music examples.

564. Collins, M. Stuart. "The Orchestral Music of Sibelius." Ph.D. diss., University of Leeds, 1973. Vol. 1, text, 473 p.; vol. 2, music examples, 430 p.

This dissertation is the only study other than Tawaststjerna's biography to explore in detail all of Sibelius's published orchestral music, from the symphonies and tone poems to the accompanied violin works and theater music. Taking the works in chronological order, Collins considers their orchestral coloring, pace, tonality, and resulting formal designs. His conclusions, which are diametrically opposed to those of such writers as Haas and Murtomäki (see nos. 445, 531, 553, and 603), suggest that in Sibelius's mind there was a clear distinction between symphony and tone poem. An added feature is a chapter entitled "Sibelius and Finnish Music," in which the author demonstrates how certain melodic and rhythmic characteristics in Sibelius's music may have been inspired by inflections of spoken Finnish or by Finnish folksong.

565. Cuyler, Louise. *The Symphony*. New York: Harcourt Brace, Jovanovich, 1973. x, 236 p. Pp. 161–66. ML1255.C9 ISBN 0-15-585076-8

By presenting Sibelius with Tchaikovsky, Dvořák, and Ives, the author places the composer squarely and solely within a nationalist context. Some cursory remarks about the seven symphonies are followed by a descriptive treatment of Symphony no. 4. Two brief music examples. A second edition, brought out in 1995, appeared too late to be included here.

566. Gerschefski, Peter Edwin. "The Thematic, Temporal, and Dynamic Processes in the Symphonies of Jean Sibelius." Ph.D. diss., Florida State University, 1962. v, 163 p. MT130.S5G47

Although the analyses have been superseded, this volume is notable for being the first, and for many years the only, dissertation in the United States on Sibelius. It was written by the son of Edwin Gerschefski (1909–1992), pianist and composer who studied in New York with Joseph Schillinger, the teacher of George Gershwin, Glenn Miller, and Tommy Dorsey. Edwin Gerschefski later became head of the Department of Music at the University of Georgia. It was he who engaged Jean Réti-Forbes on the faculty, the pianist and music historian through whom the Olin Downes papers, containing precious letters from Sibelius, were acquired by the University of Georgia in 1965.

567. Gray, Cecil. *Sibelius: The Symphonies*. The Musical Pilgrim. London: Oxford University Press, Humphrey Milford, 1935. 77 p. Reprint. Freeport, N.Y.: Books for Libraries Press, 1970. MT130.S5G7 1970 ISBN 0-8369-5283-9. Translated into Finnish by Jussi Jalas as *Sibeliuksen sinfoniat* (Helsinki: Kustannustalo, 1945).

More detailed comments about each of the seven symphonies, and with the benefit of music examples, than Gray had provided in his biography *Sibelius* (no. 156) published four years earlier. There are many references to the favorite analytical tool applied to Sibelius's music by the English during these years, the "thematic germ." Jalas's translation adds ideas of the conductor's own. Added too are photographs of a stoney-faced Sibelius and a page from Symphony no. 3.

568. Herbage, Julian. "Jean Sibelius." In *The Symphony*, 326–58. Edited by Ralph Hill. Harmondsworth, England: Penguin, 1958. MT125.S95 1958

A descriptive discussion of Sibelius's symphonies that emphasizes the idea of "coalescing fragments," the concept much in vogue among Sibelius enthusiasts around the middle of the century. The music examples, which are largely brief thematic quotations, are set at the end of the chapter. Herbage (1904–1976) belonged to the same circle as Cecil Gray and Constant Lambert and, from 1944 until 1973, produced with his wife, Anna Instone, the world-famous BBC program, "Music Magazine," on which he hosted many speakers about Sibelius.

569. Howell, Timothy B. *Jean Sibelius: Progressive Techniques in the Symphonies and Tone Poems*. New York: Garland, 1989. 288 p. ML410.S54H7 1989 ISBN 0-8240-2010-3

A dissertation, Howell's study offers an analytical perspective on the symphonies and tone poems that calls into question the widely held notion of Sibelius as a twentieth-century reactionary. He demonstrates instead how the composer formulated his own, highly original, solutions to issues in composition, with graphic analyses that are based in Schenkerian and pitch-class theories. Part I is devoted to the symphonies, with nos. 4 and 7 dealt with fully. In Part II Howell discusses the tone poems and their relationships to the symphonies. There are analytical diagrams and a short bibliography. The book lacks an index, so in order not to miss some of the several substantial discussions of a work scattered in different places, the reader must be sure to examine the entire volume.

Rev.: *Music & Letters* 73 (1992): 494.

570. Ingman, Olavi. "Sonaattimuoto Sibeliuksen sinfonioissa" [Sonata Form in Sibelius's Symphonies]. *Suomen musiikin vuosikirja 1964–65*. Helsinki: Otava, 1965, 19–34. With English summary.

A consideration of the composer's often debated treatment of sonata form, highly influenced by the analytical theories of Ilmari Krohn. Ingman believed that Sibelius followed the dynamic structural formula of sonata form quite logically until the Fifth Symphony, in the first movement of which he made a radical change. He argues that the sonata form of the Sixth Symphony's first movement is obscured by the Dorian mode, while in the Seventh Symphony, the formula is abandoned altogether.

571. Jalas, Jussi. *Kirjoituksia Sibeliuksen sinfonioista: Sinfonian eettinen pakko* [Writings on Sibelius's Symphonies: The Ethical Necessity of the Symphony (Publisher's translation)]. Helsinki: Fazer, 1988. 132 p. MT92.S63J3 1988 ISBN 951-757-163-1

Not long before his death, Jussi Jalas, husband of Sibelius's daughter Margareta, a one-time student of Ilmari Krohn, and a prominent Finnish conductor, published these writings about Sibelius symphonies in which he included chapters on *Kullervo*, the *Lemminkäinen Legends*, *Tapiola*, and the Concerto for Violin. Jalas invokes the golden mean as the basis for his analyses and uses charts to show the sections of each work. Numerous music examples are beautifully reproduced as are photographs, paintings of Sibelius (in black and white), and music facsimiles. Along with his special view of the music there are two chapters on Sibelius interpreters Robert Kajanus and Georg Schnéevoigt.

Rev.: *Finnish Music Quarterly*, 1989, no. 1: 51; *Rondo*, April 4, 1989: 51.

572. Jalas, Jussi. "Sibelius's Symphonies and the Golden Section." In *Nombre d'or et musique*, 117–20. Frankfurt-am-Main: Lang, 1988. Originally appeared as "Sibeliuksen sinfoniat ja 'Kultainen leikkaus'." *Uusi musiikkilehti*, 1955, no. 9: 17–19.

An English-language version of the idea repeatedly espoused by conductor Jalas: that the structure of Sibelius's symphonies demonstrates the *section aurea*, the golden mean. See no. 571 for the author's more expansive discussion of the idea.

573. Jordan, Alan T. "Harmonic Style in Selected Sibelius Symphonies." Ph.D. diss., Indiana University, 1984. xvii, 219 p. MT130.S5J671 1984a

A description of the harmonic style and tonal structures in Symphonies no. 1, 4, and 7, chosen because they range across Sibelius's creative life. The study, which the author describes as one of "pitch function in late and post-romantic music," uses Schenkerian ideas, reflected in graphs and terminology. There is a useful discussion of Sibelius's use of pedal point, detailed investigation of each movement with harmonic sketch of the selected symphonies, and numerous music examples. The author concludes that the role of functional harmony, the most common type of organization, remains the same throughout these three works and that a preference is shown for weakly defined tonal centers, including chords and tonalities related by a third.

574. Krohn, Ilmari. *Der Formenbau in der Symphonien von Jean Sibelius* [The Formal Construction in the Symphonies of Jean Sibelius]. Annales Academiae Scientiarum Fennicae. Series B, vol. 49. Helsinki: Suomalainen Tiedeakatemia, 1942. 218 p. ML410.S54K75F5 1942

Based on a set of idiosyncratic theories involving rhythm and phrase structure and their contribution to form, Ilmari Krohn, Finnish musicologist, composer, and one-time rival of Sibelius for a university position, analyzed the seven symphonies in such a way as to derive bar and strophic designs as well as the more conventional sonata and rondo structures. No music examples but analytical tables provide outlines for every movement of every symphony.

575. Krohn, Ilmari. *Der Stimmungsgehalt der Symphonien von Jean Sibelius* [The Atmospheric Content of the Symphonies of Jean Sibelius]. Annales Academiae Scientiarum Fennicae, Ser. B, vols. 57

and 58. Helsinki: Suomalainen Tiedeakatemia, 1945 and 1946. 2 vols. 338 p. and 437 p.

While in an earlier study (no. 574) Krohn had attempted to show the rhythmic unity of even the smallest idea in Sibelius's music, here he takes into account the larger picture in which rhythm, motive, and tonality interact. Krohn's study has acquired a certain notoriety for his inventive "Musical Visions" attached to each symphony (Symphony no. 1, for instance, is presented as "The Tragedy of Kullervo") with descriptions that threaten to turn the symphonies into tone poems and for the attempt to make Sibelius the heir to Wagner: Krohn provides a table of imaginative leitmotives (*Vaterlandsmotiv*, *Blütenmotiv*, *Funkenmotiv*, etc.) for each work. These constitute the only music examples. Krohn's symbolic ideas are based on Arnold Schering's theories of the symbolic interpretation of music, but without reference to the earlier author. For an argument on the value of Krohn's interpretation, see no. 467, pp. 71–73.

Rev.: For a sharp criticism of this work together with the author's response, see A. O. Väisänen, "Sibelius tutkimus-ongelmana," *Valvoja* 71 (1951): 60 (annotated as no. 7), and Krohn, "Sibeliuksen sinfoniojen tulkinta" [The Interpretation of Sibelius's Symphonies], *Valvoja* 71 (1951): 175–78.

576. Lambert, Constant. "The Symphonies of Sibelius." *The Dominant* [published in the U.S. as *The Gamut*] 2 (May/June 1929): 14–17.

A performance of Symphony no. 3 by the British Women's Symphony Orchestra provided this opportunity for Lambert to consider the symphonies as a whole and nos. 3 and 4 in particular. He finds in the former a revelation of the composer's real self; in the latter, his greatest achievement. Lambert stresses Sibelius's innovations of structure over innovations of façade, showing that true originality has to do with thought rather than vocabulary, and describes him as both original and one of the few inspiring figures in contemporary music.

577. Mann, Tor. *Symfonier 1–8: Partituranalyser* [Symphonies 1–8: Score Analyses]. Edited by Siegfried Naumann. 93 p. Stockholm: Kungliga Musikaliska Akademien, 1994. ISBN 91-85428-88-4. Analyses of Symphonies no. 1 and 2 were originally published separately; see nos. 600 and 605.

Because of Sibelius's often careless notation, the work of his conductors has been magnified. In an effort to achieve the composer's *klangvision*, Mann (1894–1974), an experienced Swedish conductor and *orkesterpraktikern* who was also Sibelius's personal friend, provided a commentary on matters of interpretation. Along with questions of instrumentation, dynamics, and tempi, Mann includes the occasional remark from Sibelius regarding a sound ideal. Mann intended to publish commentaries for each of the symphonies but died before completing his work, and the project was completed by Siegfried Naumann. The number of symphonies mentioned in the title is not in error: for Symphony no. 8, Naumann has assembled several letters, a concert announcement, and a sketch said to be from the Eighth Symphony.

578. Meyer, Alfred H. "Sibelius: Symphonist." *Musical Quarterly* 22 (1936): 68–86.

With a photograph of the completely bald composer by Ivar Helander, this otherwise flattering essay introduces Sibelius's music by way of examples from the seven symphonies. The author considers Sibelius's treatment of melody, rhythm, and harmony, and his ability to create the imposing out of the seemingly insignificant. Perhaps the article's chief interest today lies in its appearance in the respected *Musical Quarterly*, suggesting that in 1936 Sibelius enjoyed a measure of scholarly interest among Americans that later evaporated.

579. Murtomäki, Veijo. "Sibeliuksen sinfoniat reseptiohistorian ja klassisromanttisen perinteen valossa" [Sibelius's Symphonies in the Light of Reception History and the Classic-Romantic Tradition]. *Musiikki* 20 (1990): 5–11.

An essay arguing that, despite widely differing critical reactions, Sibelius's symphonies, like Beethoven's, continue to advance the formal unity of symphonic thought from one work to the next, a basis on which the author believes that Sibelius may well be considered history's most important symphonist.

580. Murtomäki, Veijo. "Sibelius Symphoniste" [Sibelius the Symphonist]. *Finnish Music Quarterly, Numéro special en français*, 1990: 11–22.

A review of the seven symphonies in light of the genre's history. Full-page illustrations, including a manuscript page from Symphony no. 7 sure to strike terror into the heart of the most intrepid musicologist.

581. Murtomäki, Veijo. *Symphonic Unity: The Development of Formal Thinking in the Symphonies of Sibelius.* Studia musicologica Universitatis Helsingiensis 5. Translated by Henry Bacon in cooperation with the author. Helsinki: Helsinki University, 1993. 339 p. ML410.S54M913 1993 ISBN 951-45-6406-5. The author's dissertation, the work originally appeared in Finnish as *Sinfoninen ykseys: Muotoajattelun kehitys Sibeliuksen sinfonioissa.* Helsinki: Sibelius-Akatemia. Musiikin Tutkimuslaitos, 1990. 248 + 52 p. ISBN 951-95540-6-8

A detailed study of each of Sibelius's symphonies using Schenkerian analysis. The emphasis on such traditional elements as tonality and form rather than on the more "progressive" features of tone color and texture was prompted by the author's larger goal: to demonstrate Sibelius's crucial position in the development of symphonic music after Beethoven. Music examples and useful bibliography.

Rev.: *Musiikkitiede* 2 (1990): 210–13; *Finnish Music Quarterly*, 1991, no. 1: 64–65. For a discussion between the author and Finnish critic and musicologist Tomi Mäkelä concerning the ideas in this book, see "Keskustelua sinfonisesta ykseydestä ja muotoajattelun kehityksestä Sibeliuksen sinfonioissa: Veijo Murtomäki ja Tomi Mäkelä [A Conversation About Symphonic

Unity and Formal Development in Sibelius's Symphonies: Veijo Murtomäki and Tomi Mäkelä]. *Musiikki* 21 (1991): 79–91.

582. Parmet, Simon. *Sibelius symfonier: en studie i musikförståelse* [Sibelius's Symphonies: A Study in Musical Understanding]. Helsingfors: Söderström & Co., 1955. 145 p. MT130.S5P3

Translated into Finnish by Margareta Jalas as *Sibeliuksen sinfoniat: ajatuksia musiikin tulkinnasta* (Helsinki: Otava, 1955), with an added poem, *Oodi Jean Sibeliukselle* [Ode to Jean Sibelius] written by Elmer Diktonius on December 16, 1940. Translated into English by Kingsley A. Hart as *The Symphonies of Sibelius: A Study in Musical Appreciation* (London: Cassell, 1959). 169 pp.

Parmet and his brother Moses Pergament were both conductors of Russian birth. While Moses settled in Sweden, Simon made his home in Finland where he became well known as an interpreter of Sibelius's orchestral music. Conversations with Sibelius prompted this book, whose tone is that of a reverential paean to a contemporary master. However, the analyses are shaped by Parmet's experiences as a conductor, with many observations about accents, dynamics, and tempi, and by his conviction that Sibelius's melodies owe their characteristic patterns to the structure of the Finnish language. Along with numerous music examples and a portrait of Sibelius, several concert programs are reproduced together with a facsimile of a letter from the composer to the author.

583. Pike, Lionel. *Beethoven, Sibelius, and the 'Profound Logic': Studies in Symphonic Analysis*. London: Athlone, 1978. viii, 240 p. MT125.P55 ISBN 0-485-11178-0

Beethoven's compositional process provides the point of departure for Pike's analyses of Sibelius's symphonies, and Beethoven is a reference point throughout the book as Pike studiously analyzes rhythmic elements such as pace and diminution and painstakingly describes classical tonality. A suggested link between Beethoven and Sibelius is the Fourth Symphony of

Bruckner, which is also analyzed here. Handsomely produced music examples and a short bibliography.

Rev.: *Music Review* 42 (1981): 145–47; *Nuova rivista musicale italiana* 14 (1980): 432–34.

584. Pylkkänen, Tauno. "Piirteitä Jean Sibeliuksen sinfonisesta tuotannosta" [Features of Jean Sibelius's Symphonic Production]. *Suomalainen Suomi*, 1943: 394–97.

Short, reverent survey of the seven symphonies for a cultural-political journal in which the author finds Sibelius's development to have been steady and to have preserved the Finnish national spirit like a red thread. While the symphonies rightly belong to the world, Pylkkänen says that Finns especially will find the works very close to their hearts.

585. Roiha, Eino. *Die Symphonien von Jean Sibelius: Eine formanalytische Studie* [The Symphonies of Jean Sibelius: A Form-Analytical Study]. Jyväskylä: 1941. 141 p.

A dissertation written under the direction of Ilmari Krohn, Roiha's study applies his teacher's unusual method of rhythmic and formal analysis to each of the symphonies. Although this analytical system is generally disregarded today, Roiha's work has the distinction of being the first Finnish dissertation on Sibelius. His numerous tables show types of phrases within the symphonies and outline the formal designs of every movement. Music examples illustrate the rhythmic theories. Short but interesting bibliography.

586. Salmenhaara, Erkki. "Sibelius: Die Entwicklung des Symphonikers" [Sibelius: The Development of a Symphonist]. *Österreichische Musikzeitung* 20 (1965): 148–53.

A highly regarded Finnish composer and scholar reviews Sibelius's musical development in light of issues relevant at the turn of the century, dwelling particularly on the importance of Mahler and Wagner. Reproduced are a program of the first performance of Symphony no. 7, a page from the autograph of

Symphony no. 6, and a drawing by Sibelius that appeared with one of his youthful works.

587. Simpson, Robert. *Sibelius and Nielsen: A Centenary Essay.* London: BBC, 1965. 40 p. ML390.S595S5. The revised essay appears as a chapter in the author's *Carl Nielsen: Symphonist.* London: Kahn & Averill; New York: Taplinger, 1979, 1986. ML410.N625 ISBN 0-8008-1261-1

A distinguished symphonist himself, Robert Simpson considers Sibelius's seven symphonies in the context of the genre's history, the reaction against romanticism, and the Northern symphonist Carl Nielsen, born the same year as Sibelius. Refreshingly, Simpson goes beyond thematic analysis to consider the underlying problem of movement and to elaborate upon the idea broached by Tovey, namely, that Sibelius reconciled Wagnerian dramatic pace with the cumulative energy of the sonata principle.

588. Sundberg, Gunnar. "Der Begriff Klassizität in den Symphonien von Jean Sibelius" [The Concept of Classic in the Symphonies of Jean Sibelius]. Ph.D. diss., University of Vienna, 1987. 176 p.

Defining "classicism" in its broadest sense, Sundberg finds in each of the seven symphonies different aspects of Sibelius's classicism. He characterizes no. 1 as "Late Romantic Classicism," no. 2 as "Epic Classicism," no. 3 as "Youthful Classicism," no. 4 as "Progressive Classicism," no. 5 as "New Classicism," no. 6 as "Modal Classicism," and no. 7 as "Tonal Classicism." The author concludes that Sibelius achieved a synthesis of Viennese Classicism, Tudor English music, and ideas found in works of Busoni and certain symphonists from Bruckner to Nielsen. Music examples and bibliography.

589. Tammaro, Ferruccio. *Le sinfonie di Jean Sibelius* [The Symphonies of Jean Sibelius]. Torino: G. Giappichelli, 1982. 210 p. ML410.S54T23 1982

The author, who later completed a very useful biography about Sibelius (no. 173), devotes a chapter to each of the seven symphonies. He begins, however, with a chapter on the symphony after Beethoven followed by another entitled "The National School," in which he examines the situation confronting Sibelius as a Finnish composer in Finland and as a Finnish composer, especially of symphonies, in Europe. Particularly valuable is the consideration given the composer's visits to Italy, illuminated by quotations from letters to Aino. Although difficult to obtain, this volume is well worth the effort expended, because a good portion of the material quoted from letters and from Sibelius's diary has not appeared in any other published source. The use of these materials together with Tammaro's musical discussion from the perspective of Sibelius as a symphonist who underwent a metamorphosis from late-romantic nationalist to a master of the abstract make his study an important contribution to the Sibelius literature.

590. Truscott, Harold. "Jean Sibelius." In *The Symphony*. Vol. 2, *Elgar to the Present Day*, 80–103. Edited by Robert Simpson. Harmondsworth, England: Penguin Books, 1967. 2 vols. MT125.S54

Truscott's analytical discussion appears as one chapter in a two-volume survey of the symphony from Haydn through composers of the 1950s. *Kullervo* is briefly mentioned as are selected tone poems. The description of the symphonies culminates with no. 4, which the author considers Sibelius's greatest. Music examples.

591. Vestdijk, Simon. *De symfonieën van Jean Sibelius* [The Symphonies of Jean Sibelius]. Amsterdam: De Bezige Bij; 's Gravenhage-Rotterdam: Nijgh & Van Ditmar, 1962. 262 p. MT130.S56V58

A three-part study of the symphonies that begins with biographical considerations, briefly discussing the composer in England, in Finland, and vis-à-vis such composers as Wagner and Bruckner; continues with Sibelius's handling of musical elements, from melody and rhythm through timbre and expression; and concludes with systematic discussion of the seven symphonies, to which the author, a prolific Dutch novelist with a great interest in music, brings an individual interpretation. The symphonies' principal themes are catalogued at the end of the book.

Rev.: *Suomen musiikin vuosikirja 1962–63*. Helsinki: Otava, 1963, 60–64.

Studies of Individual Works

Kullervo

See also nos. 203, 389

592. [Unsigned]. "Finnish Through and Through: *Kullervo* by Jean Sibelius." *Finnish Music Quarterly*, 1992, no. 2: 3.

Prompted by the 100th anniversary of *Kullervo*'s premiere April 28, 1892, the *Quarterly* here reproduces the original advertisement for the work from the newspaper *Päivälehti* (now *Helsingin Sanomat*) together with translations of excerpts from reviews published in the same source.

593. Kozenova, Irina. "Näkökulma Sibeliuksen Kullervoon" [A Look Into Sibelius's *Kullervo*]. Translated into Finnish from Estonian. *Musiikkitiede* 3 (1991): 97–127.

Beginning with Kullervo's story as portrayed in the *Kalevala*, the author considers the stylistic influences of such composers as Wagner and Bruckner and examines the structure by orchestral and then choral movements. There is also discussion of the composition's importance for Sibelius's later creativity.

594. Matter, Jean. "Kullervo ou comment naît un grand musicien" [*Kullervo*, or How a Great Musician Is Born]. *Schweizerische Musikzeitung/Revue musicale suisse* 107 (1967): 343–53.

A quite detailed, movement-by-movement description of *Kullervo*, mentioning orchestration, modulations, meters, and even dynamic changes at different rehearsal numbers in the score. A table of 24 music examples illustrates selected themes. Matter views *Kullervo* as a hybrid of symphony and symphonic poem. His larger message is that through this work, we witness the birth of Finnish music as well as the birth of a great composer giving voice to his people.

595. Ranta, Juho. "Jean Sibeliuksen 'Kullervo-Sinfonian' esitys, v. 1892: Vanhan miehen muistelmia" [The Performance of Jean Sibelius's 'Kullervo Symphony,' in the Year 1892: An Old Man's Memories]. *Musiikkitieto*, December 1933: 140–41.

A personal account of *Kullervo*'s historic premiere by a member of its chorus. Ranta, father of composer Sulho Ranta, recalls the soloists, the language of the rehearsals (German), and the powerful effect that Sibelius's convincing setting of the Finnish language had upon him as a Finn. Acknowledging that he may have romanticized his memories, he longs for Sibelius to release the work that it might at least be heard on radio.

596. Tarasti, Eero. *Myth and Music: A Semiotic Approach to the Aesthetics of Myth in Music, Especially That of Wagner, Sibelius and Stravinsky*. Acta musicologica Fennica 11. Helsinki: Suomen Musiikkitieteellinen Seura, 1978. 364 p. Another edition: The Hague: Mouton, 1979. ML3849.T17 1979 ISBN 90-279-7918-9. Appeared in Finnish as *Myytti ja musiikki: semioottinen tutkimus myytin estetiikasta* (Helsinki: Gaudeamus, 1994).

The first analysis of Sibelius's music using semiotics, the theory of signs and symbolism, with instructive comparisons of *Kullervo* to Wagner's *Siegfried* and Stravinsky's *Oedipus Rex*.

Rev.: *Dansk Musik Tidsskrift* 55 (1980): 84–85; *International Review of the Aesthetics and Sociology of Music* 11 (1980): 262–65; *Music Analysis* 3 (1984): 208–14; *Music Review* 44 (1983): 310–13. *Semiotica* 30 (1980): 345–57.

597. Tarasti, Eero. "Sibeliuksen Kullervo-sinfoniasta" [About Sibelius's Kullervo Symphony]. *Musiikki* 7 (1977): 1–29.

The importance of myth as a programmatic basis for musical composition together with the author's interest in semiotics form the point of departure for this discussion of *Kullervo*. A prospectus for the author's larger study, the final version has appeared in English as *Myth and Music*; see no. 596.

598. Väisänen, A. O. "Sibeliuksen Kullervo-sinfonian valta-aiheet" [The Main Themes in Sibelius's *Kullervo* Symphony]. *Kalevalaseuran vuosikirja* 33 (1953): 193–201.

A leading folk music scholar discusses main themes from each movement of *Kullervo* with comparisons to Finnish folk material, illustrated with music examples. At the time the article appeared, *Kullervo* was unpublished, unrecorded, and unavailable to the public.

Symphony no. 1

599. Dahlström, Fabian. "Eräs Sibeliuksen ensimmäisen sinfonian käsikirjoitus" [A Certain Manuscript of Sibelius's First Symphony]. *Musiikki* 8 (1978): 61–78.

Beginning with a chronology of events in the creation and early performances of Symphony no. 1, Dahlström examines the provenance of the manuscript in the possession of the Sibelius Museum and discusses differences between it and the version printed by Breitkopf & Härtel in 1902. There are music examples, including ten measures in facsimile from the manuscript.

600. Mann, Tor. *Partiturstudier: Jean Sibelius, Symfoni nr 1 e-moll, opus 39* [Score Studies: Jean Sibelius, Symphony no. 1 in E minor, op. 39]. Edited by Siegfried Naumann. Publikationer utgivna av Kungliga Musikaliska Akademien, vol. 12. Stockholm[?]: Nordiska Musikförlaget[?], 1974. MT130.S56M281

See no. 577 for annotation.

601. Normet, Leo. "Uusi ja vanha Sibeliuksen ensimmäisessä ja toisessa sinfoniassa" [Old and New in Sibelius's First and Second Symphonies]. *Suomen musiikin vuosikirja 1964–65*. Helsinki: Otava, 1965, 52–66. Translated from Estonian by Irja Harmas, with English summary.

An Estonian scholar avidly interested in the music of Sibelius, Normet discusses how Sibelius handles traditional musical elements in distinctly individual ways, from his frequent use of the diminished seventh chord, upon which he builds entire episodes, to employment of the whole-tone scale and the interval of the augmented fourth, to the hypnotic use of ostinato, pedal tones, and progressions. While these elements can be traced to earlier composers (Tchaikovsky) or practices (the *Kalevala* singers), Sibelius, rather than responding to outside influences, has employed them in his own way. The author also discusses the composer's motive technique in Symphony no. 2, which he finds to be based upon two "germ motives." In expounding upon the germ motive theory, he draws parallels between Sibelius's motive technique and two widely different repertoires: the manner of singing epic narratives from the *Kalevala* and the twelve-tone technique.

Symphony no. 2

See also no. 601

602. Goddard, Scott. "Sibelius's Second Symphony." *Music & Letters* 12 (1931): 156–63.

An enthusiastic discussion prompted by the Columbia recording of Symphony no. 2. After a description of some of the principal themes, illustrated by way of music examples, the author goes about detecting Sibelius's particular characteristics, including his manner of handling thematic material and his sensitivity to orchestral color.

603. Haas, David. "Sibelius's Second Symphony and the Legacy of Symphonic Lyricism." In *The Sibelius Companion*, 77–96. Edited by Glenda Dawn Goss. Westport, Conn.: Greenwood, 1996. ML410.S54S53 1996 ISBN 0-313-28393-1

Fresh and insightful exploration of the implications of the symphonic poem legacy of Liszt and Tchaikovsky for shaping Sibelius's Symphony no. 2 and one of the most valuable discussions available of this aspect of Sibelius's music. Russian musical aesthetics are also considered in a provocative demonstration of the interrelationship of symphony and symphonic poem at Sibelius's hands.

604. Hopkins, Antony. "Sibelius: Symphony No. 2 in D, Op. 43 (1901)." In *Talking About Symphonies: An Analytical Study of a Number of Well-known Symphonies from Haydn to the Present Day*, 126–38. London: Heinemann, 1961. 157 p. Reprint. 1977. MT125.H668

Written for the general reader. The historical information is no longer completely accurate, yet the discussion is interesting for placing Sibelius in the broad context of symphonic history from Haydn's Symphony no. 86 to Stravinsky's *Symphony in Three Movements*, for the author's explanation of why Sibelius went out of fashion, and for the observation that Liszt's B minor Sonata is the great historical precedent for Sibelius's concept of form.

605. Mann, Tor. *Partiturstudier: Jean Sibelius, Symfoni nr 2 D-dur, opus 43* [Score Studies: Jean Sibelius, Symphony no. 2 in D major, op. 43]. Edited by Siegfried Naumann. Publikationer utgivna av Kungliga Musikaliska Akademien, vol. 12, no. 2. Stockholm: Kungliga musikaliska akademien, 1977. MT130.S56M28

See no. 577 for annotation.

606. Niemann, Walter. "Jean Sibelius und die finnische Musik" [Jean Sibelius and Finnish Music]. *Signale für die musikalische Welt* 62 (1904): 185–91.

Discussion of Symphony no. 2 and *En saga* from the author's perspective on Sibelius as a purely national composer.

607. Oramo, Ilkka. "Motiivi ja muoto Sibeliuksen toisessa sinfoniassa" [Motive and Form in Sibelius's Second Symphony]. *Musiikki* 8 (1978): 1–27.

Analytical discussion emphasizing the intimate relationship of motives and their handling to the larger consideration of overall formal design. Illustrated with numerous music examples.

Symphony no. 3

See also nos. 449, 460

608. Montgomery, Alan Gene. "An Interpretive Guide to Symphony no. 3 by Sibelius." D.Mus. diss., Indiana University, 1977. v, 93 p.

Despite the title, only one chapter of this dissertation is devoted to the interpretation of Symphony no. 3. A short opening introduction is followed by a biographical chapter and a review of works based on secondary sources. Some of this material is no longer accurate in light of today's knowledge about the composer. Chapter III is a close, descriptive analysis of each movement of Symphony no. 3 with emphasis given to conducting issues. The author views the extraordinary last movement as a scherzo complete with trio, which ultimately gives way to a march. Thereafter follows a discussion of Sibelius's "stylistic continuum" in all seven symphonies, including problems of interpretation. Music examples and a bibliography, although the latter should be used with caution since it contains a number of errors.

609. Normet, Leo. "Reunamerkintöja Sibeliuksen III sinfoniasta" [Marginalia About Sibelius's IIId Symphony]. *Suomen musiikin vuosikirja 1966–1967*. Helsinki: Otava, 1967, 75–93. Translated from Estonian by Esmo Ridala, with English summary.

A consideration of Symphony no. 3 against the background of the widespread tendency in the arts to explore both the depths of the psyche and the remote past, trends evident in the first decade of the twentieth century. For the author, Sibelius possessed deep insight into the national psychology and intended to suggest with this symphony the essence of an age rather than a romanticized ideal. The discussion of the composer's handling of ostinato is also related to the national psychology. Normet sees the symphony's second movement as a set of variations, with the melodic element arising from a germ motive, and offers a "dual-form" explanation for the concluding movement. He suggests that critics should refrain from forcing this music into ill-fitting, traditional molds.

Symphony no. 4

See also nos. 260, 394, 413, 449, 530

610. Andersson, Otto. “Sibelius’ fjärde symfoni” [Sibelius’s Fourth Symphony]. *Tidning för musik* 1 (1910–11): 171–73. Reprinted in Andersson, *Studier i musik och folklore I*, 101–03. Skrifter utgivna av Svenska Litteratursällskapet i Finland, no. 408. Åbo: Svenska Litteratursällskapet, 1964. ML304.A53

A defense of Symphony no. 4 published at a time when the work was finding little understanding with audiences or critics, by one of the first persons to understand the symphony’s value. Andersson argues that in this work Sibelius created a fusion of classic, romantic, and modern elements, the ideal, he noted, for music of the future. He followed up the article with a thematic analysis; see no. 611.

611. Andersson, Otto. “Sibelius’ symfoni IV, op. 63” [Sibelius’s Symphony IV, op. 63]. *Tidning för musik* 2 (1911–12): 201–07. Reprinted in Andersson, *Studier i musik och folklore I*, 103–10. Skrifter utgivna av Svenska Litteratursällskapet i Finland, no. 408. Åbo: Svenska Litteratursällskapet, 1964.

A discussion of each movement of Symphony no. 4, giving principal themes and describing their subsequent handling. Andersson finds the individuality of this symphony’s themes more sharply defined that those of any previous work and developed with inspiration and inner logic. An early enthusiast of Symphony no. 4, Andersson predicts that the work will soon be taken to the public’s heart.

612. Bengtsson, Ingmar. “En hermenevtisk dialog som fortsätter . . . ” [“A Hermeneutic Dialogue Which Continues . . . ”]. *Juhlakirja Erik Tawaststjernalle 10.X.1976./Festskrift till Erik Tawaststjerna*, 13–27. Edited by Erkki Salmenhaara. Acta musicologica Fennica 9. Keuruu: Otava, 1976. ML55.T39 1976 ISBN 951-1-04106-1

Although Bengtsson's essay is actually an evaluation of Erik Tawaststjerna's analytical approach to Sibelius's music in his five-volume biography (no. 175), Symphony no. 4 is discussed in some detail, especially the last movement. Bengtsson praises Tawaststjerna's effort to find programmatic meaning in such "absolute" works as the Fourth Symphony (an analysis that he believes is superior in Tawaststjerna's Swedish version of the biography) and favors concentrating on the last movements of such works in order to retrieve their meanings.

613. Carlson, Bengt. "Det personliga uttrycket in Jean Sibelius' musik" [The Personal Expression in Jean Sibelius's Music]. *Nya Argus* 18 (1925): 233–34.

Apologia for Symphony no. 4, which Finnish composer Carlson (1890–1953), a pupil of d'Indy, believes has long stood in the shadow of the two first symphonies and, later, of Symphony no. 5. He sees in Symphony no. 4, as in *Voces intimae*, a deeply private expression, an artistic striving in which Sibelius has taken to heart the Socratic message: Know thyself. The gains from this struggle, he believes, are reflected in Symphony no. 5, over which reposes a calm that marches toward light and clarity.

614. Fontaine, Paul. *Basic Formal Structures in Music*. Englewood Cliffs, N.J.: Prentice-Hall; New York: Appleton-Century-Crofts, 1967. x, 241 p. Pp. 150–62. MT58.F65

Fontaine's theoretical text includes his keyboard reduction of Symphony no. 4's first movement to which he has added analytical comments about motivic relationships and sonata form structure.

615. Hill, William G. "Some Aspects of Form in the Symphonies of Sibelius." *Music Review* 10 (1949): 165–82. An abstract of Hill's study appears under the same title in the *Bulletin of the American Musicological Society*, September 1948: 41.

Despite the general title, it is Symphony no. 4 that is used to illustrate thematic interconnections and to demonstrate the composer's sonata, rondo, and variation forms. Hill's two-fold purpose was to correct erroneous claims in Cecil Gray's analyses of Sibelius symphonies and to establish that Sibelius's forms are actually modifications of traditional designs. Hill initially presented his study before the Midwestern Chapter of the American Musicological Society, May 17–18, 1947, in East Lansing, Michigan, and it is the abstract of that presentation which appears in the Society's *Bulletin*. His is the first lecture about Sibelius known to have taken place at a musicological conference in the United States.

616. Kokkonen, Joonas. "Sibelius's Fourth Symphony." In *Ihminen ja musiikki: Valittuja kirjoituksia, esitelmiä, puheita ja arvosteluja* [Man and Music: Selected Writings, Lectures, Speeches, and Criticisms], 52–60. Edited by Kalevi Aho. Helsinki: Gaudeamus, 1992. ML160.K77 1992 ISBN 951-662-554-1

An examination of the work from the point of view of the tritone by a leading Finnish symphonist. Music examples from all the movements illustrate that the work "grows organically." The full volume of Kokkonen's sayings is annotated as no. 276.

617. Murtomäki, Veijo. "Modernismi ja klassismi Sibeliuksen IV sinfoniassa" [Modernism and Classicism in Sibelius's IVth Symphony]. *Musiikkitiede* 2 (1990): 54–103.

A Schenkerian consideration of certain issues in Symphony no. 4, including "Tritone and Classical Form" with emphasis also on motivic analysis, the problem of the trio in the second movement, "Improvisation as a Form," and finales. Illustrated with musical examples and charts and a useful bibliography. The ideas are more fully developed in the author's dissertation, which has appeared in an English translation; see no. 581.

618. Nielsen, Peter Wang. "Formale og Aestetiske Aspekter i Sibelius' 4. Symfoni" [Formal and Aesthetic Aspects of Sibelius's 4th Symphony]. Århus, Denmark: 1970. 93 p.

Nielsen reviews different formal approaches to analyzing Sibelius's symphonies, beginning with Ilmari Krohn's.

Concentrating on Symphony no. 4, he provides his own analysis illustrated with charts and music examples. He also discusses how different commentators have evaluated Sibelius and addresses the topical issue of form and content. The bibliography contains references to seldom-cited Scandinavian sources.

619. Normet, Leo. "Vielä Sibeliuksen neljännestä" [Still More About Sibelius's Fourth]. *Suomen musiikin vuosikirja 1968–1969*. Helsinki: Otava, 1969, 28–45. Translated from Estonian by Heikki Enqvist with verification by Erkki Salmenhaara. English summary.

Observing that the intensive use of the tritone indicates Symphony no. 4's "tentative step toward Expressionism," Normet, who considers Sibelius too much of an epic composer to have pursued atmosphere and color as ends in themselves, identifies the symphony's two musical protagonists: the perfect fifth and the unstable tritone. He discusses in turn each of the Symphony's four movements from the points of view of formal structure and the role played by the two contending intervals. No music examples but letter diagrams and measure numbers outline the formal schemes.

620. Pennanen, Ainomaija. "The Fourth Symphony: A State of Mind." *Finnish Music Quarterly*, 1990, nos. 3–4: 44–47.

Comments on the structure and interpretation of Symphony no. 4 by three prominent Finnish conductors, Esa-Pekka Salonen, Jukka-Pekka Saraste, and Leif Segerstam.

621. Rubbra, Edmund. "Sibelius's Fourth Symphony." *Musical Times*, February 1934: 127–28.

Thoughtful remarks by a pianist and writer (b. 1901) who, at mid-twentieth century, was one of England's leading symphonists. Illustrated with a few brief music examples.

622. Rydman, Kari. "Sibeliuksen neljännen sinfonian rakenneongelmista" [On The Structural Problems of Sibelius's Fourth Symphony]. *Suomen musiikin vuosikirja 1962–63*. Helsinki: Otava, 1963, 17–32. With Swedish summary.

Believing that traditional analytical methods have led to strange and artificial results where Symphony no. 4 is concerned, Rydman offers an analysis based on the opening motive, its tritone projections, and its Lydian qualities. While the evolution of the "motto motive" can be found in all movements, he finds the first and third movements particularly complicated. There is a discussion of other analytical views, especially those of Cecil Gray and Eino Roiha, with charts and music examples that illustrate the author's method.

623. Similä, Martti. "Studio per practica: tutkielma Sibeliuksen IV sinfoniasta" [Study Through Practice: Essay on Sibelius's IVth Symphony]. *Uusi musiikkilehti*, 1957, no. 6: 9–13, 21.

A movement-by-movement discussion of Symphony no. 4 by an experienced conductor and Sibelius interpreter. The author describes harmonic and dynamic events and illustrates some of the main themes with music examples.

624. Tarasti, Eero. "Aika, avaruus ja aktorit Sibeliuksen 4. sinfoniassa" [Time, Space, and Actors in Sibelius's 4th Symphony]. *Musiikkitiede* 3 (1991): 39–74.

A semiotic analysis of each movement of the Fourth Symphony, in which parallels are drawn to *Parsifal* and "program narratives" are established for every measure in the symphony.

625. Tawaststjerna, Erik. "Sibelius' 4. Sinfonie: Schlussphase und Vollendung" [Sibelius's 4th Symphony: Final Phase and Completion]. *Beiträge zur Musikwissenschaft* 16 (1974): 97–115.

A discussion of the completion of Symphony no. 4 in the light of Sibelius's diary entries, personal letters, and responses to its performance. The author also considers the work's impressionistic and expressionistic features against a background of contemporary artistic and social trends. Essentially the same information may be found in Tawaststjerna's biography (no. 175); see the chapter entitled "Fourth Symphony" in volume 2 of the English translation. Music examples.

626. Tawaststjerna, Erik. "Sibelius vid tiden för fjärde symfonins tillkomst" [Sibelius at the Time of the Creation of the Fourth Symphony]. *Musikrevy* 30 (1975): 116–19.

A description of the composer's activities around the time of the Fourth Symphony, particularly the trips to Göteborg, Berlin, and Riga, giving diary entries and illustrations. The material is taken from the author's biography (no. 175), the chapter entitled "The Fourth Symphony," volume 2 of the English translation. This Swedish-language version, however, has the advantage of preserving the composer's original language in diary entries.

Symphony no. 5

See also no. 613

627. Bisgaard, Lars. "Musikalsk hermeneutik på hierakisk grundlag: Bidrag til en musikalsk faenomenologi, II" [Musical Hermeneutics on a Hierarchical Basis: Contributions to a Musical Phenomenology, II]. *Dansk Årbog for Musikforskning* 17 (1986): 69–92.

This second of a two-part article includes a close look at Sibelius's Symphony no. 5, interpreted as a biological and universal birth process, by means of the author's "cyclic-hierachical" method of musical analysis. The method, based on a hierachical theory of music and incorporating ideas from the Danish composer Per Nørgård (b. 1932) and the Czech-American psychologist Stanislav Grof (b. 1932), is supposed to facilitate interpretation of a formal structure according to ideas of astrology as well as psychology. Music examples, diagrams, and bibliography.

628. Hepokoski, James. *Sibelius: Symphony No. 5*. Cambridge, England: Cambridge University Press, 1993. xi, 107 p. ML410.S54H4 1993 ISBN 0-521-40143-7

Placing Sibelius's Fifth Symphony in the context of early twentieth-century compositional issues, the author uses the composer's diary entries, musical sketches, and revisions together with his own penetrating insights to reveal new dimensions of the work. Hepokoski introduces a fresh analytical perspective into the literature with his concept of "rotational form" and provides new English translations of selected passages from Sibelius's diary based on the quotations in Erik Tawaststjerna's *Jean Sibelius* (no. 175). The last chapter considers different recordings of Symphony no. 5, giving particular attention to divergences of tempos. Music examples.

Rev.: *Music & Letters* 75 (1994): 483–84; *Musical Times* 134 (1993): 709.

629. Jalas, Jussi. "Sibeliuksen V sinfonian jälkiosien orgaanisesta yhteydestä" [About the Organic Connection in the Last Movement of Sibelius's Fifth Symphony]. In *Ihminen musiikin valtakentässä: Juhlakirja Professori Timo Mäkiselle 6.6.1979*, 133–36. Edited by Reijo Pajamo. Jyväskylä Studies in the Arts 11. Jyväskylä: Jyväskylän Yliopisto, 1979. ML55.M2 1979 ISBN 951-678-166-7

Conductor Jalas challenges Gerald Abraham's assertion (in no. 557) that the second movement of Sibelius's Symphony no. 5 is unusually simple, almost naïve. He demonstrates that the essential materials for this symphony's great Finale are in fact contained in its slow movement. No music examples but page and measure numbers from the score are cited.

630. Kauko, Olavi. "Sibelius ja aika" [Sibelius and Time]. In *Kuvastimessa . . . durch einen Spiegel . . . Joonas Kokkonen: Juhlakirja Joonas Kokkoselle 13.11.1981*, 129–35. Edited by Timo Mäkinen, Lassi Nummi, and Timo Teerisuo. Savonlinna: Savonlinnan Kirjapaino Osakeyhtiö, 1981. ISBN 951-95745-1-4

A consideration of temporal relationships in Symphony no. 5 with implications for Golden Section analysis. Music examples.

631. Kuusisto, Taneli. "Ydinmotiivin asema Sibeliuksen V sinfoniassa" [The Position of a Germ Motive in Sibelius's 5th Symphony]. *Rondo*, 1965, no. 6: 10–13.

An attempt to demonstrate that a single motivic idea forms the basis for Symphony no. 5, without, however, using music examples.

632. Nørgård, Per. "Om Sibelius' og Carl Nielsens femte symfonier" [On Sibelius's and Carl Nielsen's Fifth Symphonies]. *Dansk Musiktidsskrift* 40 (1965): 111–13.

Two Fifth Symphonies written so closely in time inevitably invite comparison, and the discussion here, written by an eminent Danish composer, centers on motivic technique in the two works. Whereas Nielsen (whose Fifth Symphony dates from 1921–1922) is described as having explored intervallic alteration (here called *deformationer*), Sibelius (whose Fifth Symphony was begun in 1915) used traditional material in an objective, symmetrical way, which is compared to the atonal structures of Schoenberg and Webern. The author contends that such a view calls for a re-evaluation of Sibelius's status as a national romantic.

633. Tovey, Donald Francis. "Sibelius." In *Essays in Musical Analysis*. Vol. 2, *Symphonies, Variations, and Orchestral Polyphony*, 121–29. London: Oxford University Press, Humphrey Milford, 1935. MT90.T6E8

Tovey's genial analyses of the Third and Fifth Symphonies have influenced Anglo-Saxon writers on both sides of the Atlantic, from William Henderson and Olin Downes to Robert Simpson and Arnold Whittall. Tovey raises the central question of how to transfer the vast movement of Wagnerian music-drama to instrumental music; according to him, Sibelius built a musical scheme out of fragments, subverting the expectations of conventional sonata form in the process. It was Tovey who designated the majestic, slow-moving theme of the Fifth Symphony's last movement as Thor's hammerstrokes. His images return again and again to haunt the literature on Sibelius.

Symphony no. 6

See also no. 497

634. Elliot, J[ohn] H[arold]. "The Sixth Symphony of Sibelius." *Music & Letters* 17 (1936): 234–36; also in *Music and Dance* (1936): 234–36.

An essay (no music examples or documenting notes) mainly devoted to Symphony no. 6, which the author says is not held in the same esteem in England as are other Sibelius symphonies. While touching on the composer's wider reputation and on the nature of the symphonies as a whole, he characterizes Symphony no. 6 as the "most recondite and baffling" and wonders whether it perhaps represents the fundamental Sibelius.

635. Gray, Cecil. *The Sibelius Society [Analytical Notes]*. Vol. 3. *String Quartet, Symphony no. 6*. [N.p.]: The Sibelius Society, n.d. 20 p.

Descriptive notes with music examples printed to accompany the Sibelius recordings issued by Walter Legge's subscription society. The material on Symphony no. 6 is identical to the discussion of the work in Gray's *Sibelius: The Symphonies* (no. 567).

636. Pike, Lionel. "Sibelius' Debt to Renaissance Polyphony." *Music & Letters* 55 (1974): 317–26.

An exploration of counterpoint, modality, and imitation in Sibelius's Symphony no. 6. The author attributes these features to Sibelius's knowledge of Renaissance polyphonic practice and suggests that by using such techniques and through his skillful handling of ambivalences inherent in the Dorian mode, the composer created a new kind of symphonic argument. The discussion is essentially the same as the final chapter of the same author's *Beethoven, Sibelius and the 'Profound Logic'* (no. 583). Music examples.

Symphony no. 7

See also nos. 418, 445

637. Berglund, Paavo. *A Comparative Study of the Printed Score and the Manuscript of the Seventh Symphony of Sibelius*. Acta musica V. Studies published by the Sibelius Museum. Turku: Institute of Musicology, Åbo Akademi, 1970. 67 p. MT130.S5B5

Conductor Berglund, an outstanding interpreter of Sibelius's music, discovered so many discrepancies between the Seventh Symphony's printed score (Wilhelm Hansen, 1925, 1946) and the orchestral parts that he undertook to reconcile the differences by a study of the symphony in manuscript. The results appear here in the form of a measure-by-measure list of corrections and interpretive comments. Two charts address dynamics and *divisi* markings from pages 64 to 68 of the published score.

638. Kujawsky, Eric. "Double-perspective Movements: Formal Ambiguity and Conducting Issues in Orchestral Works by Schoenberg, Sibelius and Carter." D.M.A. diss., Stanford University, 1985. iv, 237 p. ML457.K85 1990

A discussion of Sibelius's Seventh Symphony, Liszt's B minor Sonata, Schoenberg's Chamber Symphony, and Elliott Carter's Concerto for Orchestra, for all of which the author has invented the term "double-perspective movements." He compares these and other similarly constructed movements and offers observations about conducting. Music examples sweep from Beethoven to Webern; there is a short bibliography, but no up-to-date sources on Sibelius.

639. Kilpeläinen, Kari. "Sibelius's Seventh Symphony: An Introduction to the Manuscript and Printed Sources." In *The Sibelius Companion*, 239–272. Edited by Glenda Dawn Goss. Westport, Conn.: Greenwood, 1996. ML410.S54S53 1996 ISBN 0-313-28393-1. An earlier version of the study appeared in Finnish as "Jean Sibeliuksen 7. sinfonian musiikillisista lähteistä ja teoksen synnystä niiden valossa." *Musiikki* 20 (1990): 39–72.

The most closely argued and carefully researched investigation ever made of Symphony no. 7. The author examines the genesis of the work through systematic study of the composer's sketches and drafts, uncovers connections with other works, and offers fresh analytical perspective based on his findings. Fully documented, including many music examples from unpublished sketch material.

640. Murtomäki, Veijo. "Materiaali, muoto ja tonaalisuus Sibeliuksen VII sinfoniassa" [Materials, Form, and Tonality in Sibelius's VIIth Symphony]. *Musiikki* 18 (1988): 23–71.

This discussion, which deals primarily with the Seventh Symphony's form and tonality, is developed and given more fully, in English, in the author's dissertation; see no. 581.

641. Väisälä, Olli. "Sibeliuksen VII sinfonian melodisen aiheiston sukulaisuussuhteista" [On the Family Relationships in the Melody of Sibelius's Seventh Symphony]. *Näkökulmia musiikkiin, SIC 3*, 191–202. Edited by Kari Kurkela. Helsinki: Sibelius Academy, 1990. ML160.N22 1990 ISBN 951-370040-2

A demonstration of the close relationship of the Seventh Symphony's famous trombone theme to other materials in the work. As the "continuously sounding model" in Sibelius's mind, the trombone theme, identified here as the reason for this symphony's existence, embodies the abstract idea that governs the entire composition. The idea is manifest in thematic material as well as in the vision for the different sections. Music examples.

Symphony no. 8

642. Kilpeläinen, Kari. "Vielä hieman Sibeliuksen 8. sinfoniasta" [Still a Little More About Sibelius's Eighth Symphony]. *Synkooppi* 10 (1989): 27–33.

The most careful and up-to-date consideration available of the evidence surrounding the Eighth Symphony. The author provides documentation for many of Sibelius's activities that seem to be connected to the work, from periods of living and presumably working in the Hotel Karelia to receipts for copying and binding, to the composer's own remarks. Although the author points out that the fate and character of the symphony remain a mystery, he has succeeded in identifying what is fact and what is fiction in the puzzle that surrounds the work.

643. Parmet, Simon. "Den åttonde symfonins gåta" [The Riddle of the Eighth Symphony]. *Nya Argus* 50 (1957): 246–48, 262–62. Reprinted in *Con amore: Essäer om musik och mästare* (Helsingfors: Söderström & Co., 1960). Appeared in Finnish as "Kahdeksannen sinfonian

arvoitus," in *Sävelestä sanaan* (Helsinki: Werner Söderström Osakeyhtiö, 1962), pp. 79–93.

Conductor Parmet reviews Sibelius's claims about the Eighth Symphony, mentioning a letter in his possession in which Sibelius speaks of a symphony in three movements, meaning possibly no. 7 or no. 8. He discusses the composer's opposition to the avant-garde, his perfectionism, and his self-criticism, characteristics manifest in the number of works withdrawn. Although the facts surrounding Symphony no. 8 can be found elsewhere, Parmet's article is interesting as the testimony of a musically knowledgeable contemporary on the mystery of this enigmatic work.

644. Tawaststjerna, Erik. "The Fate of the Eighth Symphony." Extract from *Sibelius V*. Translated by Erkki Arni. *Books from Finland* 23 (1989): 104–05.

Erik Tawaststjerna recounts conversations with family members, passages from Sibelius's diary, and extracts from letters in the search for an explanation for the fate of the Eighth Symphony. The material is taken from Volume 5 of the author's Sibelius biography (no. 175), which presently exists only in Finnish. Some of the same information may also be found (in English) in another Tawaststjerna article; see no. 645.

645. Tawaststjerna, Erik. "Sibelius's Eighth Symphony: An Insoluble Mystery." *Finnish Music Quarterly*, 1985, nos. 1–2: 61–70; 1985, nos. 3–4: 92–101.

A two-part article, taken from the author's biography (no. 175), which discusses evidence for the Eighth Symphony from surviving letters, particularly those exchanged between Sibelius, Serge Koussevitzky, and Olin Downes, and quoting a receipt for the copying of some of its pages. The chronology is somewhat misleading, as interviews, letters, and ideas exchanged over the course of years are here compressed in time. The discussion actually begins with *Tapiola*, the circumstances of its commission, and Sibelius's state of mind as he composed and revised the score. Aino Sibelius's story is reported, of how her husband burned a laundry basket of manuscripts during the 1940s, among which was presumably the Eighth Symphony. Illustrated with numerous photographs.

7. MUSIC FOR THE THEATER

See also nos. 134, 366, 534, 671

646. Andersson, Otto. *Jean Sibelius och Svenska Teatern* [Jean Sibelius and the Swedish Theater]. Åbo: Förlaget Bro, 1956. 39 p. Reprinted in *Studier i musik och folklore I*, 87–100. Skrifter utgivna av Svenska Litteratursällskapet i Finland, no. 408. Åbo: Svenska Litteratursällskapet, 1964. ML304.A53

The founder and director of the Sibelius Museum originally delivered these words on December 8, 1955, as a lecture during a celebration at the Swedish Theater. In the essay printed here, Andersson peruses the composer's activities in Helsinki's Swedish Theater, beginning with music for Adolf Paul's play *King Christian II* in 1898. The survey continues through the production of Mikael Lybeck's *The Lizard* (*Ödlan*) in 1910. Not all of the information is correct: Sibelius's *Pan and Echo* (*Pan ja kaiku*), for instance, was not composed for Hoffmansthal's *Electra* as Andersson states.

647. Appelgren, Stig. "Jungfrun i tornet, från karelsk jullek till opera: Tema med variationer av Johannes Häyhä, Rafaël Hertzberg och Jean Sibelius" [*The Maid in the Tower*, From Karelian Christmas Play to Opera: Theme with Variations by Johannes Häyhä, Rafaël Hertzberg and Jean Sibelius]. *Budkavlen* 65 (1986): 72–85.

Examining a Karelian Christmas play as a source for the story of Sibelius's early opera, the author compares a version by Johannes Häyhä, a doctor in Karelia, with the libretto by Sibelius and Hertzberg. He places both versions in the wider context of Northern literary traditions, quotes the libretto of each, includes pictures of the three creators, and supplies a short bibliography rich in sources for folklore research.

648. Aspelin-Haapkylä, Eliel. *Suomalaisen teatterin historia* [History of the Finnish Theater]. 4 vols. Suomalaisen Kirjallisuuden Seura, no. 115. Helsinki: Suomalaisen Kirjallisuuden Seura, 1906–1909. PN2859.F5A8

Scattered references to Sibelius in volume IV of this detailed history mention musical works composed by Sibelius for Finland's National Theater, from *The Origin of Fire* (*Tulen synty*) to *Death* (*Kuolema*). A source useful for establishing a literary and theatrical context during the time when much of Sibelius's incidental music was written and for identifying key figures in Helsinki's musical and theatrical life, of whom the author, whom Sibelius knew personally, was one.

649. Fontaine, Paul. *Basic Formal Structures in Music*, 66–68. Englewood Cliffs, N.J.; New York: Appleton-Century-Crofts, 1967. MT58.F65

A keyboard reduction of "Miranda" from *The Tempest* is offered as an illustration of the expansion of elementary three-part form, A-B-A2-B2-A3.

650. Frenckell, Ester-Margaret von. *ABC för teaterpubliken* [ABC for Theater Audiences]. Helsingfors: Söderström & Co., 1971. 291 p. + illustrations. ISBN 951-52-0023-7

Although a general history, Frenckell's book provides a valuable look into the personalities and activities of a world in which Sibelius was very active. She identifies such personalities as Victor Castegren and Konni Wetzer, theater directors under whom Sibelius conducted, and discusses the folk theater and its connections to Helsinki's Swedish Theater. The bibliography is especially useful for the citation of little-known documents. Well illustrated with a good index.

651. Furuhjelm, Erik. "Sibelius' musik till 'Pelléas och Mélisande'" [Sibelius's Music to *Pelléas and Mélisande*]. *Finsk musikrevy* (April 1905): 147–51.

A rather superficial introduction to Sibelius's incidental music for Maeterlinck's play. Music examples show principal themes.

652. Härkönen, Leo. "Sibeliuksen musiikki Adolf Paul'in näytelmään Kuningas Kristian Toinen" [Sibelius's Music to Adolf Paul's Play King Christian II]. *Musiikkitieto*, 1934, nos. 9–10: 138–40.

A detailed synopsis of Paul's story followed by a description of Sibelius's music.

653. Härkönen, Leo. "Sibeliuksen musiikki Maeterlinck'in näytelmään Pelleas ja Melisande" [Sibelius's Music to Maeterlinck's Play Pelléas and Mélisande]. *Musiikkitieto*, 1933, no. 10: 99–101.

A summary of Maeterlinck's plot, based on a German translation of the play from 1897, and a description of Sibelius's suite arranged from the incidental music. The author issues a call for studies to explain both the historical background and the musical importance of Sibelius's scores.

654. Kilpeläinen, Kari. "Two Sibelius Discoveries." *Fazer Music News*, 1994, no. 8: 2–3.

An article written in conjunction with the first publication of two Sibelius works, *The Lizard* (*Ödlan*) and *Suite for Solo Violin and String Orchestra*, both of which remained in manuscript until the 1990s. Kilpeläinen provides essential background and places the works within the broader context of the composer's oeuvre.

655. Lüchou, Marianne. *Svenska Teatern i Helsingfors: Repertoar, Styrelser och teaterchefer, Konstnärlig personal 1860–1975* [The Swedish Theater in Helsinki: Repertoire, Boards and Theater Directors, Artistic Personnel, 1860–1975]. Helsingfors: Stiftelsen för Svenska Teatern, 1977. 327 p. PN2859.F53H448 ISBN 951-52-0387-2

An illustrated reference book, listing the repertory of the Swedish Theater in Helsinki chronologically, beginning in November of 1860. Also given are producers and directors, leading actors and actresses, and, when music was involved, composers and conductors. Sibelius's connections to this theater began as early as 1898 when he conducted the music to Adolf Paul's play *King Christian II* and continued through the premiere of the work that came to be known as *Finlandia*, performances of *Belshazzar's Feast*, *Pelléas et Mélisande*, and various other compositions. Along with dates and personnel information, there are welcome indices of personal names, titles of plays, the names of guest theater and dance troupes, and illustrations.

656. Ranta, Sulho. "Jean Sibelius ja näyttämön musiikki" [Jean Sibelius and Music for the Stage]. *Uusi musiikkilehti*, 1955, no. 9: 37–39.

Summary review of works written by Sibelius for the theater with five illustrations from various productions, including one showing Sibelius's daughter Ruth Snellman in the ballet pantomime *Scaramouche*.

657. Roiha, Eino. "Sibeliuksen Karelia-sarjan historiallista taustaa" [About the Historical Background of Sibelius's *Karelia Suite*]. *Kalevalaseuran vuosikirja* 33 (1953): 161–69.

Details of the historical origin of one of Sibelius's best-known works. Although the *Karelia Suite* familiar to most listeners today consists of an Overture (op. 10), and an Intermezzo, Ballade, and *Alla marcia* (op. 11), its initial form was quite different. Roiha traces how Sibelius was involved in composing music for seven tableaux depicting scenes from Karelian history, an event sponsored by the Viipuri Student Association as a fund-raising venture in the fall of 1893. He also discusses political and literary aspects important to the whole production, including the participation of such important figures as Larin Paraske, who was brought from Porvoo to sing in the first tableau, and Werner Söderhjelm, Sibelius's friend, who read the prologue.

658. Rosas, John. "Sibelius' musik till skådelspelet Ödlan" [Sibelius's Music to the Play *The Lizard*]. *Suomen musiikin vuosikirja 1960–61*. Helsinki: Otava, 1961, 49–56. With Finnish summary.

Discussion of the incidental music to Mikael Lybeck's play *The Lizard* (*Ödlan*) based on Sibelius's manuscript. For years part of Lybeck's estate, the music manuscript was discovered by Harold E. Johnson in 1957–1958 and acquired by the Sibelius Museum in 1960. Rosas quotes excerpts from it here.

659. Salmenhaara, Erkki. "Jean Sibelius and the *Tempest*." *Finnish Music Quarterly*, 1993, no. 4: 35–41.

Historical background to Sibelius's last work for the stage, together with an evaluation. The article, which is especially valuable for the quotations from contemporary letters, also includes color pictures of the production of *The Tempest* in Savonlinna, Finland, and a short discography.

660. Tammaro, Ferruccio. "Mélisande dai quattro volti" [The Four Faces of Mélisande]. *Nuova rivista musicale italiana* 15 (1981): 95–119.

A comparison of the musical settings of Maurice Maeterlinck's *Pelléas et Mélisande* by Debussy, Schoenberg, Fauré, and Sibelius. Tammaro considers the factors that led four composers of different musical and cultural backgrounds to compose music for the same play. He finds that Debussy and Schoenberg are opposites in aesthetic and artistic expression, while Sibelius and Fauré represent a midpoint between these two poles.

661. Tawaststjerna, Erik. "Sibeliuksen Myrsky-musiikki op. 109" [Sibelius's *Tempest* Music, op. 109]." Translated into Finnish by Erkki Salmenhaara. *Musiikki* 6 (1976): 3–13. Also printed in *Ihminen musiikin valtakentässä: Juhlakirja Professori Timo Mäkiselle 6.6.1979*, 61–68. Edited by Reijo Pajamo. Jyväskylä Studies in the Arts 11. Jyväskylä: Jyväskylän Yliopisto, 1979. ML55.M2 1979 ISBN 951-678-166-7

An essay originally read as a program commentary to a radio broadcast of Sibelius's music to *The Tempest*. There is a general discussion of the background and the musical setting and quotations of parts of Shakespeare's text taken from Paavo Cajander's famous translation into Finnish.

662. Tawaststjerna, Erik. "Sibelius' Finlandia: A Symbol of Press Freedom." Helsinki: n.p., 1971. 12 p. Originally appeared in the *Helsingin Sanomat*.

The author describes the historical and political circumstances surrounding the composition of *Finlandia*, briefly touching on other patriotic works from the same period and mentioning the role of Axel Carpelan in suggesting the title of the work.

8. WORKS FOR VIOLIN

See also nos. 48, 389, 391, 392, 519, 654

Concerto for Violin

663. Bronstein, Raphael. *The Science of Violin Playing*. 2d edition. Neptune, N.J.: Paganiniana Publications, 1981. 253 p. ISBN 0-87666-638-1

A method for the violin whose last chapter presents "technical analyses" of ten complete violin concertos, Sibelius's included (pp. 119–40). Practical and interpretive directions for virtually every measure of the concerto run parallel to the score of the solo violin part edited by Bronstein. Russian born, the editor began performing on the violin at the age of ten, studied with Leopold Auer, and began a teaching career as Auer's assistant. He views the concerto as a succession of pictures ranging from the image of a peacefully swimming swan to the violence of giants hurling rocks and thunderbolts.

664. Kloiber, Rudolf. *Handbuch des Instrumentalkonzerts* [Handbook of Instrumental Concertos]. Wiesbaden: Breitkopf & Härtel, 1973, revised 1983. 2 vols. Vol. II: 209–13. MT125.K599 ISBN 3-7651-0052-8.

A listener's guide to the Violin Concerto, with principal themes from each movement preceded by a short summary of the composer's life and a brief history of the work.

665. Lindgren, Minna. "I've Got Some Lovely Themes for a Violin Concert" [sic]. *Finnish Music Quarterly*, 1990, nos. 3–4: 24–31.

A review of the history of the Concerto and discussion of the musical reasons that led to its revision, which included eliminating an unoriginal rhythmic theme, a cadenza, and many virtuoso elements. The revisions are viewed as being consistent with the attitude of a composer whose relentless self-criticism and tendency toward compression are well known. There is a facsimile of a portion of the letter from which the title comes and two pages showing the cadenza that was later excised. The title is a correct translation of Sibelius's faulty Finnish formulation of the term for concerto.

666. Salmenhaara, Erkki. "The Violin Concerto." In *The Sibelius Companion*, 103–19. Edited by Glenda Dawn Goss. Westport, Conn.: Greenwood, 1996. ML410.S54S53 1996 ISBN 0-313-28393-1. An abbreviated version of this article appears as "Where a Genius Worked," in *Nordic Sounds*, 1991, no. 1: 16–18.

A close look at the history of Sibelius's Violin Concerto, including the composer's personal connections to the instrument; the critical responses to the first performances, especially in Helsinki, with valuable translations of substantial portions of contemporary reviews; and attention given to the nature of and the reasons for the revisions. The author also considers the work's subsequent performance and recording history. Well documented, furnishing corrective details to certain aspects of Sibelius's life and work.

667. Siukonen, Leena. "Sibeliuksen viulukonsertto: muodon ja teemojen rakenteen tarkastelua" [Sibelius's Violin Concerto: An Investigation into Formal and Thematic Structure]. *Musiikki*, 1951, nos. 3–4: 17–20.

An analysis of each of the Concerto's three movements according to the rhythmic and structural theories of Ilmari Krohn. A type of sonata form is outlined for the first movement and rondo forms for the remaining two.

Other Violin Works

668. Ignatius, Anja. "Sibeliuksen viulusävellysten agogiikasta ja dynamiikasta" [Agogics and Dynamics in Sibelius's Violin Compositions]. *Pieni musiikkilehti*, 1965: 16–18.

The first Finnish violinist to record Sibelius's Concerto for Violin (in 1943) offers a performer's perspective on the composer's violin works.

669. Kilpeläinen, Kari. "Two Sibelius Discoveries." *Fazer Music News*, 1994, no. 8: 2–3.

Background to the *Suite for Solo Violin and String Orchestra*, op. 117. For full annotation, see no. 654.

670. Salmiala, Seija. "Ajatuksia Jean Sibeliuksen serenadeista ja humoreskeista" [Thoughts About Jean Sibelius's Serenades and Humoresques]. *Pieni musiikkilehti*, 1975, no. 3: 17–21.

A consideration of the *Serenades*, op. 69, and *Humoresques*, opp. 87 and 89, against the background of Sibelius's "three periods," with parallels drawn to other composers' works. Illustrating her points with music examples, the author remarks on the difficulty of programming these compositions, because they are chamber-like yet demand a full orchestra. She therefore suggests the idea of concerts specifically designed for these works.

9. VOCAL WORKS

Although it is the symphonic music that has circled the globe many times over, vocal music occupied an extremely important place in the compositional life of Jean Sibelius. Along with more than 100 solo songs there are melodramas, choral compositions, and even attempted operas. The wider dissemination of these works, however, has been limited, first, by the language of the texts, which are mostly in Finnish or Swedish, and second, by the often topical nature of much of the music.

To understand these works requires at the very least some sensitivity to Finland's great literary tradition. It is a tradition that has been enriched by writings in both of the country's languages. It is also a tradition that nourished Sibelius from his earliest days, and its pertinence is therefore biographical as well as musical. The composer was a devoted admirer of such writers as Finland's great Swedish-language poet Johan Ludvig Runeberg (1804–1877); with other literary figures he became personal friends. The present section therefore begins with sources for study of the literary aspects of the vocal music, including a literary history (no. 671), followed by investigations into the relationship of Sibelius's music to poets and writers. Runeberg's importance is aptly reflected in the many entries devoted to this figure. Unfortunately, the relationships of other writers important to Sibelius, such as Karl August Tavaststjerna, have yet to be given due consideration.

Articles and studies devoted first to solo songs and then to choral music follow these literary references. An early essay in the United States on the songs was Virgina T. Pyle's "The Song-style of Jan [sic] Sibelius" (D.M. treatise, Florida State University, 1972. 27 p. + unnumbered music examples). This short tract, however, which surveys the composer's life and works and adds descriptive remarks about four songs (op. 17, no. 6; op. 36, no 1; op. 60, nos. 1 and 2), is not a dissertation and thus has been omitted from the entries below.

Where the choral music is concerned, there is an important social dimension to bear in mind. Much, if not most, of Sibelius's music for chorus was created at the behest of one or another of Finland's choirs. The histories of these ensembles sometimes intertwined in fascinating ways with the composer's own. In view both of these connections and of the scarcity of scholarly studies of the choral music, it seemed important to include below those histories of choral ensembles that illuminate connections to Sibelius's life and work.

* * *

Literary History

671. Laitinen, Kai. *Suomen kirjallisuuden historia* [The History of Finland's Literature]. Helsinki: Otava, 1991. 666 p. PH301.L28 1991 ISBN 951-1-11775-0. Translated into Swedish by Kerstin Lindqvist and Thomas Warburton as *Finlands litteratur* (Helsingfors: Söderström & Co., 1988). 422 p. PH301.L2818 1989 ISBN 951-52-1159-X

A history of Finland's literature in both the Finnish and Swedish languages in which the author shows connections between the two bodies of writing and gives salient features of genres and movements. The two editions are not identical, the Swedish version being considerably shortened and only the Finnish edition including a useful chronology of Finland's historical and literary events. Some details about one of the most important institutions with which Sibelius had connections, the Swedish Theater, are not quite accurate; for corrections, see George C. Schoolfield's review in *Swedish Book Review* where the reader will also find bibliography for further reading and study.

Rev. of the Swedish edition: *Swedish Book Review*, 1989, no. 1: 103–105.

672. Mustelin, Olof. *Euterpe: Tidskriften och kretsen kring den* [*Euterpe*: The Publication and the Circle Around It]. Skrifter utgivna av Svenska Litteratursällskapet i Finland, no. 398. Helsingfors: Svenska Litteratursällskapet i Finland, 1963. An edition was also published in Åbo by Holger Schildts Förlag, 1963. 415 p. AP48.E8M8

One intriguing part of Sibelius's life concerns his involvement with the so-called Euterpists, a group of intellectuals in Helsinki who formed a cultural society just as the new century dawned. Many of the Euterpists wrote poetry that Sibelius set to music, one (Karl Flodin) was a leading music critic, and the group's periodical *Euterpe* (see no. 369) published reviews of Sibelius's music and a work list. Mustelin provides a rich background for this aspect of the composer's life, portraying the Euterpists' formation, their ideals, and their activities, and placing Sibelius within a larger social and cultural context. Facsimiles show select archival material and pages from *Euterpe*; a bibliography lists the archives consulted.

Sibelius and the Poets

673. Flodin, Karl. *Om musiken till Runebergs dikter* [About the Music to Runeberg's Poetry]. Helsingfors: [n.p.], 1904. 56 p. Also published in *Johan Ludvig Runebergs 100 årsminne: Festskrift den 5 Februari 1904*, 250–304 (Helsingfors: 1904). PT9786.Z5J6

A survey of Runeberg poems that had received musical settings by the early twentieth century. Although not as complete as the Forslin bibliography below (no. 675), the evaluations and other, sometimes lengthy, remarks accompanying some of the Sibelius settings are of interest, since they come from one of Finland's leading critics. A concluding section mentions compositions inspired by Runeberg poems.

674. Forslin, Alfhild. "Konstnärsgemenskap hos Sibelius och Runeberg" [Artistic Relationship between Sibelius and Runeberg]. *Finsk tidskrift* 177–78 (1965): 404–15.

A look at the connections and parallels between Sibelius and Runeberg with a discussion of Sibelius's settings of this poetry. Although there are no music examples, the points are illustrated with well-chosen quotations from the poems skillfully used to illuminate aspects of Sibelius's character.

675. Forslin, Alfhild. *Runeberg i musiken: Bibliografi med kommentarer och historisk översikt* [Runeberg in Music: Bibliography with Commentary and Historical Overview]. Svenska Litteratursällskapet i Finland, no. 367. Åbo: Åbo Tidnings och Tryckeri Aktiebolag, 1958. 365 p. ML80.R87F77

This valuable book catalogues the settings of Runeberg's words to music, not only by Sibelius but also by other nineteenth- and twentieth-century composers. The author has thereby provided not only a bibliographical tool but also useful perspective on Sibelius's choice of Runeberg's texts in relation to his contemporaries. The commentary provides publication information for each setting and references to reviews and articles, occasionally even including quotes from Sibelius's family letters. Illustrated (including a facsimile of a page from *The Morning {Morgonen}*) and containing an excellent bibliography and an index to the musical settings by first lines and titles.

676. Fougstedt, Nils-Eric. "Jean Sibelius' Runeberg-tonsättningar" [Jean Sibelius' Runeberg Compositions]. *Finlands Röda Kors' "Julhälsning 1945*." N.p.: Finlands Röda Kors, 1945: 7, 27–28.

Brief survey of the texts by Runeberg that Sibelius chose to give musical settings with author Fougstedt's reflections on the attraction of this poet for the composer. Accompanied by a caricature of Sibelius by Antti Favén dated 1936.

677. Fougstedt, Nils-Erik [sic]. "Sibelius tonsättningar till Rydberg-texter" [Sibelius Compositions to Texts by Rydberg]. *Musik-världen* 1 (December 1945): 16–17.

A short but useful consideration of Sibelius's attraction to the Swedish poet Viktor Rydberg (1828–1895). The author, a fine conductor who led the Radio Symphony Orchestra and an occasional composer, identifies the most representative of the Rydberg texts chosen by Sibelius for musical setting and provides an excerpt from the concluding chorus of one of them, *Snöfrid*.

678. Oksala, Teivas. "Runebergin ja Sibeliuksen Bardi" [Runeberg's and Sibelius's *Bard*]. *Kanava* 15 (1987): 429–30.

Speculations on whether Sibelius had in mind Runeberg's poem *The Bard* when he composed the tone poem of the same title. The author reproduces the poet's Swedish verses together with a Finnish translation by Tarmo Manelius taken from the 1987 publication of Runeberg's *Dikter I*.

679. Pfaler, Sylvia von. "Sånger av Sibelius till ord av Runeberg" [Songs by Sibelius to Words by Runeberg]. *Finsk tidskrift* 138 (1945): 254–64. Also published in *Suomen laulunopettajain yhdistyksen vuosikirja/Sånglärarföreningens i Finland årsbok* 5 (1956): 6–13.

A review of five of Sibelius's best-known solo song settings of Runeberg texts (*Fågelfängaren, Blommans öde, Den första kyssen, Flickan kom ifrån sin älsklings möte*, and *Norden*). The poet's verses are given, followed by a short description of the music.

Solo Songs and Related Studies

See also nos. 91, 372, 392

680. Batka, Richard. "Sibelius als Liederkomponist" [Sibelius as Song Composer]. *Kunstwart* 20 (1907): 457–459.

A sympathetic, if romanticized, view of Sibelius's songs, which the author finds expressive of the elegiac character of the Finnish people and the embodiment of their close connection to nature.

681. Borg, Kim. "How To Sing Them: Some Thoughts on the Interpretation of Sibelius' Songs." *Finnish Music Quarterly*, 1990, nos. 3–4: 58–61.

Remarks "from the inside out," so to speak, by a well-known Finnish bass who has performed this repertory often (and who was related to Sibelius on his mother's [Maria Charlotta Borg] side). Borg gives a "short list" of his favorite Sibelius songs that he considers widely effective.

682. Borg, Kim. "Zur internationalen Verbreitung der Lieder von Sibelius" [On the International Dissemination of Sibelius's Songs]. *Österreichische Musikzeitschrift* 20 (1965): 153–56.

An articulate plea for more frequent performance of Sibelius's songs. The author provided lists of selected songs that he considered especially appropriate for audiences outside Scandinavia.

683. Clifford, Carole. "Jean Sibelius: The Influence of Nature and Nationalism on the Songs of Opus 36 and Opus 37." D.Mus. diss., Florida State University, 1993. iv, 30 p. text, 30 p. music + bibliography. ML410.S54C5

A dissertation that begins with a biographical review based on secondary sources; much of the information is accurate, although it is mistakenly concluded that "Sibelius was primarily Swedish" (p. 8) and that he rejected the influence of Wagner (p. 3; see nos. 175 and 467 for informed studies of these issues). The heart of the document, however, is a song-by-song description of text and stylistic characteristics found in opp. 36 and 37, which are reproduced in the Appendix. The bibliography includes articles about Sibelius's songs found in current-events publications and a list of recordings.

684. Desmond, Astra. "The Songs." In *The Music of Sibelius*, 108–36. Edited by Gerald Abraham. New York: Norton, 1947. ML410.S54A5

A less than enthusiastic general survey in which the author recognizes the importance of singing the songs in the language Sibelius composed them.

685. Djupsjöbacka, Gustav. "Jean Sibelius, Op. 50: In the Spirit of German Lied." *Finnish Music Quarterly*, 1988, no. 4: 34–37.

A discussion of six of the composer's nine songs to German texts by an exceptionally fine pianist who is fully experienced in performing Sibelius's music. Illustrated with a photograph and music examples.

686. Karila, Tauno. "Vesimaisemat Jean Sibeliuksen, Oskar Merikannon ja Yrjö Kilpisen yksinlaulujen melodiikassa" [Water Imagery in Melodies of the Solo Songs by Jean Sibelius, Oskar Merikanto, and Yrjö Kilpinen]. Diss., Helsinki University, 1954. 211 p. ML390.K186V5

A rather cumbersome analysis in which songs by three leading Finnish song composers, selected for their water images, are first categorized as strophic, declamatory, or those in which the accompaniment helps to create the line. Graphs beneath the texts for each song use a system of letters, A, E, D, U, to indicate whether the melodic line is horizontal, rising, descending, or undulating followed by numbers signifying the duration of the direction and interval structure. A section of commentary groups the songs by type of water scene such as calm surface, surface waves, running water, and so on. Some 35 of Sibelius's songs are subjected to scrutiny.

687. Karttunen, Antero. "Sibeliuksen yksinlauluista" [On Sibelius's Solo Songs]. *Rondo*, 1965, no. 6: 18–20.

Short survey that groups the songs generally into early, middle, and late periods and ends with a list of suggested recordings.

688. Karttunen, Antero. "Sibelius yksinlaulujen säveltäjänä" [Sibelius as Composer of Solo Songs]. *Kirkko ja musiikki*, 1965, no. 5: 16–17. The article appeared in Swedish as "Sibelius som kompositör av solosånger." *Musikrevy* 21 (1966): 205–07, and in German as "Sibelius als Liederkomponist." *Sibelius-Mitteilungen*, February 1966: 10–13.

The songs are discussed in three periods with important characteristics mentioned. There are small differences between the articles, including the facsimile of the piano miniature *Granen* that appears only in the *Musikrevy*.

689. Katila, Evert. "Jean Sibelius laulusäveltäjänä" [Jean Sibelius as a Song Composer]. *Valvoja* 24 (1904): 215–25.

Survey of Sibelius's song production against the background of nineteenth-century European and Finnish composition. The author, Evert Katila (1873–1945), was a music critic who had studied under Sibelius at the Helsinki Orchestra School and who wrote pioneering Finnish-language reviews for *Päivälehti*, *Uusi Suometar*, and *Helsingin Sanomat*.

690. Keane, Robert. "The Complete Solo Songs of Jean Sibelius." Diss., University of London, 1993.

According to the author's abstract, a copy of which was provided by the Sibelius Museum, Sibelius's many and diverse songs share compositional techniques with the major works. It is stated that the songs, when examined through the sketches, show Sibelius to be "primarily a melodic composer, concerned more with harmonic articulation of his ideas than with structure."

691. Keane, Robert. "'Höstkväll': Two Versions?" *Finnish Music Quarterly*, 1990: 62–65.

Discussion based on primary sources of *Autumn Evening*.

692. Keane, Robert. "Sibelius' Orchestral Songs." *Nordic Sounds, NOMUS*, 1990, no. 4: 3–5.

A useful article on the originally orchestrated songs.

693. Kilpeläinen, Kari. "Jean Sibeliuksen *Julvisa*-laulun op. 1, nro 4 nuottikuvasta" [Concerning the Versions of Jean Sibelius's Song *Julvisa*, op. 1, no. 4]. *Musiikkitiede* 5 (1993): 94–122.

An important examination of the manuscript and printed sources for Sibelius's setting of Topelius's text ("Giv mig ej glans, ej guld, ej prakt"), which exists both for soloist and for men's chorus. The author lists discrepancies among the versions and includes a facsimile of Fazer's print of the solo song.

694. Krohn, Ilmari. "Jean Sibeliuksen 'Timantti hangella'" [Jean Sibelius's *Diamond on the March Snow*]. *Uusi musiikkilehti*, 1955, no. 9: 10–14.

Krohn applies his peculiar analytical methods to Sibelius's setting of Josef Julius Wecksell's *The Diamond on the March Snow* (*Demanten på marssnön*), addressing the overall structure along with rhythm, melody (including an interval count), harmony, and texture. Illustrated with tables but no music examples.

695. Nyberg, Paul. "Tillägg till Porträtterna av fru Lenngren av Zachris Topelius" [Supplement to *Porträtterna* of Mrs. Lenngren by Zachris Topelius]. *Lucifer*, 1949: 6–9.

Valuable background to the text of Sibelius's melodrama *The Countess's Portrait* (*Grevinnans konterfej*). During the eighteenth century, the Swedish poet Anna Maria Lenngren, known for her gentle satires of complacent bourgeouis attitudes and read in both Sweden and Finland, wrote a substantial poem entitled *Porträtterna*. Her poem inspired the nineteenth-century Finland-

Swedish writer Zachris Topelius to create an even lengthier and more dramatic version in which the Countess addresses a portrait of her younger self, "to gentle music," instructs Topelius. These are the words for which Sibelius later composed his melodrama. Nyberg reproduces a portion of Topelius's supplementary poem, which was apparently intended for a soirée in 1872 in Sibelius's hometown of Hämeenlinna.

696. Rautavaara, Sini. "'Die Rautawaara: The Countess.'" *Finnish Music Quarterly,* 1989, no. 2: 40–48.

An affectionate, illustrated biographical sketch of Finnish soprano Aulikki Rautawaara (1906–1990), including remarks on her performances of Sibelius's songs.

697. Rautavaara, Sini. "Sibeliuksen 'Svarta rosor': laulun viisi tulkintaa" [Sibelius's *Black Roses*: Five Interpretations]. *Synteesi* 7 (1988): 86–89.

Of three sopranos often connected to Sibelius, Ida Ekman, Maikki Järnefelt, and Aulikki Rautawaara, the last named performed with a restrained elegance different from the late romantic school of singing represented by the other two and in a manner admired and approved by the composer. The author compares these singers' different renditions of Sibelius's famous setting of lines from *Black Roses* (*Svarta rosor*) and adds the interpretations of two recent leading soloists, Jorma Hynninen and Tom Krause, whose performances tend to be closer to Rautawaara's. Especially valuable are the music examples that give the differences among all five singers' versions of mm. 1–5 and mm. 30–33. Sources include interviews with Aulikki Rautawaara and recordings, listed in the short but worthwhile bibliography.

698. Rosas, John. "Jean Sibeliuksen viisi joululaulua opus 1" [Jean Sibelius's Five Christmas Songs opus 1]. Translated from Swedish by Ilpo Tolvas. *Pieni musiikkilehti*, 1975, no. 4: 4–6.

One of the first discussions of the problem of Sibelius's curious opus numbering, of which the Five Christmas Songs provide an excellent example: written between 1895 and 1913, the songs were collectively assigned the opus number 1 in the composer's personal work lists. Rosas explains the songs' background in an article welcoming their new publication by Fazer in 1975.

699. Rudder, May de. "Mélodies de Jean Sibelius." *Le guide musical* 52 (1906): 9–11. Translated into Swedish as "Sånger af Sibelius." *Finsk musikrevy* 2 (1906): 54–58.

A general, somewhat romanticized discussion of some of Sibelius's vocal works, beginning with the choral *Song of the Athenians (Athenarnes sång)* but dealing mostly with a selection of solo songs from a collection translated into French by Jacques d'Offoël. There are no music examples, and the piece is more interesting for presenting a French perspective on Sibelius than for its musical insights.

700. Saarenpää, Toivo, trans. *Sibeliuksen lauluja säveliin sovittaen suomentanut* [Sibelius's Songs Translated According to the Music]. Helsinki: Werner Söderström Osakeyhtiö, 1922. 60 p.

Not a study, but the texts of twenty Sibelius songs composed to verses by Oscar Levertin, Ernst Josephson, Gustaf Fröding, Johan Joseph Wecksell, Johan Ludvig Runeberg, Victor Rydberg, Karl August Tavaststjerna, and Adolf Paul, translated and adapted into Finnish.

701. Siikaniemi, Alku. "Jean Sibelius, laulujen mestari: muisteloita ja vaikutelmia" [Jean Sibelius, Master of Songs: Memories and Impressions]. *Valvoja* 35 (1915): 625–36.

Personal rather than scholarly, these are impressions of Sibelius's songs and choral music with a few piano compositions mentioned in passing. Accompanied by a biographical summary.

702. Sirén, Valerie. "The Songs." In *The Sibelius Companion*, 171–200. Edited by Glenda Dawn Goss. Westport, Conn.: Greenwood, 1996. ML410.S54S53 1996 ISBN 0-313-28393-1

An insightful discussion of the song repertoire, which gives due consideration to the poets and their texts and to singers—both those for whom Sibelius composed and those whom he heard. The singers of *Kalevala* poetry in particular seem to have made a powerful impact on the composer, and the author emphasizes the importance of their performance style for singers of Sibelius's songs. She also demonstrates the wide range of styles within the composer's repertoire, from the traditional *romans* to the abstract, the humorous, and even the erotic, and suggests how the songs may be grouped into three style periods. Music examples.

Choral Ensembles

703. Andersson, Otto. *Finlands-svenska musikfester under femtio år* [Fifty Years of Finland's-Swedish Music Festivals]. Åbo: Förlaget Bro, 1947. 405 p. ML37.F5A5

Andersson's is the first book-length study of the festivals that have so enriched Finland's musical life and prompted such Sibelius works as *People from Land and Sea* (*Män från slätten och havet*) and *Song of the Athenians* (*Athenarnes sång*). Illustrated, with an appendix listing members of various ensembles and covering the period 1897–1947. Unfortunately, there is no index, so the reader must dip into each chapter to gather information.

704. Dahlström, Fabian. *Akademiska sångföreningen 1838–1988: 150-årsjubileumsskrift med historik* [Academic Song Society 1838–1988: 150-year Jubilee Publication with a History]. Helsingfors: Akademiska sångföreningen, 1988. 348 p. ML421.A34D2 1988 ISBN 951-99926-34

The oldest men's chorus still in existence in Finland, Akademiska sångföreningen has played a role in the country's musical life since its founding by Fredrik Pacius in 1838. In this jubilee publication, the former Director of the Sibelius Museum supplies a well-researched history of the organization to which Sibelius's father had belonged and of which Sibelius was an honorary member. The composer wrote several works for the ensemble; these are given in the chorus's repertory list together with the dates each was performed.

705. Kilpiö, Markku. "The Story of the Finnish Choir: Social Institution and Human Instrument." *Finnish Music Quarterly*, 1987, no. 2: 2–9.

A helpful English-language introduction to the choir tradition in Finland to which Sibelius's contributions, although not investigated here, were substantial.

706. *100 år med MM: 1878–1978* [100 Years with The M{erry} M{usicians}: 1878–1978]. Edited by Torsten Paulig, Roger Bergman, Kaj Duncker, and Gustav Thulé. Jyväskylä: K.J. Gummerus, 1978. 352 p.

MM, which stands for Muntra Musikanter (The Merry Musicians), is a successful and élite mens' choir founded in 1878 by G. Sohlström. Based in Helsinki, the choir has been a vital part of its country's musical life, performing and commissioning choral works from prominent composers including Sibelius. Along with a history of the ensemble, the volume includes such useful information as a well-documented calendar of the choir's activities, with repertory performed; matriculation lists naming members of various kinds (Sibelius, for example, became an associate member of the choir in 1896 and an honorary member in 1915); and brief biographical information, often unavailable elsewhere, about the members.

707. Ruutu, Martti. "YL:n synnyn vuosikymmenet" [The Decades {Since} the Birth of YL]. In *Sata, Sata, Sata . . . Ylioppilaskunnan Laulajat 1883–1983*. Part I, 124-92. Edited by Veijo Ilmavirta. Helsinki: Ylioppilaskunnan Laulajat, 1983. ML269.8.H42S3 1983 ISBN 951-99446-5-6

Ylioppilaskunnan Laulajat, known as YL, or, in English, the University Singers, is the Finnish-language men's chorus of Helsinki University and Finland's oldest Finnish-language choir. In this chapter, Ruutu traces the beginnings of an organization in which Sibelius's choral music often played a part. His study, which quotes programs and contemporary reviews, provides a framework for the conditions in which Sibelius created such memorable works as *The Boat Journey* (*Venematka*) and *Song of My Heart (Sydämeni laulu*).

708. Smeds, Kerstin, and Timo Mäkinen. *Kaiu, kaiu, lauluni: Laulu- ja soittojuhlien historia* [Echoing, Echoing, My Song: A History of Singing and Playing Festivals]. Helsinki: Otava, 1984. With Swedish summary. 165 p. ML37.F5S6 1984 ISBN 951-1-07886-0

A richly illustrated history of the festival tradition that stretches right back to 1881 when the Society for Culture and Education (*Kansanvalistusseura*) staged a song festival in Jyväskylä, Finland. Since a number of Sibelius's choral compositions owe their origins to the festival custom, the composer figures rather often in these pages. Among the abundant iconographical material is a facsimile of the first page of Sibelius's manuscript copy of *People from Land and Sea* (*Män från slätten och hafvet*). There is also an index and an excellent bibliography.

709. *Suomen Laulu vierailla mailla* [Suomen Laulu on World Travels]. Helsinki: Werner Söderström Osakeyhtiö, 1936. 272 p.

An illustrated account of Suomen Laulu, established as a male choir by Heikki Klemetti in 1900, for which Sibelius's choral music was staple fare. The choir eventually became mixed and today even boasts a children's choir. Repertory presented on major tours from 1900 to 1933 is given together with extensive reviews from the cities visited, all translated into Finnish. A useful source for performance and reception history.

710. *YL Amerikassa* [YL in America]. Helsinki: Kivi, 1939. 256 p. ML304.8.H5Y69

A history of American tours by the choir known as YL (identified in no. 707). Among its most successful was the visit in 1937 when the choir was to perform Sibelius's *Origin of Fire* (*Tulen synty*) with Serge Koussevitzky and the Boston Symphony Orchestra. The score, however, disappeared en route to Boston.

This and other events are told in the volume, which also includes a section (pp. 240–55) of English-language reviews from American papers, although there are no documenting notes.

711. *Ylioppilaskunnan Laulajat: 6.4.1883–6.4.1953* [The University Singers: April 6, 1883–April 6, 1953]. Helsinki: Ylioppilaskunnan Laulajat, 1953. 336 p. ML304.8.H5Y69y

An illustrated account of fifty years of the choir known in Finland as YL, this volume is a collection of articles by different writers on aspects of the chorus and its history. One contribution discusses the chorus's journey to the United States in 1938; another reviews connections with composers such as Sibelius. A chronological program repertory gives the literature sung in Helsinki in the years 1934 to 1953. When used in conjunction with the program repertory in the book annotated as no. 712, a more complete picture of choral activity emerges.

712. *Ylioppilaskunnan Laulajat 50 vuotta* [The University Singers 50 Years]. Helsinki: Suomalaisen Kirjallisuuden Seura, 1933. 384 p. + 18 unnumbered pages.

Includes a chronological list of concerts given in Helsinki from 1883–1933 with the repertory sung at each together with short articles on composers connected to the choir. A list of music for men's choir printed in Finland before 1900 gives titles and printed sources for many of Sibelius's choral works. A complementary catalogue to no. 711.

The Choral Music

See also nos. 65, 199, 372, 378, 393, 396, 428, 699

713. Dahlström, Fabian. "Kantatens senare öden" [The Cantata's Later Fate]. *Klinga visa, sjung fiol: Finlands Svenska sång- och musikförbund 1929–1979*, 21–22. Helsingfors: FSSMF Förlag, 1983. ML27.F5F54 1983 ISBN 951-99448-6-9

In conjunction with an essay by Erik Tawaststjerna (see no. 730), Dahlström discusses how Sibelius's setting of Jarl Hemmer's *Song of the Earth* (*Jordens sång*), composed for the inauguration of Åbo Academy, escaped the fate of so many inaugural works, which are seldom heard after the event for which they are commissioned. He shows that the cantata was incorporated into the repertory of Helsinki's Swedish Oratorio Choir conducted by Bengt Carlson, subsequently performed numerous times, and made into various arrangements.

714. Dahlström, Fabian. "Onko Sibeliuksen kuoroteos 'Taiteelle' olemassa?" [Does Sibelius's Choral Work 'Taiteelle' Exist?]. *Pieni musiikkilehti*, 1985, no. 3: 16.

It was originally thought that the thrilling final chorus of Sibelius's *Snöfrid*, composed in 1900, would be appropriate to perform for the inauguration of Finland's National Theater together with *The Origin of Fire* (*Tulen synty*), which had been especially commissioned for the occasion. However, Rydberg's Swedish words posed a problem, since the Theater's main goal was to present drama in the Finnish language. *Snöfrid* was therefore given Finnish words by Volter Kilpi, beginning *Riennä taide!* At issue is what constitutes a different work, and the discussion is based on manuscripts in the Sibelius Museum.

715. Dahlström, Fabian. "Sibelius' Works for Mixed Chorus." *Fazer Music News*, Spring 1993: 1–3.

Brief but welcome review of works seldom discussed, perhaps because many were intended for amateur groups. Dahlström points out that Sibelius was the first "to adopt an authentic Finnish declamation in choral music" and provides some historical background for the genesis of certain choral compositions.

716. Fantapié, Henri-Claude. "Sibelius' Cantatas." *Fazer Music News*, 1992, no. 4: 14–15.

A short discussion of the background and musical features of four choral works, *Song of Väinö* (*Väinön virsi*), *Hymn to the Earth* (*Maan virsi*), *Song of the Earth* (*Jordens sång*), and *My Own Land* (*Oma maa*), which Sibelius composed between 1918 and 1926.

717. Goddard, Scott. "The Choral Music." In *The Music of Sibelius*, 137–40. Edited by Gerald Abraham. New York: Norton, 1947. ML410.S54A5

Descriptive survey hampered by the unavailability of scores of the choral works at the time of writing.

718. Haapanen, Toivo. "Jean Sibeliuksen Sydämeni laulu" [Jean Sibelius's *Song of My Heart*]. In *Pilvilaiva: Aleksis Kivi ajan kuvastimessa*, 28–43. Helsinki: Otava, 1947. PH355.S82Z5ap

A detailed discussion of *Song of My Heart* (*Sydämeni laulu*) and Sibelius's rhythmic, harmonic, and melodic choices in light of the poetic structure of the lines taken from Aleksis Kivi's famous novel *Seven Brothers*. The work, which was written for the men's choir YL (see no. 707), is reproduced in facsimile.

719. Hyökki, Matti. "Jean Sibelius, Op. 84: Unknown Songs for Male Voice Choir." *Finnish Music Quarterly*, 1987, no. 2: 10–15.

An examination of the five songs of op. 84 with the suggestion that their Swedish texts might partly account for their neglect among Finnish choirs. The works in question are *Mr. Lager and the Fair One* (*Herr Lager och Skön fager*), *On the Mountain* (*På berget*), *A Dream Chord* (*Ett drömackord*), *Eternal Eros* (*Evige Eros*), and *At Sea* (*Till havs*). The discussion includes music examples and a list of songs for male voice choir *a cappella*.

720. Karila, Tauno. "Sana ja sävel Jean Sibeliuksen kuorotyylissä" [Word and Tone in Jean Sibelius's Choral Style]. *Valvoja* 65 (1945): 397–401.

A short essay mostly devoted to a discussion of Sibelius's choral works to texts from the *Kalevala* and the *Kanteletar*. No music examples, but the author makes interesting observations about the composition of *Hail, O Moon!* (*Terve kuu*), although not without error. The work was created for the choir called Suomen Laulu or "SL," but the text reads "YL," which stands for Ylioppilaskunnan Laulajat. It was the choir's particularly fine, low bass singers who wanted a vehicle to display their voices that helps to account for the exceptionally low compass of the piece.

721. Klemetti, Heikki. "Aleksis Kiven teksteihin tehtyjä sävellyksiä" [Compositions to Texts of Aleksis Kivi]. *Suomen musiikkilehti*, 1934: 207–10; also published in *Sulasol*, 1984, no. 1: 4–6; 1984, no. 2: 7.

A review of some of the choral settings of the great Finnish writer Kivi's texts, including Sibelius's *Song of My Heart* (*Sydämeni laulu*). Klemetti recalls the time when the composer, then living on Liisankatu in the center of Helsinki, wrote the work which Klemetti himself premiered in the fall concert of YL. Music examples, including a facsimile of the three opening bars of Sibelius's manuscript.

722. Laitinen, Kai. "Vielä 'Ateenalaisten laulusta'" ['The Song of the Athenians' Again]. *Parnasso* 40 (1990/5): 313.

A response to no. 728. Laitinen adds two sources to the discussion of the *Song of the Athenians*' text, its background, and the figure of Tyrtaeus, a character in Rydberg's original poem whose obscure origins make it possible for both Athenians and Spartans to claim him.

723. Levón, Eino. "Vähässä paljon seisoo" [In a Little Stands a Lot]. *Suomen musiikkilehti*, December 1935: 188–89.

The author tells how the three-voice *Nostalgia* (*Kotikaipaus*), the manuscript of which is reproduced in facsimile, originated after his three daughters serenaded Sibelius one evening. Although anecdotal, it gives an idea of the composer's working methods. Another version of the story was told later in *Suomen Kuvalehti*, 1953, no. 8: 30–31, again with a facsimile, although this time less well reproduced.

724. Maasalo, Armas. "Miten Sibeliuksen Oma maa syntyi" [How Sibelius's *Oma maa* Was Born]. *Musiikkitieto*, 1944, nos. 9–10: 143. Also published in *Uusi musiikkilehti*, 1955, no. 9: 35–36, and *Kansalliskuoro 50-vuotias* (Hyvinkää: 1958), 105–07.

A personal memoir by the conductor who premiered the cantata *My Own Land* (*Oma maa*), which was commissioned by the National Chorus (Kansallis-Kuoro) for the ensemble's ten-year celebration in 1918. Maasalo remembers the composer working on the score in the quiet of the hospital in Lapinlahti, where Sibelius's brother Christian was director. He also reprints Helsinki music critic Evert Katila's response to the first performance.

725. Pajamo, Reijo. "Maakuntalaulumme" [Songs of Our Provinces]. *Sulasol*, 1984, no. 3: 12–13; 1984, no. 4: 33–34; 1985, no. 1: 40–41.

A review of compositions connected with different provinces in Finland among which is Sibelius's *Song for the People of Uusimaa* (*Uusmaalaisten laulu*), composed to a poem by teacher Kaarlo Terhi (1872–1921). The author explains the work's poetic and musical origins and provides music examples of this and other choral works by such composers as Emil Genetz, Oskar Merikanto, and Leevi Madetoja.

726. Pesola, Väinö. "Jean Sibelius kuorosävellystensä kuvastimessa" [Jean Sibelius Reflected in His Choral Compositions]. *Uusi musiikkilehti*, 1955, no. 9: 46–48.

Right worshipful reflection on the titles Sibelius composed for chorus with photographs of the sauna at Ainola and Sibelius with a cigar. The author, born in 1886, was one of the leading choral conductors in Finland, a product of the Orchestra School and the Helsinki Music Institute, and a composer of many works, especially humorous ones, for male and mixed choirs.

727. Politoske, Daniel. "The Choral Music." In *The Sibelius Companion*, 201–20. Edited by Glenda Dawn Goss. Westport, Conn.: Greenwood, 1996. ML410.S54S53 1996 ISBN 0-313-28393-1

The most expansive discussion of the choral music available. The author proceeds by type of ensemble and connects the histories of many works to episodes in the composer's life. Music examples include welcome excerpts from choral scores that are difficult to obtain outside Finland.

728. Ruusunen, Aimo. "'Ateenalaisten laulu' onkin spartalainen?" [Is 'Song of the Athenians' Really Spartan?] *Parnasso* 40 (1990/3): 174.

An argument that the text of the famous *Song of the Athenians* (*Athenarnes sång*) may better fit the historical situation of Sparta than Athens. The author points out that the poet of the verses, Viktor Rydberg, never wrote an independent poem by this title; rather the text comes from his lengthy *Dexippos*, in which no specific tribe or race is mentioned. The author theorizes that Rydberg adapted warlike Sparta's situation to Athens in his text, into which Finns read their own oppressive circumstances, and which Sibelius and Eino Leino, through his translation of the words into Finnish, elevated into Finland's patriotic hymn.

729. Stenius, Hanna. "Små minnen från *Snöfrids* uruppförande" [Little Memories of the First Performance of *Snöfrid*]. *Tidning för musik* 5 (1915): 211–12.

A personal reminiscence of rehearsals of *Snöfrid* in 1900, a work being prepared for performance by Robert Kajanus's choir and orchestra under the direction of "Aunt Thérèse," choral director Thérèse Hahl (1842–1911). Sibelius's presence at one rehearsal caused a great stir and a certain amusement when he showed reluctance to accompany the choir at the piano.

730. Tawaststjerna, Erik. "Sibelius' kantat Jordens sång" [Sibelius's Cantata *Song of the Earth*]. In *Klinga visa, sjung fiol: Finlands Svenska sång- och musikförbund 1929–1979*, 16–21. Helsingfors: FSSMF Förlag, 1983. ML27.F5F54 1983 ISBN 951-99448-6-9

A discussion of the origin of the cantata *Song of the Earth* (*Jordens sång*), which Sibelius composed for the inauguration of the Swedish-language university in Turku, Åbo Academy. The essay and two of the music examples are taken from the author's biography (no. 175), although here, a facsimile of the opening measures of Sibelius's manuscript is reproduced.

Index of Compositions

Index of Authors, Editors, and Translators

Subject Index

SEE ALSO THE HEADINGS IN THE TABLE OF CONTENTS